THE
AWAKENED LIFE

ALCHEMY

DENNIS WILLIAM HAUCK

Publishing: Mike Sanders
Senior Acquisitions Editor: Janette Lynn
Art Director: William Thomas
Copy Editor: Rick Kughen
Cover Designer: Jessica Lee
Book Designer/Layout: Ayanna Lacey
Indexer: Celia McCoy
Proofreader: Christina Guthrie

Published by Penguin Random House LLC
001-322104-SEP2021
Copyright © 2021 by Dennis William Hauck

International Standard Book Number: 978-161564-999-0
Library of Congress Catalog Card Number: 2021931008

23   22   21   5   4   3   2   1

Interpretation of the printing code: The rightmost number of the first series of numbers is the year of the book's printing; the rightmost number of the second series of numbers is the number of the book's printing. For example, a printing code of 21-1 shows that the first printing occurred in 2021

Printed in the United States of America

Reprinted and updated from *The Complete Idiot's Guide to Alchemy*

For the curious
www.dk.com

Contents

Part 3: **Applying the Principles of Alchemy in Your Life   111**

Introduction

My initiation into alchemy came while I was attending the University of Vienna. I had gone there to study mathematics in the tradition of Viennese logician Kurt Gödel. However, within three months of my arrival, I was sidetracked into an ancient and mystical discipline of which none of my professors approved.

Four hundred years earlier, Vienna and nearby Prague were at the heart of European alchemy, and hundreds of alchemists flocked to the area. I was unaware of Vienna's rich alchemical tradition until I stumbled into a basement room in the university library that was full of old alchemy books.

The old Fraktur texts were difficult to decipher, but it was the strangely profound drawings that resonated with me. Whatever was going on in those drawings seemed more real than anything that was going on in my life at the time, and I wanted to be part of it. I resolved to learn as much as I could about alchemy and began studying the dusty old manuscripts.

My intense interest in alchemy seemed to open a channel in me, and I began seeing alchemical imagery in my dreams and everywhere I went in Vienna. It was as if alchemy was taking an interest in me. Old treatises, engravings, and alchemical symbols somehow found their way into my life. Finally, a chemistry professor gave me the name of a practicing alchemist who might be willing to teach me more.

The alchemist's name was Merus Favilla. He practiced alchemy in Prague for more than 20 years, and he lived and breathed the ancient art. Although I was elated when he took me on as an apprentice, the way he taught was different from anything I had ever experienced. He never organized his teachings and only spoke of broader principles when he was inspired by a particular outcome or event. He encouraged chaos and freethinking and despised expectation and the "smugness of knowing." Merus believed his state of mind—the way he observed an experiment—could influence its outcome.

Yet Merus never thought of himself as a wizard or magician. He was a deeply mystical man who hid his true nature from the world. His Latin craft name, *Merus Favilla*, hints at his deeply held beliefs. His name means "the truth (or value) in the still-burning embers of the dead."

"The light that survives in the ashes," he once explained, "is awareness itself that we all take for granted." For him, understanding the value of consciousness was the key to doing alchemy. I soon learned that this idea was a common thread in alchemy. The fabled Philosopher's Stone was the alchemists' symbol for purified consciousness and heightened awareness. As the Belgian alchemist Gerhardt Dorn (1520–1584) put it: "You must transmute yourselves from dead stones into living Philosophical Stones."

Unlike dry academic disciplines, alchemy comes alive within you if you are ripe for it. And it can grow into something that is more than the sum of its parts. That is when the true secret teachings begin and when unexpected transformations happen. There is some sort of energetic connection to the principles of alchemy that is synergistically empowering to a person's consciousness. True alchemists know exactly what I am talking about, and by the time you are done with this book, I hope you will, too.

So, let *your* apprenticeship begin now! Start the work as a novice, like card Zero (The Fool) on the transformational path of the Tarot, which depicts a free-spirited vagabond who carries everything he needs in his knapsack. Forget anything you thought you knew about alchemy and alchemists. You are now awakening to a new way of understanding and a new path of enlightenment. Free your mind. And don't worry—you have everything you need hidden inside you. Just come as you are.

How This Book Is Organized

The objective of this book is to teach you the alchemists' coded language so you can work with the powerful principles they used and apply them in your own life. We will go right to the heart of this ancient and complicated tradition with no unnecessary secrecy, no pompous theorizing, and no special allegiance to any particular tradition or organization. The goal is to glean the essence of what the alchemists were talking about and unveil the universal methods of transformation they discovered.

Following the style of the alchemists, major philosophical concepts are capitalized to differentiate them from their mundane meanings. For example, "sulfur" refers to the flammable yellow chemical that is also known as brimstone, while "Sulfur" refers to the underlying principle of fire, passion, and energy that the alchemists associated with that substance. Similarly, the terms "Above" and "Below" are philosophical concepts related to our ideas of Heaven and Earth.

The material in this book is divided into five sections:

Part 1, Discovering the Hidden Roots of Alchemy, traces how the craft developed from the mythic writings of godlike beings into the philosophical treatises of the Alexandrian alchemists. From alchemy's origins in ancient Egypt to the founding of the Great Library, the basic tenets of alchemy were well developed long before the heyday of the medieval alchemists.

Part 2, Working in the Inner Laboratory, describes what went on in alchemists' workshops. They devoted all levels of mind, body, and spirit to the Great Work and suffered through the same agonizing transformations as the materials in their experiments. The secret connection between mind and matter—established through meditation and prayer—was essential to making tinctures and elixirs and transforming base metals into noble ones.

Part 3, Applying the Principles of Alchemy in Your Life, reviews the fundamental concepts of alchemy and shows how they are part of all we experience in the world. These primordial principles are embedded in the fabric of creation and are expressed on all levels of reality, from our bodies and personal psychology to the evolution of the stars and galaxies. Awareness of these archetypal patterns helps us understand and manage the chaotic forces that surround us.

Part 4, Performing the Operations of Alchemy, reveals the secret processes alchemists used to achieve their transformations. These universal operations worked simultaneously on all levels of reality—the physical, the mental, and the spiritual. You will learn how the principles are applied in lab work, healing and rejuvenation, personal psychology and relationships, and social and planetary alchemy.

Part 5, Understanding Alchemical Consciousness, points to the key to unlocking the mysteries of alchemy, as well as personal transformation and psychology, biology and the life sciences, and quantum physics and cosmology. Not only were alchemists the first chemists, they were the first doctors and healers, the first psychologists, and the first explorers of a science of consciousness. From their wisdom, we offer a cosmological model of the role of consciousness in the universe.

Resources

There are some useful tools for further study at the end of this book. Appendix A, Recommended Resources, includes a list of books, websites, and organizations. Appendix B is a glossary of alchemical terms. Finally, there is a comprehensive index of the contents of this book.

Acknowledgments

I want to thank the International Alchemy Guild (IAG) for allowing me to access their extensive archives and graphics files in the preparation of this work. I am also forever indebted to Merus Favilla for his patience while guiding a stubborn mathematician into the Greater Mysteries.

Trademarks

All terms mentioned in this book that are known to be or are suspected of being trademarks or service marks have been appropriately capitalized. Alpha Books and Penguin Group (USA) Inc. cannot attest to the accuracy of this information. Use of a term in this book should not be regarded as affecting the validity of any trademark or service mark.

DISCOVERING THE HIDDEN ROOTS OF ALCHEMY

The roots of alchemy are buried in the shifting sands of ancient Egypt. According to legend, alchemy developed from the teachings of divine visitors who came to Egypt more than 10,000 years ago. One of the visitors, named Thoth, is considered the first alchemist, as well as the father of mathematics, music, astronomy, and agriculture. He recorded the wisdom of the godlike visitors and sealed his writings in two great pillars that became known as the Pillars of Hermes. Greek historians report that the pillars were rediscovered thousands of years after the Great Flood and were hidden away in an isolated temple in western Egypt. The city of Alexandria was founded to study and translate the sacred texts, and from there, the spiritual technology of alchemy spread throughout the world. By examining the lives and environments of those early alchemists, we get a deeper understanding of alchemical principles and how they evolved in different cultures.

Your Initiation In Alchemy

Just what is alchemy? This question can present a bewildering variety of answers because alchemy is at the root of so many different traditions and disciplines. And that's unfortunate, for the simplest thing about alchemy is its definition. So, to avoid confusion in your study of this subject, remember this basic definition right from the start: alchemy is the art of transformation.

Alchemy is about how one thing is changed into another, and the goal of alchemy is to perfect or evolve the substance at hand. Alchemists try to change something that is inferior, imperfect, or unacceptable into something that is better, more perfect, and closer to what they desire.

It does not matter whether we're talking about metals, chemicals, or herbs or whether we're talking about our bodies, minds, or souls. Nor does it matter whether we're talking about chemistry, biology, medicine, religion, sociology, politics, software, or psychology. The word "alchemy" is always about how to accomplish some sort of creative transformation.

So, there you have it. You've already made a giant leap toward understanding alchemy, and you've only just begun! Alchemy might seem confusing and arcane and even deliberately misleading sometimes, but once you understand the alchemists' symbolic, coded language, their words will all fall into place.

Why Study Alchemy?

Why should you spend your time trying to penetrate the alchemists' language and learn the age-old secrets of alchemy? What relevance does alchemy have today?

Surprisingly, this ancient discipline, which dates back more than 2,500 years, has much to offer the modern world. The universal principles discovered by alchemists apply to all levels of the physical, mental, and spiritual transformation. Alchemical techniques will help you make the transformations you desire, regardless of whether you are working in an artist's studio or a boardroom, in a lab developing healing medicines working in a clinic as a therapist, or working in the inner laboratory of your own soul and spirit.

The ancient art of transformation reveals the hidden chemistry of change that underlies an enormous variety of subjects ranging from psychological transformation and personal relationships to the formation of stars and planetary systems. In fact, the principles of alchemy have achieved more respect today from the general public and among scholars than at any time in the last 400 years.

While putting the "alchemist" job title on your resumé might not bring in a flood of offers, thinking of yourself as a practicing alchemist in the workplace and everyday world can bring unexpected rewards and advancement. So, let's look at the different kinds of modern alchemy and see how they can help you get ahead in the world.

The Kinds of Alchemy

Because in the most basic terms, alchemy is the art of transformation, the best way to study the different aspects of alchemy is to focus on what is being transformed.

Spiritual Alchemy

The most popular reason for studying alchemy today is to reconnect with deeper spiritual realities. In this approach to alchemy, the gold of the alchemist is not the common metal gold; instead it is an inner spiritual gold. Using meditation to penetrate the symbolic imagery of alchemy, the seeker attempts to transform the dark, heavy, karmic lead of the soul into the bright, purified, and incorruptible gold of spirit. Much of this book is devoted to this topic, and we will begin learning the techniques of spiritual alchemy in Part 2.

Psychological Alchemy

Alchemy not only gave birth to chemistry, but it also gave birth to modern psychology. Alchemists were the first to treat psychological problems as chemical imbalances in the body. They believed the archetypal powers of the planets and metals were expressed in humans as our basic instincts and emotions, and these could be transformed into the nobler aspects of awakening and enlightenment through alchemical processes.

Swiss psychologist Dr. Carl Jung (1875–1961) is credited with returning alchemy to its rightful stature in academia with his development of depth psychology, which he based on the universal symbols of alchemy that appeared in his patients' dreams. Jung made the ancient operations of alchemy viable tools in helping his patients achieve psychological wholeness.

Psychological alchemy will be a recurring thread throughout this book. We go into some detail on these techniques in Part 4.

Artistic Alchemy

Throughout history, alchemy has had a tremendous influence in the creative arts. Early Egyptian alchemists were experts at capturing essences in oils and perfumes and applying colors from metal oxides to jewelry and sculptures. Today, many artists working with metal, glass, enamels, clay, and other media consider themselves part of the alchemical tradition.

Alchemical art tends to use materials in ways that make them appear to be something else, thus revealing their essences in unexpected ways. We can also find similar transformative staging in alchemical literature, music, and even software games.

Many filmmakers follow the principles of alchemy to add psychological depth and archetypal power to their films. Workers from Paramount Studios even set up an "Alchemy in Film" panel in the late 1990s to assist writers in understanding alchemy. Films like *2001, 2010, Like Water for Chocolate, The Fifth Element, The Matrix, Revelation, Fullmetal Alchemist, The Da Vinci Code*, and the *Harry Potter* series, are just a few examples where the creators have made conscious use of alchemy in the plotline.

The key to creative alchemy is being able to free the mind from conventional thinking and assumptions. Being able to see new patterns requires letting the inner light of imagination shine in new and unexpected directions. Alchemists called this crucial stage "fermentation," and you will learn how to use it when we begin working with the operations of alchemy in Part 4.

Social Alchemy

In the last century, many concepts of alchemical philosophy became tools in movements and organizations driven by the desire to reform social and cultural conditions. These crucibles of change centered on educational, religious, and political institutions and included civil rights, free speech, voting rights, LGBTQ rights, economic inequality, women's rights, bureaucratic reforms, and peace efforts. Part of the desire to raise social awareness and provide community support originates from hundreds of Hermetic organizations, such as the Freemasons, Golden Dawn, OTO, Rosicrucians, Gnostics, and similar groups.

Alchemical methods of dissolving bureaucracy and bringing organizations back to life have found many applications in business and government. Often, the leaders of movements in racial equality, economic equity, political justice, and other reform efforts borrow alchemical terms and principles to change the status quo. The common goal of social alchemists is to transform the consciousness and attitudes of people. We explore the power of social alchemy further in Part 5.

Practical Alchemy

Most of the work in practical alchemy deals with producing tinctures, elixirs, tonics, oils, balms, and other compounds that capture healing energy. More advanced laboratory work focuses on mineral alchemy and transmuting the metals commonly associated with changing lead into gold. Laboratory alchemy reached its heyday in Europe in the Middle Ages, but in the last 50 years, laboratory work has staged a noticeable resurgence, as people and companies offer more alchemical products for sale.

In Part 2, you will learn how to make a spagyric tincture with emphasis on the mental and spiritual participation needed to make an alchemized medicine.

Therapeutic Alchemy

During the last century, we have seen the proliferation of a new breed of alchemical practitioners who focus on ancient healing modalities. Techniques such as alchemical hypnotherapy, dream therapy, and shamanic journeying use imagery to direct or stimulate healing energy.

Oriental alchemical arts like yoga, aikido, Tai Chi, Chi Kung, tantra, acupuncture, and reiki have seen a profound increase in Western culture. Alchemical bodywork, such as chiropractic, Rolfing, Feldenkrais, bioenergetics, and polarity therapy, have their origin in the work of eighteenth-century alchemists seeking to isolate the life force.

Modern holistic disciplines such as homeopathy, herbology, naturopathy, Ayurveda, Chinese medicine, aromatherapy, and reflexology trace their origins in ancient alchemical teachings, and even New Age astrologers, numerologists, and Tarot readers owe their livelihoods to Egyptian and Babylonian alchemists. We study some of these fascinating traditions in more detail in Part 5.

Quantum Alchemy

The quantum world envisioned by modern scientists is a re-expression of ancient alchemical principles. According to theoretical physicist Dr. Fred Alan Wolf, quantum physics is the New Alchemy, and the two disciplines share many fundamental principles, such as the idea that consciousness is a force in nature.

Also, alchemy has had a tremendous influence in other sciences, such as geology, botany, biology, and of course, chemistry. We will probe deeper into this breakthrough work in Part 5.

The Perennial Philosophy

The wide variety of possible alchemical transformations can seem bewildering to new students of alchemy. But remember, alchemy deals with universal principles that must work on all levels of reality. For an alchemist, there is no real distinction between the different kinds of transformation. This is because the myriad objects and possibilities in our world are all manifestations of just one thing—the One Mind at the source of creation. Everything has the signature of its creator, and by focusing on this single divine spark in everything, the alchemist hopes to reveal the primordial essence of a substance or situation and guide its growth to a natural state of perfection.

This fundamental concept is part of a powerful and persistent ancient philosophy that is the reason for the endurance of alchemy through the ages. The alchemists referred to it as the "One True Philosophy of the Whole World" and believe it was first revealed to humanity in ancient Egypt. It is also known as the "Perennial Philosophy" because, down through history, it has always resurfaced in some form despite attempts by orthodox authorities to suppress it.

*To perform their transformations, alchemists attempt to understand and
connect with the unseen reality behind the manifested world.*
(From L'atmosphère: Météorologie Populaire by Camille Flammarion, 1888)

The basic idea of the Perennial Philosophy is that there are certain universal truths
common to all cultures and systems of knowledge. German mathematician Gottfried
Leibniz (1646–1716) first used the term in this sense when he defined it as the eternal
philosophy that underlies all religions. The term was further refined by twentieth-
century philosopher Aldous Huxley (1894–1963) to mean the most basic and
everlasting universal truths sensed by all human beings that seem true in all areas of
human endeavor.

In other words, down through history, people in many different cultures and times have
experienced similar feelings about the nature of reality and the meaning of existence.
Differences arise only when some authority attempts to control or adapt these basic
ideas into a rigid system of behavior. In this view, the world's governments and
religions are constantly fighting each other over minor, cultural variations in the same
basic belief system. Unlike dogmatic religion, which encourages these petty sectarian
disputes, the Perennial Philosophy states that there are as many roads to the divine
mind as there are people in the world.

The three fundamental tenets of alchemy and the Perennial Philosophy of which it is part are:

1. The material world is not the only reality. A hidden level of reality exists that determines our world. The physical world is a projection of a higher Mind that cannot be grasped by the senses. Only the higher faculties of the human mind and spirit can resonate with it.

2. The basic duality of material versus nonmaterial realities is mirrored in human beings. Our material bodies are subject to the physical laws of birth and death; our nonmaterial bodies or souls carry the essence of who we are and are not subject to decay or loss. This eternal divine spark is known to alchemists as the Fifth Element or Quintessence.

3. All human beings possess the capacity to perceive these separate levels of reality, both in themselves and in nature, but we are taught to ignore the subtle clues to this greater awareness. The perception and application of this ultimate truth is the natural goal of human beings and the purpose of our existences. Awakening to this higher purpose is the first step in the Great Work of alchemy.

What makes alchemy different from other traditions that are part of the Perennial Philosophy is that alchemy attempts to apply this wisdom in practical ways in the everyday world. No other discipline has taken such a down-to-earth and in-your-face approach to working with mystical principles.

Unfortunately, that approach got a lot of alchemists burnt at the stake by authoritarian kings and religious leaders. But their sacrifices also make alchemy a uniquely powerful discipline—a combination of religion and science that makes a lot of sense to people trying to remain true to themselves in the modern world. You can find more about being alchemists in today's world in Part 5 (Understanding Alchemical Consciousness).

Becoming an Alchemist

In the past, becoming an alchemist began with a long apprenticeship or training period that traditionally involved a specific path of initiation. In the ancient mystery schools, the teachings were arranged into three levels of mastery:

1. The *Philosophicum* (or knowing what is really there)

2. The *Theoreticum* (or knowing how it works)

3. The *Practicum* (or knowing how to do it)

Obviously, initiatory alchemy was a very personal process that usually involved a one-on-one relationship with an adept or master alchemist that lasted many years.

Not surprisingly, modern teaching of alchemy takes place at a faster pace on all three levels of initiation at once. On the philosophical level, the objective is to achieve an awareness of the lower and the higher worlds in which the alchemist works. The goal of the theoretical work is to understand how to interact and control the unseen energies of those realms. The practical work is concerned with learning the personal and laboratory techniques of transformation and is, in turn, presented in three phases: the Plant Work, the Mineral Work, and the Animal Work.

There are workable alternatives for people seeking initiation in alchemy other than years of apprenticeship to a practicing alchemist. The first option is self-study, in which this book can serve as your guide. The fact is ancient alchemical manuscripts are no longer hidden away on the shelves of medieval libraries. Most of these works have been republished or are available on the Internet. Online collections and other sources of original texts are listed in Appendix A (Recommended Resources).

Other options to learn alchemy include attending alchemy conferences and webinars or taking courses online. A complete list of schools offering courses in alchemy also can be found in Appendix A.

In this chapter, we mapped out the first steps in your initiation into alchemy. We defined alchemy in simplest terms as the art of transformation and looked at how the principles of this ancient craft can be applied in the modern world. The applications are personal transformation (psychological and spiritual work), artistic creation, social reform, the sciences, healing modalities, and producing alchemical products.

We also learned that alchemy is part of the Perennial Philosophy, the basic tenet of which is that there are certain universal truths common to all cultures and belief systems. In addition, we offered a few options for learning alchemy with recommended resources. In the next chapter, we will begin our work in earnest with the establishment of a sacred laboratory space in which to perform the Great Work.

The First Alchemists

The roots of alchemy are buried in myth and mystery that goes back more than 10,000 years. Ancient Egyptian scrolls describe "visitors from the firmament" who came to the Nile Delta and shared their knowledge of the universe and taught humans writing, mathematics, science—and the art of alchemy.

The first alchemy books in recorded history appeared almost simultaneously in Egypt, Mesopotamia, India, and China more than 2,000 years ago, and historians date the birth of modern alchemy to that period. This was the era of the great library at Alexandria, and ships visiting the busy Egyptian port carried alchemical manuscripts around the world. However, those early writings quote even more ancient texts and refer to a lost tradition that goes back to the dawn of civilization.

All we can say with certainty is that by 800 C.E., the principles of alchemy were widely known by philosophers, priests, and craftsmen in civilized nations around the globe. Hundreds of parchment scrolls, clay tablets, papyri, and manuscripts existed that dealt with alchemical principles and processes. Yet, to this day, the true source of that knowledge remains unknown.

Although references to alchemical principles are found in Egyptian scrolls dating back to 1500 B.C.E., the original canon of texts from which those principles were derived has vanished. The alchemy manuscripts that have survived are remarkably similar in style and seem to originate from a common source. All those texts are written in a strange, convoluted style with obscure references to preexisting concepts and are filled with secret ciphers for which no explanation is given.

The Gods of Alchemy

Despite the difficulty in pinning down the historical source of alchemy, the answer to the question of where alchemy came from is almost unanimous among alchemists. Alchemists agree that their art originated in Egypt during a time known as *Zep Tepi*, which is an ancient Egyptian phrase meaning "the First Time." It refers to an epoch more than 12,000 years ago when divine beings arrived "through the Void" to settle in Egypt. The gods shared their wisdom and civilized the primitive humans. In this tradition, alchemy is literally a gift from the gods.

According to legend, the contingent of godlike beings settled in Egypt and exhibited an advanced technology that enabled them to transform matter. These beings were the first alchemists. It is said they practiced their art in Hormanouthi in a small temple hidden near the Nile River.

According to hieroglyphic texts, the visitors originated from "different levels in the firmament," and their bodies were more evolved than humans. Whether for purposes of breeding or out of sheer lust, the visitors began having children with young Egyptian women. The children of these unions were described as giants ("titans") who eventually had dominion over the Earth and its creatures.

Surprisingly, the idea of angelic visitors lusting after humans more than 12,000 years ago is part of many religious traditions. Genesis 6:1–5 describes fallen angels who wanted to have children with the daughters of men. In exchange, they taught men magic and metallurgy and how to make tinctures to capture the essence of plants. The story is elaborated in considerable detail in the Old Testament apocryphal *Book of Enoch*.

Who were these mysterious visitors? Zosimus, the father of Greek alchemy who lived in Alexandria around 300 C.E., wrote that fallen angels who had children with humans taught alchemy and "all the secret arts of nature" to mankind, and he insisted the legends predated history and were literally true. The Christian writer Tertullian (155–240 C.E.) and many early Hermetic writers spoke of this same race of superhumans and their interactions with humans. The alchemist Clement of Alexandria (150–215 C.E.) said the visitors "laid bare the secrets of the metals, understood the virtues of plants, the force of magical incantations, and their learning even extended to the science of the stars."

In an ancient Egyptian text called "Isis the Prophetess to Her Son Horus," Isis begins teaching her son the principles of alchemy and tells him how she acquired her skills. She had gone to the temple in Hormanouthi to learn the sacred art and met one of the visitors who was overcome by physical desire for her. Isis offered to satisfy his hunger if he would disclose the secrets, but he refused. Eventually, she met another visitor named Amnael who agreed to her demands, and Isis was initiated into the mysteries of alchemy.

According to legend, Isis, her brother and sister, her husband Osiris, and five other divine beings settled in Heliopolis, which became the center for alchemy in Egypt. The myths of Isis and Osiris help explain the mysteries of alchemy and are retold many times in the writings of alchemists. We cannot determine whether these ancient myths contain any literal truth, but there is no doubt that alchemists felt they imparted deep wisdom about the true origin of their craft.

Thoth: The Father of Alchemy

Thoth was one of the godlike beings who lived in Egypt during the time of *Zep Tepi*. However, there is an important difference between Thoth and all the other gods of Egypt. Thoth is the archetypal representation of mind who exists on all levels of time and space, in Heaven, on Earth, and In-Between.

Thoth, as a symbol of mind and consciousness, has always existed and always will. He spoke the first Word of creation, and all he has to do is name a thing to bring it into existence. Thoth brought the first gods into being, yet he is content to serve both the gods and mankind. Thoth is the divine intermediary between Heaven and Earth (or spirit and matter) that makes alchemy possible. Medieval alchemists attributed the powers of Thoth to the Roman god Mercury, the messenger god of inspiration and divination who carries the caduceus.

The Egyptians considered Thoth the first scribe; he is considered to be the inventor of language and writing who recorded the ancient teachings in hundreds of books. Because of this, Thoth is the father of many disciplines, including alchemy, mathematics, agriculture, music, magic, religion, science, and medicine.

Most of the scrolls attributed to him were preserved in the great library at Alexandria. In the writings, Thoth presents alchemy as a unique spiritual science—a merging of soul and spirit that requires a balanced blending of heart, body, and mind.

Most often depicted as a man with the head of an ibis (a tall wading bird with a long, curved beak), Thoth was also associated with baboons and apes, which is taken as a symbol of his divine mission to raise our animal nature to new levels of awareness. Thoth was known as the "Revealer of the Hidden" and "Lord of Rebirth" and was considered the initiator of human evolution.

One of Thoth's scrolls from which fragments remain is called *The Book of Breathings,* which teaches humans how to become gods through spells and control of the breath. Thoth is also considered the author of *The Book of the Dead,* which guides the departed through the underworld into the eternal light. It is said the lost *Book of Thoth* was written in his own hand and consisted of strange symbols that elevated the reader's consciousness to directly experience the "presence of the gods." The book allegedly revealed the true story of the creation of humankind and described an afterlife in the stars for those who followed his teachings.

The Pillars of Hermes

According to legend, Thoth preserved his canon of writings inside two great pillars just before the Great Flood inundated the world. Thousands of years later, the pillars were rediscovered. According to existing texts written by Egyptian priests around 1550 B.C.E., one of the pillars was discovered outside the city of Heliopolis, and the other was unearthed near Thebes.

The massive columns were covered with sacred hieroglyphics. When first discovered, they were referred to as the "Pillars of the Gods of the Dawning Light." Both pillars were eventually moved to a secret temple dedicated to the "First Gods of *Zep Tepi.*" Some texts indicate that this location was the Temple of Amun in Siwa, which is the oldest temple in Egypt. Only priests and pharaohs were allowed to view the sacred objects and scrolls.

The sacred Thothian texts were periodically put on public display and have been mentioned by credible sources throughout history. The Greek legislator and writer Solon (630–560 B.C.E.) studied them firsthand and noted that they memorialized the destruction of an ancient, advanced civilization. The great historian Herodotus (484–413 B.C.E.) encountered the two pillars in a secret Egyptian temple he visited in 400 B.C.E. "One pillar was of pure gold," wrote Herodotus, "and the other was as of emerald, which glowed at night with great brilliancy." Because Hermes is the Greek name for Thoth, he named them the "Pillars of Hermes."

The mysterious Pillars of Hermes were reportedly viewed by Alexander the Great, Achilles Tatius, Dio Chrysostom, and Laertius, and other Roman and Greek historians have described them in detail. In *Iamblichus: On the Mysteries*, Thomas Taylor quotes one ancient writer who noted that the two pillars were created before the Great Flood. The Alexandrian scribe Manetho recorded that the pillars contained 36,525 manuscripts written by Thoth, although it should be noted that this figure is the exact number of days in 100 years, which symbolized ultimate completion to the Egyptians.

The Emerald Tablet

When opened, Thoth's pillars were said to contain not only many sacred manuscripts but also a marvelous artifact that has become known as the *Tabula Smaragdina* ("Emerald Tablet"). The green crystalline tablet carried a succinct summary of the Thothian writings and outlined a new philosophy of the "Whole Universe."

Replica of the original Emerald Tablet based on descriptions in Alexandrian texts.
(From Rosicrucian Alchemy Museum, San Jose, California)

The priests of Amun kept the tablet and other texts in hiding, but its words filtered down into other writings. Phrases from the Emerald Tablet can be found in the Papyrus of Ani (1250 B.C.E.) and in chapters from the *Book of the Dead* (1500 B.C.E.), the Berlin Papyrus No. 3024 (2000 B.C.E.), and other religious scrolls dating between 1000 and 300 B.C.E. One papyrus known as "An Invocation to Hermes," which dates from Hellenic Egypt, actually refers to the tablet: "I know your names in the Egyptian tongue, and your true name as it is written on the Holy Tablet in the holy place at Hermopolis, where you did have your birth."

Not until Alexander the Great (356–323 B.C.E.) conquered Egypt and became its Pharaoh in 332 B.C.E. did knowledge of the tablet's existence spread. Historical documents show that Alexander traveled to Siwa, where he reportedly retrieved the writings of Thoth and the tablet. He then took the items with him to Memphis, Egypt and then on to Hermopolis.

The Treasures of Alexander

The Pillars of Hermes were said to contain more than 300 scrolls in addition to the Emerald Tablet. Reports indicate that Alexander moved them to the Temple of Heliopolis in 332 B.C.E. and put them on public display. Researcher Manly P. Hall found fragments of a letter from one traveler who had seen the Emerald Tablet in Heliopolis. "It is a precious stone, like an emerald," wrote the man, "whereon these characters are represented in bas-relief, not engraved into the stone. It is esteemed above 2,000 years old. Plainly, the matter of this emerald had once been in a fluid state like melted glass, and had been cast in a mold, and to this flux the artist had given the hardness of a natural and genuine emerald, by his art."

Hermetic scholars believe that Alexander built the great library at Alexandria primarily to house and study the Thothian materials, and the writings of a scribe from the Temple of Heliopolis confirmed that view. His name was Manetho (circa 300 B.C.E.), which means "Gift of Thoth," and he was one of the first scribes allowed access to the contents of the pillars. He wrote that the writings were more than 9,000 years old and contained the sum of all knowledge.

Unfortunately, only a few of Manetho's works survived the burning of the great library at Alexandria. Some of his letters to Ptolemy II survived, as well as one of his books, called *Sothis*. In that book, Manetho wrote: "After the Great Flood, the hieroglyphic texts written by Thoth were translated from the sacred language into Greek and deposited in books in the sanctuaries of Egyptian temples."

Manetho wrote that the magical *Book of Thoth*, written in the hand of Thoth himself, was kept in a locked gold box in the inner sanctuary of the Temple at Hermopolis, and only one priest at a time was entrusted with the key. According to some historians, an occult brotherhood known as the "Sons of Horus" was formed before the Arab invasion of Egypt to preserve Thoth's book and his other teachings, as well as the complete works of Manetho. The alchemist Clement of Alexandria was given access to the secret documents in about 170 C.E., but that is the last recorded reference to this original material.

The Fate of the Emerald Tablet

When Alexander left Egypt in 331 B.C.E., he headed north to Cappadocia and Mesopotamia. According to some reports, he took the treasures from the Pillars of Hermes and stored them in an underground cavern in Cappadocia. Supposedly, he was going to pick them up on his return journey home to Macedonia. Alexander went on to conquer all the remaining territory from Babylonia to India but died on the return trip in 323 B.C.E. Alexander's final wish was to be buried near the temple at Siwa in Egypt, but his tomb has never been found.

The legend picks up again in Cappadocia in 32 C.E., when a young boy named Balinas was exploring caves outside the city of Tyana and allegedly discovered the ancient texts hidden by Alexander. The precocious lad took a five-year vow of silence as he absorbed the materials and then sought out teachers versed in Hermetic philosophy to complete his education. He became known as Apollonius of Tyana and was renowned for his magical skills and healing abilities.

Apollonius (15–100 C.E.) is said to have returned the tablet to Alexandria in about 70 C.E. and made the enlightened city his home. He wrote most of his books in Alexandria, though he continued to travel the world, inspiring many people he met with his great wisdom.

As for the Emerald Tablet, a few reports indicate that it was buried for safekeeping in a vault on the Giza plateau in about 400 C.E., but no trace of it has ever been found. The earliest surviving translation of the Emerald Tablet is in the Arabic *Book of Balinas the Wise on Causes*, which was written in about 700 C.E. Several Arabic translations made their way to Europe with the Moorish invasion of Spain in 771 C.E.

The first Latin translation appeared in 1140 C.E. in a book by Johannes Hispalensis called *Book of the Secrets of Creation*. After the alchemist Albertus Magnus issued several more translations in the mid-1200s, the Emerald Tablet spread like wildfire.

Most European alchemists had a copy and often referred to "the secret formula" it contained.

The Legend of Thoth/Hermes

In the history of alchemy, the line between myth and reality has always been blurred. To the Egyptians, Thoth, the father of alchemy, was a divine being, the custodian of all knowledge, and the intermediary between Heaven and Earth. Many modern authors have looked at the legends and surmised that Thoth was a survivor from the lost continent of Atlantis, while others have suggested he might have been an extraterrestrial visitor.

One thing is sure: The mythic status of Thoth cannot be denied. In fact, nearly every ancient culture has some mythic figure that can be associated with Thoth. The Romans identified him with Mercury, their winged god who carried messages between gods and men.

To the Greeks, Thoth became Hermes, a priest, philosopher, and alchemist who lived in Egypt at about the time of Moses. His Latin name, Hermes Trismegistus, means "thrice greatest Hermes." Some writers say this refers to the idea that his writings were created by three different Egyptian teachers—a philosopher, a priest, and a king.

Many medieval alchemists believed Hermes Trismegistus was a real person who lived for centuries and traveled throughout the world. Indeed, because so many later authors wrote under his name, it might have seemed like Hermes lived for hundreds of years. Nevertheless, historical documents trace his presence in Ceylon, India, and Babylonia, where the Arabs venerated him as the first person to have shared his knowledge of the art of alchemy. The oldest written reference to his name is in a papyrus of notes from a meeting of the Ibis Cult near Memphis in 172 B.C.E.

The mythic image of Thrice-Greatest Hermes is of an ancient mage, a gentle and kind man much more accessible than Thoth. Despite his humility, he possessed a unique mastery of all three levels of reality—the physical, the mental, and the spiritual.

Thirteen manuscripts known as the *Corpus Hermeticum* are attributed to Hermes. These alchemical and esoteric teachings from the Alexandrian period were not known in the West until 1471 C.E., when the Italian astrologer Marsilio Ficino (1433–1499) translated them into Latin.

The Staff of Hermes

The primary symbol of Hermes is the caduceus, a staff with two serpents entwined in opposite directions around it. Snakes were considered the most fundamental life form, and because they shed their skins were thought to possess the secret of immortality. The coiled serpent symbolizes the divine fire or reservoir of life force in the body. The caduceus is often shown with two wings, which represents the purified or ascended life force.

The caduceus bears a striking resemblance to the double-helix of proteins that make up DNA, which is the basic blueprint of all life. Several modern authors have suggested that this similarity is a clue that Thoth or someone associated with him manipulated our genetic structure to speed up human evolution within the last 40,000 years.

There is a strange Greek legend that relates how Hermes came to possess the caduceus. One day, a Greek seer named Tiresias was hiking on Mount Kyllene and discovered two snakes copulating alongside the road. In an effort to separate the snakes, he stuck his walking staff between them. Immediately, Tiresias was turned into a woman and remained so for seven years, until once again, he found two copulating serpents and separated them with his staff. At that moment, Tiresias transformed back into a man.

The magical staff, complete with the entwined snakes, was considered too dangerous for anyone to use and was hidden in a cave on Mount Kyllene. The cave, marked by an upright stone phallus, would eventually become the birthplace and home of Hermes. While still a young man, he found the caduceus and eventually learned to harness its power for healing.

Today, Hermes' staff has become the chief logo of the medical profession, and there are certainly more representations of the Hermetic symbol in the world today than at any other time in history. Scholars insist it all began with the mythic Greek healer god Asclepius, who adopted the caduceus to symbolize healing, though the mythic connection goes back much farther to the original Hermes–Thoth. The Ebers Papyrus, a 68-foot-long scroll that is the oldest surviving book in the world, tells us: "Man's guide is Thoth, who bestows on him the gifts of speech, who makes the books and illumines those who are learned therein, and the physicians who follow him, that they may work cures."

Hermetic Philosophy

The esoteric teachings of Thoth and Hermes make up the philosophical foundations of alchemy, and these ideas are summarized in the Emerald Tablet. Take a moment to read the tablet and try to absorb its meaning. It often helps to rewrite the tablet in your own words. Nearly every medieval alchemist from Albertus Magnus to Isaac Newton had his own version of the Emerald Tablet that guided them in their work.

The Emerald Tablet

In truth, without deceit, certain, and most veritable.

That which is Below corresponds to that which is Above, and that which is Above corresponds to that which is Below, to accomplish the miracles of the One Thing. And just as all things come from One Thing, through the thoughts of One Mind, so do all created things originate from this One Thing, through Adaptation.

Its father is the Sun, its mother the Moon. The Wind carries it in its belly; its nurse is the Earth. It is the origin of All, the consecration of the whole Universe; its inherent strength is perfected if it turns into Earth.

Separate the Earth from Fire, the Subtle from the Gross, gently and with great Ingenuity. It ascends from Earth to Heaven and descends again to Earth, thereby combining within Itself the powers of both the Above and the Below.

Thus, will you obtain the Glory of the Whole Universe. All Obscurity will be clear to you. This is the greatest Force of all powers because it conquers every Subtle thing and penetrates every Solid thing.

In this way was the Universe created. From this comes many wondrous Applications because this is the Pattern.

Therefore, am I called Thrice Greatest Hermes, having all three parts of the knowledge of the Whole Universe. Herein have I completely explained the Operation of the Sun.

The first principle presented in the Tablet is known as the Doctrine of Correspondences, which describes a vertical relationship between spirit or energy in the realm Above and matter or manifestation in the realm Below. A powerful envisioning of this vertical axis of reality can be found in a treatise in the *Corpus Hermeticum* called the "Divine Pymander" (or "Divine Mind"). Attributed to Hermes Trismegistus, the text describes his meeting with the One Mind and what it revealed to him about the nature of reality.

The Tablet goes on to elaborate on the nature of the One Thing, which alchemists interpret as the First Matter or primordial stuff of creation. The first two sentences of this paragraph present the Four Elements in the order of Fire, Water, Air, and Earth.

Associated with each of the elements are alchemical operations: Calcination (Fire), Dissolution (Water), Separation (Air), and Conjunction (Earth). We will learn more about the operations of alchemy in Part 4.

The fourth paragraph is the most mystical part of the Emerald Tablet and reveals how to enter the spiritual realm using the alchemical operations of Fermentation (spiritizing matter) and Distillation (a purifying circulation of rising vapors and falling condensate).

The fifth paragraph describes the Quintessence (Fifth Element) that is created by following these instructions. In the next section, we learn this process is a universal Pattern that governs transformation on all levels. It is not only the secret pattern embedded in Nature, but it also is the formula that alchemists follow in the Great Work.

Note that when the tablet refers to the "Universe," it is talking about the physical universe in which we live. When it speaks of the "Whole Universe," it is referencing both the material universe Below and the spiritual universe Above.

The final paragraph identifies the author as Hermes Trismegistus ("Thrice Greatest Hermes"). Free of the cycle of rebirth and existing outside time, he has grasped the "Operation of the Sun" or the inner workings of the Whole Universe.

The Tabula Smaragdina Engraving

Perhaps the easiest way to grasp the principles expressed in the Emerald Tablet is by viewing them pictorially. Renaissance alchemists spent many hours meditating on the Hermetic symbols depicted in a stunning engraving called *Tabula Smaragdina*, which is Latin for "Emerald Tablet" (see the following figure). Created by artist Matthieu Merian, it was first published in 1618 in Daniel Mylius's *Opus Medico-Chymicum* (*The Medical-Chemical Work*).

Let's examine this engraving a little closer to gather some basic insights into the meaning of the Emerald Tablet. The first thing you notice about this engraving is its sharp division into Above and Below sections. The Above is the spiritual realm of light and divine union, while the Below is the manifested realm of matter and duality.

Next, we see two great suns rising over the horizon Above. The larger sun in the background is the ineffable One Mind, whose rays encompass the whole universe. In front of this is a smaller sun known as "Mind the Maker." This we can think of as the mind of nature or the physical laws of the created world.

"Mind the Maker" is an important and controversial Hermetic concept that would have gotten you burnt at the stake if you had spoken of it in the Middle Ages. It implies that

God does not directly participate in our world. Instead, the Word of God was projected into our reality like a template or computer program—what the Emerald Tablet calls the Pattern. In the drawing, these crystallized thoughts of God are represented by the angelic messengers embedded in the smaller sun.

This humanistic concept does not mean the alchemists did not believe in God. On the contrary, they sought to reveal and perfect the original divine light in everything. This is the true nature of the Great Work, and it begins Below in the duality of matter. We see the duality of our material existence in the division of the Below into left and right sections. On the left is the daytime realm of Solar energy and masculine symbols. On the right is the nighttime realm of Lunar energy and feminine symbols.

The Emerald Tablet engraving presents the Hermetic principles in terms of the symbols of alchemy.
(By Matthieu Merian in Daniel Mylius' Opus Medico-Chymicum, 1618)

At the center of the Below is the hermaphroditic Hermes, who wields two starry axes. He has cut the chains that bind us to the world Below and realizes the full power of the archetypal forces Above.

At the heart of the engraving is a bull's-eye target depicting the One Thing of the universe. This is the plethoric chaos that is the origin of all created things. The seven layers of this sphere must be peeled away like an onion to reveal the secret at its core, which is marked with the alchemists' cipher for Mercury. We will learn more about this hidden essence at the heart of chaos in Part 4.

In this chapter, we explored the mythic roots of alchemy in ancient Egypt and discovered a group of divine visitors responsible for the education and evolution of the human species. One of the visitors, Thoth, was the first alchemist, and some of his teachings—notably the Emerald Tablet–have survived to this day. In the next chapter, we will see how Thoth's teachings became a part of Egyptian magic and follow their influence on the development of alchemy.

Egyptian Magic and Alchemy

The word alchemy derives from the Arabic phrase *Al-Khemia*, which means "from the land of Khem." *Khem* is an Egyptian term for "black" that describes the fertile black soil found in the Nile River delta. But in many writings, *Al-Khemia* also referred to the mysterious and secretive black arts or magical tradition of the Egyptians. Our word "chemistry" did not appear until the seventeenth century, and it derives from the same root but is associated with only the laboratory side of the alchemist's work.

The Land of Khem was also the birthplace and home to alchemy for at least 5,000 years. Specifically, scholars consider Egyptian alchemy to span the centuries from 5000 B.C.E. to 350 B.C.E. This was followed by a period of Greek alchemy in Egypt from the arrival of Alexander the Great in 332 B.C.E. to the Arabian invasion in 642 C.E. Arabian alchemy flourished for another 500 years before the heyday of alchemy began in Europe.

Alchemy and Theurgy

At the same time the principles of alchemy were emerging in the writings of Alexandrian scholars, the ancient Egyptian cult of Heka evolved into an organized collection of beliefs and practices that became the basis for modern magic. Heka magic consists of spells and incantations that appeal directly to the gods for their help.

Every god of Egypt had their own special spells, but the most powerful god was Heka himself, who often took on the form of a young boy. He was the source of the boundless energy and creativity necessary for any lasting transformation. Written spells, talismans, and amulets from the Heka cult date back to 4500 B.C.E., and it was actively practiced in Egypt until about 500 C.E.

In the open intellectual climate of Alexandria, there was a merging of Heka practices with the Neoplatonist philosophy of Plotinus (204–270 C.E.) that gave birth to a spiritualized magic known as "theurgy" ("divine working"). The Theurgists described reality as a series of emanations from the One, an ineffable presence outside the universe that was sometimes referred to as "The Good." From the One (called *To Hen* by the Greeks) emanates the Divine Mind (*Nous* or consciousness). From the Divine Mind proceeds Soul (*Psyche*), which includes both individual and world soul. Finally, Soul is the seed of Nature (*Physis* or physical manifestation).

The whole basis of Theurgy is that one can follow the divine emanations back to their source. In other words, a person can evoke and even direct the divine energies by a purifying their own consciousness to the level of the divine mind through meditation, rigorous prayer, fasting, and devotional rituals. Plotinus called the union of the inner divinity of the soul with the Divine Source *henosis*, and he created a school where methods of meditation were taught to help his pupils achieve that state.

The Syrian philosopher Iamblichus (250–325 C.E.), who came to Alexandria to study philosophy, expanded theurgy to include ceremonial practices intended to bring divine energies into the everyday world through the heightened consciousness of the magician. For him, ceremonial magic was a psychospiritual tool that bridged the higher or astral identity of the magician with the Divine Source.

Iamblichus believed all physical creation was equally divine because it was all contained within the One Mind. He made the Platonic idea of the soul's descent or embodiment in matter a central part of his philosophy. In *Theurgia: De Mysteriis Aegyptiorum* ("Theurgy: On the Egyptian Mysteries"), he wrote: "The theurgic discipline leads the soul to the Creator of the world and frees it of everything pertaining to the realm of matter by uniting it with the Sole Eternal Reason or *Logos*."

According to Iamblichus, the source of the Sole Eternal Reason (Logos) is the transcendent, incommunicable Monad or "One" outside of our space and time that cannot be understood by humans. Next is the Dyad, the duality of existence that stands between the One Mind and the myriad of created things. Hermeticists call this the "Mind of Nature" or "Mind the Maker." For Iamblichus, the Monad was the domain of original thought, while the Dyad was the domain of the objects or results of thought. We will explore these concepts in more detail when we build our model of alchemical consciousness in Chapter 22.

The Great Work in Alchemy and Theurgy

Under the Neoplatonist influence in Alexandria, alchemy and theurgy evolved as separate disciplines that shared the same goals of the Great Work. Isolating and purifying the soul, or spiritual essence of plants and minerals, was always part of practical lab work in alchemy. But now the emphasis was on the human soul and the evolution and perfection of the soul of the whole universe.

The powerful new Science of Soul that was developed in Alexandria was a unique blend of practical chemistry, psychology, spirituality, and magic. Both alchemists and theurgists believed all matter, including humankind, was alive with the divine signatures of its creator. Bodies slowly evolved toward a perfect expression of that divine intent, and the alchemists' goal was to speed up this natural process to resurrect the spiritual essences trapped in matter and cause that which already exists in a latent state to become active and grow.

"The Great Work is, above all things, the creation of man by himself," noted French magician Eliphas Levi in his book *Transcendental Magic* (1958). "That is to say, the full and entire conquest of his faculties and his future; it is especially the perfect emancipation of his conscious will, assuring full power over the Universal Magical Agent. This Agent, disguised by the ancient philosophers under the name of the First Matter, determines the forms of modifiable substance, and we can really arrive by means of it at metallic transmutation and the Universal Medicine."

The concept of the First Matter (Prima Materia) was central to both theurgy and alchemy, and it united their practitioners in the Great Work. Like alchemists, theurgists believed the First Matter is the primordial chaos that contains all possibilities. It is an unorganized state of energy or proto-matter that is the same for all substances and exists in an invisible state between energy and matter. The First Matter emerged from chaos and is controlled by the light of consciousness (Logos) from the One Mind.

The Alexandrian Enlightenment

Philosophers, alchemists, magician-sorcerers, and spiritual leaders from around the world visited Alexandria to consult the library's scrolls and confer with other scholars. Even the earliest Greek texts from Alexandria are full of references to Chinese, Indian, Babylonian, Hebrew, and Persian writers and their traditions. Eastern influences of meditation, mind development, Vedic astrology, and Oriental magic are obvious in the writings of the Alexandrians. This high-minded merging of philosophies invigorated and strengthened alchemy, enabling it to survive the coming Dark Ages and bloom again in medieval Europe.

The first alchemist of record in Alexandria was Bolos of Mendes, a sorcerer who lived there in about 300 B.C.E. He was a follower of Democritus (circa 400 B.C.E.), a Greek philosopher who originated the atomic theory of matter. Bolos wrote important treatises on the techniques of tingeing metals, chemistry, and astrology, and he presented a system of sympathetic magic based on how deeply aware the sorcerer could become of the hidden forces of nature.

In Bolos' most influential work, *On Natural and Mystical Things,* he describes the discovery of an ancient text hidden within a great column that dealt with the universal harmony of nature. Many believe this is the first recorded reference to the Emerald Tablet.

Bolos is credited with creating a practical science of alchemy by joining philosophy and theory with practical demonstrations and experimentation. He identified four areas of practical experimentation: Gold, Silver, Precious Stones, and Dyes. A passage from Bolos' *On Natural and Mystical Things* became a fundamental motto of alchemists for the next 2,000 years: "Nature rejoices in Nature; Nature conquers Nature; Nature masters Nature."

Ostanes of Medes (circa 300 B.C.E.) was another sorcerer-alchemist from Alexandria who was a contemporary of Bolos. The Persian alchemist was one of the first to identify the elixir of life, which he described as a "divine water" that cured all maladies. Ostanes had a great influence on early alchemists and is mentioned many times in early scrolls as a respected authority. He personally taught other alchemists—including Pseudo-Democritus, who wrote many early alchemical texts. Ostanes would eventually become the personal alchemist for Alexander the Great.

The most famous and revered of the Alexandrian alchemists was Zosimus of Panopolis (circa 250 C.E.). Arabian alchemists referred to him as "the universal wise man with the brilliant flame." Zosimus worked closely with his sister Theosebeia doing experiments, and he wrote a 28-volume alchemy encyclopedia. Fortunately, most of his encyclopedia survived the burning of the Great Library of Alexandria and provides us with much of our knowledge of how the ancients practiced their craft.

Zosimus wrote many other books, including *The Book of Images*, and he wrote many important commentaries on magic, astrology, and theology. Like Bolos, Zosimus noted that alchemy had its roots in sacred hieroglyphs engraved on ancient pillars, but he emphasized that it was absolutely forbidden to divulge the exact texts to the uninitiated.

Zosimus was a member of the Gnostics, an early group of Christians formed in the first century. He believed that one could only obtain true knowledge of the divine by direct experience and not from religious authorities. He felt that the Great Work of alchemy was to perfect the alchemist himself and that such work would bring out the divinity in both man and nature. With Zosimus, Alexandrian alchemy took a new direction that emphasized its mystical principles.

As we learned in the previous chapter, another important figure in Alexandria was Manetho, a priest and scribe who lived there during the reigns of Ptolemy I (367–283 B.C.E.) and Ptolemy II (323–246 B.C.E.). Records indicate Manetho supervised many important religious projects in Egypt and lived for more than 80 years. Among Manetho's surviving books are *The Sacred Book, On Antiquity and Religion,* and the *Digest of Physics.* He also wrote an encyclopedia of Egyptian history that is considered the most complete and authoritative on record.

Manetho's name literally means "Gift of Thoth," but he was also known by the name *Maani Djehuti,* which means "I have seen Thoth." Manetho was instrumental in translating and interpreting the ancient scrolls attributed to Thoth and is believed by some to have been the first translator of the Emerald Tablet.

Two female alchemists in Alexandria earned the lasting respect of alchemists down through the ages. The first, Maria Prophetissa (also known as Mary the Jewess), lived in about 200 B.C.E. She invented many early alchemical devices, including the *Bain Marie* ("Mary's Bath"), which is a double-boiler water bath that evenly distributes heat to substances. Maria also invented the kerotakis apparatus, a closed vessel in which thin leaves of copper and other metals were exposed to the action of various vapors, such as sulfur and mercury. She discovered hydrochloric acid and was famous for Mary's Black, which she formed by fusing sulfur with a lead-copper alloy.

Maria Prophetissa was famous for her prophetic sayings that stressed the unification of opposing forces. "Invert nature," she advised, "and you will find that which you seek." Another of her sayings was, "Join the male and the female, and you will find what is sought." She is also famous for this mystical dictum that describes the progression of alchemical transformations: "One becomes two, two becomes three, and by means of the third and fourth, it achieves unity; thus the two are but one."

Maria Prophetissa unites the powers Above and Below to reveal the Quintessence, symbolized by the five, five-petal flowers.
(From Symbola Aureae Mensae by Michael Maier, 1617)

The second famous female alchemist in Alexandria and a contemporary of Maria Prophetissa was Kleopatra, who should not be confused with Cleopatra the Hellenic Queen of Egypt. This Kleopatra is credited with inventing the chief laboratory apparatus of alchemists down through history—the alembic or still head. Distillation enabled alchemists to purify substances into their most essential components and is the most important operation in chemistry.

Kleopatra's philosophical writings on alchemy stressed the importance of bringing inanimate substances and chemicals to life, and she compared the work of alchemy to the creation of a fetus in the womb.

Greek Philosophy and Alchemy

Not only were the Alexandrian alchemists inventing new equipment and improving ancient techniques, but they also fundamentally altered alchemical philosophy. Most of these new ideas came from Greek philosophers.

The philosophy of Plato (429–347 B.C.E.) that matter was fashioned into its forms by qualities imposed on it from an archetypal realm of ideals also fueled the alchemists' belief in the transformation of the metals. The Greeks taught that the microcosm and macrocosm obeyed the same set of universal laws and that heavenly bodies could influence events on Earth. In the Emerald Tablet, the idea of the macrocosm is represented by the word "Above" and the idea of the microcosm is represented by the word "Below." The philosophy here is that "All Is One"; that is, the same laws apply to all levels of reality.

Aristotle (385–322 B.C.E.), who was Alexander's instructor in alchemy, was deeply respected in Alexandria and his theory of the Four Elements found full expression among the alchemists there. Aristotle's belief that nature strives toward perfection is clearly part of the alchemical idea that all metals grow toward the perfection of gold within the bowels of the earth.

Another Greek idea that became part of the philosophy of alchemy was the belief that nature itself is alive and aware, and it participates in changes in its environment. In other words, there is a celestial consciousness embedded in the world responsible for the changes we experience. Thus, the alchemists considered all matter to be alive with an intrinsic intelligence. Any substance could be transformed and perfected if that indwelling spirit—sometimes called the Magisterium—could be purified and resurrected.

The Concept of Transmutation

One of the biggest philosophical changes in alchemy took place during the Greek period in Egypt near the end of the fourth century B.C.E. and had to do with the transformation of metals. Today, we refer to the permanent transformation of one metal into another as *transmutation*. However, it is apparent from surviving manuscripts that the Egyptians judged metals by the physical qualities of color, hardness, texture, and weight, and if a metal looked like gold, they considered it to be gold.

As mentioned earlier, the Egyptians were unsurpassed in the arts of dying fabrics, tinting glass and gemstones, and tingeing metals. To change the colors and textures of metals, they dipped them into acids and other chemical solutions, alloyed them with various metals, gilded them with gold, or treated them with a variety of polishes and secret compounds. When changing the appearance of metals, however, the Egyptians were not consciously faking things. They really believed the metals could be changed into one another by manipulating their visible qualities. For instance, in the Leiden

Papyrus, an alchemical scroll written in 727 B.C.E., there are numerous recipes for the coloring and gilding of metals, but the concept of actual transmutation does not arise.

Starting in about 50 B.C.E., however, a distinct change in the way alchemists described the transformation of metals can be found in the Alexandrian texts. The practical recipes on tingeing and gilding metals were gone. Instead, changes in the physical appearance of metals were interpreted in spiritual terms, and the mystical connection between the alchemist and their work became crucial to the success of the work.

In a long commentary to the librarian of the Serapeum in Alexandria, the alchemist Synesius (373–414 C.E.) tried to summarize the development of this fundamental change in attitude among alchemists. Although the metaphysical methods he described are rather obscure, there is no doubt alchemists of the new millennium were convinced their spiritual techniques produced real and permanent transformation of the metal itself and not just its appearance. The concept of alchemical transmutation was born.

Destruction of the Alexandrian Texts

While alchemy flourished around the world at the beginning of the first millennium, the deteriorating political climate in Egypt had already spelled disaster for the Great Library at Alexandria.

The first assault came because of a conflict between the Egyptian co-ruler Ptolemy XIII and his sister Cleopatra. The Roman ruler Julius Caesar arrived in 48 B.C.E. to resolve the conflict and named Cleopatra the sole ruler. But her brother blockaded the port of Alexandria and war broke out, resulting in the Great Library catching fire with an estimated 400,000 manuscripts lost. The 300,000 remaining manuscripts at the Great Library were then moved to an adjoining temple called the Serapeum and to a center for scholars known as the Museum.

What remained of the library survived another three centuries. Then in 270 C.E., the Queen of Syria invaded Egypt and occupied Alexandria for two years before the Romans drove her out. During the occupation, the Museum was partly destroyed and more books were lost.

By 275 C.E., the mystical and secretive writings of alchemists in Alexandria had caught the attention of Roman authorities. Finally, in 290 C.E., Emperor Diocletian decreed the destruction of all manuscripts on alchemy in Egypt, which resulted in a further loss of precious original works on alchemy.

Then in 312 C.E., Christianity became the official religion of the Roman Empire, and in 391 C.E., Emperor Theodosius banned all pagan sects. Christian zealots immediately attacked the Serapeum temple library, destroyed nearly all the books, and turned it into a Christian church.

The Museum survived until 415 C.E., when Christian mobs dragged Hypatia, the last librarian, out into the street and accused her of being a heretic and teaching Greek philosophy. Using abalone shells, they scraped the flesh from her body while she was still alive.

What remained of the Great Library of Alexandria consisted of fewer than 30,000 volumes, which were moved into a small building for safekeeping. The final straw for the library came when the Arabs conquered Egypt in 642 C.E., and Caliph Umar instructed his men to burn all the remaining books.

Alchemy in Asia

Alchemists in China and India, who had been inspired by the writings of the Alexandrians, made great strides in their craft. From 300 B.C.E. onward, alchemy spread rapidly throughout Asia. It should be remembered, however, that both Chinese and Indian alchemy were well developed centuries before the rise of Alexandria.

Alchemy had surfaced in China in about 500 B.C.E. and had its roots in Taoism, a system of philosophy that originated with a Hermes-like sage known as Lao Tsu. His teachings became the basis for a tradition of inner alchemy that focused on the transformation of the practitioner's life force (known as *Chi*). The basic premise of this kind of biological alchemy is that humans have only a limited supply of the life force in their bodies. This leaks away through the day-to-day activities of living, but it is possible to accumulate the life force and live for centuries if one understands alchemy. Lao Tsu's alchemy must have worked, for many reports say he lived nearly 200 years. His followers developed a huge body of writings that consisted of more than 1,500 manuscripts. Of these, about 500 deal with alchemy.

Taoist alchemy rests on the same basic principles revealed in the Emerald Tablet, and there are many possible explanations for these similarities. According to legend, the Egyptian Hermes traveled throughout Asia and lived in what is now Ceylon for some time. There are even some references to Hermes' presence in ancient Indian religious texts. In terms of the Emerald Tablet, the life force or Chi is the One Thing, which is transformed by the "meditation of One Mind." This idea shows up in Taoist alchemy in the Chi follows mind principle. By learning to focus the light of consciousness, the practitioner hopes to transform and control the life force.

Taoist alchemical texts discuss recipes for creating various mineral elixirs, provide descriptions of alchemical apparatus, and give rituals and meditations for purification and focusing of the mind of the alchemist. Taoist alchemists also experimented with the life-giving properties of gold, cinnabar (a sulfur-mercury ore), jade, pearls, lapis lazuli, rubies, and many other minerals, as well as thousands of herbs.

By 300 B.C.E., Chinese alchemists were attempting to transmute base metals into gold but not necessarily for material wealth like so many of their counterparts in the West. The Chinese were focused on extending life and saw gold as an essential ingredient in the much-sought Golden Elixir of Immortality.

One of the most famous Chinese alchemists was Ko Hung (283–343 C.E.). As a child, he was trained in the strict moral doctrines of Confucianism but embraced Taoism as a young man. He became an alchemist and spent the rest of his life searching for the elixir of life. His gentle philosophy was a blend of Confucian ethics and Taoist mysticism that he described in a monumental work called *He Who Holds to Simplicity*.

In one of his alchemical treatises, Ko Hung described the three kinds of alchemy practiced in China. The first, he said, concerned the preparation of a drinkable gold liquid that produced longevity. The second was about producing an artificial cinnabar or red stone that could be projected to perfect any substance instantly. The final kind of alchemy concerned the actual transmutation of base metals into physical gold.

Like the Chinese, the Indian alchemists were conscious of accumulating the life force, which they symbolized as kundalini, a serpent of vital energy coiled at the base of the spine. Also, like the Chinese, Indian alchemists associated medicinal gold solutions with longevity and immortality.

Sanskrit texts mentioning alchemical methods and the elixir of life date back to 1000 B.C.E., but very few original alchemy manuscripts from India still exist. We know the alchemical tradition flourished in India from 900 to 1300 C.E. However, except for an oral tradition that survives in the Tamil communities in southern India, all that remains today is a popular system of health tonics and elixir therapy called *rasayana*.

Rasayana is a Sanskrit word that literally means the path (yana) of the elixir (rasa). It is considered the rejuvenation branch of the ancient Indian health tradition of Ayurveda, which is another Sanskrit word meaning knowledge (veda) of the life force (ayur). Rasayana alchemists still make mercury cures, gem elixirs, herbal tonics, and other alchemical products sold throughout modern India.

By 1100 C.E., both Chinese and Indian alchemists were clearly becoming less concerned with practical lab work and more focused on the spiritual techniques of transformation. The metals had become identified with various parts of the human body, and the purified essences the alchemists sought to work with were to be found within. The outer laboratory became the inner laboratory.

In fact, Taoist adepts began seeing themselves as spiritual metals whose duty was to work their transmutations in a world of base metals or common mortals. Among Taoist alchemists, there was tremendous optimism that changing the world was possible. But even as the spirit of alchemy soared to new heights in the Orient, it was nearly extinguished in the West during the Dark Ages.

How the Arabs Saved Alchemy

Although the Arabs destroyed what remained of the Great Library of Alexandria, they were ultimately responsible for preserving alchemical knowledge. As the Arabs established a new civilization throughout Persia, Palestine, Syria, Egypt, Arabia, Asia Minor, North Africa, and eventually Gibraltar and Spain, they assimilated a great deal of diverse cultures in a short period of time and were eager to acquire those cultures' knowledge. From its founding around 750 C.E., Baghdad became a center of learning, and manuscripts from all around the world made their way to the city.

While a handful of the Alexandrian manuscripts made their way to Constantinople, most of the more important works ended up in Arabia. Many Alexandrian scrolls had already been translated into Arabic, and others were smuggled out of Egypt after Emperor Diocletian's decree of 290 C.E.

In about 400 C.E., a mystical group of Christians known as the Nestorians saved many alchemical manuscripts by taking them to Persia and Arabia for safekeeping. The Sabeans of Harran, a Syrian group of astronomers and alchemists, translated many Alexandrian alchemy texts into their native dialect before they were exiled to Mesopotamia in 489 C.E.

Knowledge of alchemy had spread through Babylon to the Orient in about 500 C.E. and finally reached Europe with the Moorish invasion of Spain in 711 C.E. At its peak, the Muslim occupation of Europe encompassed Spain, Gibraltar, and most of Portugal and southern France. Cordoba, in Spain, became the new center of alchemical knowledge, and Muslim, Jewish, and Christian alchemists and mystics all flocked to the city.

Notable alchemists who came to Cordoba to live and work included Muhammad ibn Umail (900–960), Maslamah ibn Ahmed (950–1007), and Moses ben Maimon (1108–1204) (also known as Robert of Chester). Like Alexandria, the crossbreeding of ideas in Cordoba resulted in a flood of new ideas. Jewish texts like the *Zohar* ("Book of Splendor") and the *Sepher Jetzirah* ("Book of Formation") gave birth to the Kabbalah, and many lost alchemy manuscripts were retrieved after they were translated back into Latin from Arabian. Finally, with the Crusades, the Templars and other travelers who went to fight for the Holy Land further dispersed the Arabian texts throughout Europe.

The Babylonian Hermes and Arabian Alchemy

The Muslims knew the legend of Thoth, the Hermes of the Greeks, and called him Hirmis or Idris. According to Arabian legend, Hermes was exiled from Egypt and came to Babylon to teach. The Babylonian Hermes wrote at least 15 new books on alchemy and magic, including *The Great Epistle of the Celestial Spheres*.

Many works by Greek philosophers were among the Arabian alchemical translations. Plato, or "Aflatun," was considered by Arabians to be a great alchemist who invented several devices for use in the laboratory. According to the Arab tradition, Pythagoras (known as "Fithaghurus") acquired his knowledge of mathematics and alchemy from the scrolls found in the Pillars of Hermes. Pathagoras' *Book of Adjustments* became immensely popular among Arabian alchemists.

There were also translations of the works of a teacher of Socrates named Archelaos (circa 350 B.C.E.), to whom Arabs attribute the great alchemical treatise *Turba Philosophorum*. Also, translations exist of the oral teachings of Socrates, who was considered a practicing alchemist who successfully generated an artificial life form. Socrates never publicly admitted to being an alchemist and was opposed to writing down any alchemical treatises for fear they would fall into the wrong hands.

Aristotle, who the Arabs called "Aristu," was revered as a great alchemist and scholar. Aristotle wrote a book on alchemy for his student, Alexander the Great, which by order of Heraclius, was translated into Syrian in 618. Several works by Aristotle survived only in Arabic, including a discourse between him and Alexander called *Epistle of the Great Treasure of God*. The book has three chapters entitled "About the Great Principles of Alchemy," "Alchemic Operations," and "The Elixir." In it, Aristotle reviews the alchemical writing of Hermes, Asclepius, Pythagoras, Plato, Democritus, and Ostanes.

The other writings of the Alexandrian alchemists also became popular in Arabia, and many translations were made. The works of Bolos of Mende and Zosimus were especially popular. A group of Hermetic Muslims called the Brothers of Purity compiled an encyclopedia of alchemical theory and practice in the years between 909 and 965 that consolidated the diverse teachings.

The first Muslim alchemist, Khalid ibn Yazid (660–704), was initiated into alchemy by Morienus, a Christian hermit and alchemist who flourished in the 650s. His student, Khalid, wrote several original treatises on alchemy. Khalid's castle became a vibrant center for alchemy in the seventh century, with visiting alchemists sharing their books and discussing their ideas with each other.

One influential Arabian alchemist was Al-Razi (866–925), who is known in the West as Rhazes. He was a Persian alchemist and physician who taught in Baghdad, and he was an even more prolific writer than Jabir and authored 33 books on natural science, mathematics, and astronomy and 48 more on philosophy, logic, and theology. He authored 21 books on alchemy, including his influential *Compendium of Twelve Treatises* and *Secret of Secrets.*

Rhazes was a very accurate and systematic experimenter who produced the first classification of metals, chemicals, and other substances. He was also known as a compassionate teacher and humanitarian who personally distributed gifts to the poor and nursed the sick back to health with his own preparations.

Not all alchemists fared well in the Arabian lands. Al-Tughari, a widely respected alchemist born in 1063, worked as a civil servant, but politics proved to be his undoing, and he was publicly executed in 1121. Before he died, Tughari wrote many important books and poems on alchemy. He claimed to have gotten his esoteric knowledge directly from Hermes, and indeed, his work is very sophisticated and can only be understood by advanced students. Tughari's most famous work is *The Lamps and the Keys,* in which he presents ancient Hermetic teachings and theories of alchemy.

Thanks to Arabian alchemy, the basic laboratory methods of distillation, sublimation, dissolution, calcination, and crystallization were greatly improved and better understood. The refining of metals and alloys was also perfected. Overall, the greatest contribution was the development of chemical apparatus and experimental techniques. The Arabs were meticulous and untiring in their experimentation and made careful written observation of their results. They designed their experiments to gather information and answer specific questions, which represented the true beginning of the scientific method.

Jabir's Gibberish

The greatest Arabian alchemist was Jabir ibn Hayyan (721–815), who wrote an astonishing number of books that dealt with every aspect of alchemy. Among his most important works are *Book of the Kingdom, Little Book of the Balances, Book of Mercury,* and *Book of Concentration.* He also translated dozens of alchemy manuscripts and saved many original texts that had been lost when the Great Library of Alexandria was destroyed.

Jabir was a fanatical experimenter, and his practical guides to alchemy included the refining of metals; preparation of steel; dying of cloths and leather; the making of varnishes to protect cloth and iron; writing with gold ink from pyrites; glassmaking using manganese dioxide; distilling acetic acid from vinegar; and producing lead carbonate, arsenic, and antimony from their sulfides. Jabir corrected experimental errors and references in the works of Pythagoras, Plato, Aristotle, and other Greek philosophers and developed his own complex numerological system of scientific alchemy.

But Jabir was so careful to conceal the true principles of alchemy that his works rarely made sense to outsiders, and the term "gibberish" originally referred to his writings. Nonetheless, to the initiated, Jabir is still held in the highest esteem.

Jabir believed the metals formed from two primeval forces or exhalations deep in the bowels of the earth. The dry exhalation became Sulfur, and the wet exhalation was Mercury. The various metals then formed by differing purities and concentrations of Sulfur and Mercury, and gold formed from the purest and most balanced combination of these two primordial elements. To transform base metals into gold, one must purify and balance their Sulfur and Mercury. He also popularized the idea of a Philosopher's Stone that would instantly combine the Sulfur and Mercury essences of base metals to make gold. Jabir spent the rest of his life trying to find it.

Jabir's Sulfur-Mercury Theory of the metals was the single greatest advance in alchemical philosophy of the Arabian era. Alexandrian alchemists had planted the seed with their observations of the actions of sulfur and mercury compounds in the kerotakis apparatus. The preparation of cinnabar (a brilliant red sulfide of mercury) was made by the union of sulfur and mercury in the apparatus, and this process always held a powerful fascination for the Greek alchemists who considered sulfur and mercury "tincturing spirits" because of their ability to color and alloy the metals. This was the first inkling that sulfur and mercury were more than just common substances.

Jabir combined the kerotakis observations with Aristotle's theory that the Elements Earth and Water give rise to smoky and vaporous exhalations deep in the earth. The earthy smoke consisted of Earth burning (changing into Fire), and the watery vapor was Water evaporating (changing into Air).

Jabir added to Aristotle's theory the idea that sulfur and mercury formed as byproducts of these elementary exhalations. The range of metals was created when sulfur and mercury recombined in various degrees of purity and proportion. Jabir theorized that the two "tincturing spirits" of sulfur and mercury acted like two dyes that could be mixed to produce a range of colors, or in this case, a range of metals.

The treatises of Jabir became widely known in Europe under his Latin name Geber, and his works were translated into Latin in the fourteenth century by someone historians now refer to as "Pseudo-Geber." Unfortunately, Pseudo-Geber became so enthused about the original Jabir's work that he decided it would not hurt if he published a few of his own books under the illustrious name of Geber. So be forewarned: while Jabir is always Jabir, Geber is not always Jabir.

In this chapter, we peered deeper into history to understand the development of the concepts of alchemy from the perspective of the people and circumstances involved. This kind of living history is the best way to get a real understanding for the philosophical development of alchemy. Much of the story of alchemy centered on Alexandria, the great shining beacon of enlightenment in the ancient world. When that light was finally extinguished around 600 c.e., it marked the beginning of the 500-year-long Dark Ages. In the next chapter, we conclude our examination of the development of alchemical concepts as the light of Alexandria is rekindled in the Middle Ages and Renaissance.

CHAPTER
4

The Rebirth of Alchemy in Europe

After the outpouring of inspired alchemical manuscripts in Alexandria, the craft of alchemy went into a dormant phase and was actively pursued only in Arabia and the East. The West was in the grip of the Dark Ages, a period of stagnate intellectual growth and lack of innovation that lasted from the destruction of the Alexandrian Library and fall of the Roman Empire (476 C.E.) to the beginning of the second millennium (1000 C.E.).

Arabian invaders brought alchemy back to life in Europe through the infusion of Alexandrian manuscripts and commentaries they brought with them when they crossed over from Morocco in 711 C.E. Although they occupied Spain for more than 700 years, the Islamic rulers proved very tolerant, and Spain soon became a haven for Jews and other persecuted minorities. The new rulers also encouraged learning in what some historians refer to as a mini renaissance in Europe.

The Emerald Tablet and other alchemy manuscripts were first translated into Latin in the early 1100s and quickly spread throughout Europe. Scholars eagerly embraced the new ideas, which resulted in a wide dissemination of alchemy manuscripts. However, alchemy proved to be a complex tradition full of special jargon and symbolic images, and the ancient craft was not so easily deciphered.

Try as they might, early students of alchemy failed to grasp the deeper meanings of the new ideas and most preferred literal interpretations that did not require too much thought. In the cryptic, multilevel language of alchemy, interpreting anything literally spells disaster, so before long, European alchemists were trapped in a quagmire of gibberish and contradictory concepts. Only one literal fact seemed clear, and that was that alchemy was about making gold. The early alchemists' feverish attempts to transform base metals into gold resulted in the discovery of acids, alcohols, alloys, and hundreds of new compounds.

This practical tradition of laboratory work was the precursor to modern chemistry, but there was a deeper spiritual tradition in alchemy that took longer to resurface in Europe. In Alexandria, during the last 50 years B.C.E., a more metaphysical view of alchemy based on spiritual and psychological work began to emerge. This Hermetic interpretation combined the fire of nature with the fire of the mind as the single agent of change in the universe. These teachings were summarized in the Emerald Tablet, which describes the relationship between the One Mind of the universe and the One Thing of the manifested world.

The fundamental struggle between empirical alchemists (who believe knowledge comes only from sensory experience) and metaphysical alchemists (who believe knowledge is conceptual and can arise in independently in consciousness) fueled the spread of alchemical ideas. Alchemy became the leading intellectual movement in Europe. Many universities replaced the works of Aristotle with texts attributed to Hermes, and even the Catholic Church honored Hermes Trismegistus as one of its founders. It was the heyday of alchemy.

The First European Alchemists

The first translation of an Arabian alchemy manuscript in Europe was the *Book of the Composition of Alchemy* by Morienus, who had lived in the seventh century. In 1144, Robert of Chester, who had translated the *Koran* and introduced algebra and other Arabian teachings to the West, translated Morienus' book into Latin.

Soon after Robert's translations began circulating, the floodgates opened, and by 1200, Europe was inundated with hundreds of Arabian books. So much translating was going on that the Archbishop of Toledo in Spain founded a new college completely devoted to making Latin translations of Arabian works. One of his translators, Gerard of Cremona (1114–1187), single-handedly translated 76 manuscripts, including important alchemy books by Avicenna and Jabir.

Many writers were also ready to interpret the confusing alchemy texts for the eager Europeans. Writers, such as Vincent of Beauvais and Bartholomew the Englishman, added long commentaries to the Latin translations of Arabian alchemy works, and other authors wrote whole books trying to explain what the Arabs were saying. Jewish scholar Moses Maimonides (1135–1204) wrote a popular commentary on alchemy entitled *Guide for the Perplexed.*

Before long, Europe was producing its own alchemists. The first of these was a Swabian monk by the name of Albertus Magnus ("Albert the Great"), who lived from 1193 to 1280. Albertus was a true genius, so skilled in all forms of knowledge that he was called *Doctor Universalis.* He became an adept in alchemy, and his lab work resulted in the discovery of potassium, lye, and many other useful compounds.

Albertus Magnus points to the creation of the hermaphrodite as part of the Great Work of alchemy.
(From Viridarium Chymicum by Daniel Stolzius von Stoltzenberg, 1624)

Through his meticulous observations of the metals, Albertus became aware of the regular repetition of their properties. He created the first periodic table in which the characteristics of the elements repeat in an eightfold cycle. "The metals are similar in their essence, and differ only in their form," he summarized. "One may pass easily from one to another, following a definite cycle."

Albertus taught at several universities, including universities in Freiburg, Cologne, and Paris, and he initiated many other Europeans into alchemy. One of his students was

St. Thomas Aquinas, who became one of the world's greatest philosophers. Aquinas popularized the works of Aristotle and wrote a monumental compendium of religious philosophy called *Summa Theologica*. He is also thought to have created the influential text *Aurora Consurgens* ("The Rising Dawn"), which is an alchemical interpretation of the biblical "Song of Songs."

Aquinas was a prolific writer, but after having a mystical experience in December 1273, he never wrote another word. As a result, several of his most important works end abruptly in the middle of a paragraph. He told his fellow monks that during meditation he had seen a vision of Sophia, the divine feminine principle suppressed by the patriarchal Church. He said he had found the Philosopher's Stone in the silent wisdom of Sophia, and after that profound experience, everything he had written seemed irrelevant.

The Wizardry of Roger Bacon

Educated at Oxford and Parisian universities, Roger Bacon was another medieval genius who mastered numerous disciplines. Like Leonardo da Vinci, Bacon created drawings and models of airplanes, helicopters, tanks, submarines, and other inventions centuries ahead of his time. He drew one of the first complete maps of the world and created the more exact Gregorian calendar we still use today. He also built early microscopes and telescopes and constructed a towering observatory that survived for centuries.

Bacon was initiated into alchemy by a mysterious Frenchman named Master Peter, whom Bacon often referred to as the "Lord of Experimentation." Others suggest that Albertus Magnus initiated Bacon in Paris, but whoever taught him, Bacon quickly became Europe's leading alchemist. He shared formulae for numerous useful compounds, including gunpowder, and produced powerful tinctures and elixirs. He is also said to have achieved successful transmutations of the metals.

In *Mirror of Alchemy*, Bacon described his practical view of alchemy: "Alchemy is a science teaching how to transform any kind of metal into another through the use of the proper medicine. Alchemy therefore is about how to make and compound a certain medicine, called the Elixir, such that when it is cast upon metals or imperfect bodies of any kind, it fully perfects them in the very projection. The first principles of this Elixir can be found in nature and are called Sulfur and Mercury, and all metals and minerals are begotten of these two. But I must tell you that nature always intends and strives to the perfection of gold, yet there are many accidents coming between the metals that change their purity."

Unfortunately, Bacon was so far ahead of his time that his contemporaries believed he was in league with the devil, and his antisocial behavior did not help dispel the rumors. He was said to have created a talking head of brass that revealed dark secrets to him and a mirror in which he could see into the future.

Although he was a Franciscan monk with a Doctorate in Divinity from Oxford, Bacon was constantly in trouble with the Church, which kept a close eye on his activities. Finally, in 1257, a Church court accused him of practicing sorcery and placed him under house arrest in Oxford for the rest of his life.

Pope Clement IV released him from his sentence in 1267 on the condition that Bacon write down all his knowledge in one book. The result was a vast compendium of mathematics, science, and philosophy called the *Opus Majus* ("The Major Work"). In it, Bacon summarized all branches of science and proposed they were all part of a single true philosophy that had been lost to mankind.

But Bacon continued to criticize the Church and even declared that the ancient civilizations of Egypt and Greece were morally superior to the Christian world. Not surprisingly, he was sentenced to prison for heresy in 1278 but was released 14 years later by the head of the Franciscan order after Bacon shared certain alchemical secrets with him. In his typically defiant fashion, Bacon immediately began work on *Compendium Theologiae,* a book about the theological errors and faults of Catholicism. His superiors were incensed at his impudence, but because he had an ally in the head of the Franciscan order, he avoided prison this time.

But the Church never forgave Roger Bacon, and his works are still banned. When he died in 1294, his fellow monks nailed all the books in his library to their shelves and left them to rot unopened.

Alchemy and the Church

Roger Bacon's run-ins with Church authorities were typical of the relationship between alchemists and religious authorities in the Middle Ages and Renaissance. To avoid conflicts, some alchemists deliberately concealed their work in Christian terminology. For example, the word "Christ" was often used to refer to the Philosopher's Stone. Other alchemists stopped publishing their ideas or went into hiding.

The Church was always suspicious of alchemists' preoccupation with meditation and spiritual development. The chillingly unsympathetic position of the Church was read into court records in 1687, during the heresy trial of Miguel de Molinos (1628–1696). Molinos was an advocate of meditation and quiet contemplation, but he crossed the line when he asserted that anyone could practice prayer and meditation in the presence of God in the privacy of their own chambers.

According to the representative of the Pope, the only duty of the Church was to preserve ritual and maintain the physical presence of the Church and not to invoke the spiritual enlightenment of individuals. The Church banned all Molinos' writings and sentenced him to life in prison, where he died nine years later.

Of course, the Church's fury was not directed just against alchemists and people seeking spiritual development. Anyone who healed with herbs or extolled the virtues of natural cures was accused of practicing the Black Arts. The Church had declared that the devil caused all disease, which could only be cured by exorcisms performed by priests. Anyone else was interfering with the will of God.

The Conscious Universe of Giordano Bruno

One alchemist who could not be silent was mathematician and alchemist Giordano Bruno (1548–1600). Fascinated by the nature of consciousness and how memories were formed, he created a geometry of language to clarify thought processes. Bruno gave public lectures on the principles of the Emerald Tablet, describing the tablet's "Operation of the Sun" as the grand symbol of all natural processes. He boldly asserted that the sun was the center of the cosmos, in direct violation of Church dogma. Then he went so far as to assert that consciousness was part of the fabric of the universe, which contained many other worlds that harbored intelligent life.

That declaration was too much for the Church, and in 1576, they attempted to arrest him on charges of heresy. Bruno, who was a Dominican priest, got wind of the action against him and fled, but the Church pursued him across Europe as he continued to publish his heretical manuscripts. Finally, the priests of the Inquisition caught up with him in 1592 and began a seven-year trial. During the long proceedings, they listed every single blasphemous statement Bruno ever made and demanded he recant each one. When he refused to recant something, they tortured him mercilessly. Still, he refused to take back anything he had said or written. When the Inquisitors realized they could not break him, they sentenced him to death, and on February 8, 1600, a gag was tied tightly around Bruno's tongue to silence him, and he was burned alive in public.

Black Death and the Rise of Medical Alchemy

It has been estimated that more than three million people were burned at the stake during the Middle Ages. Girls could be tortured for witchcraft from the age of 9, and boys from the age of 10. Homosexuals were sometimes thrown into the fires of burning witches. The Church also proclaimed that all cats were demons to be burned along with witches. Cats were imprisoned alive in the walls of buildings to ward off evil spirits, and at Easter, cats were locked in wicker baskets and thrown into bonfires.

These Church practices are said to have killed so many cats that the rat population surged, which contributed to the rapid spread of the Black Death (bubonic plague) in the fourteenth century. Nearly half the population of Europe perished—including at least one Pope and hundreds of Inquisitors.

The Black Death had another unforeseen consequence. It gave rise to the great need for medicines, and alchemists were at the cutting edge in the search for new cures. Alchemists produced many herbal tinctures and tonics that provided relief to diseased people, and the silver and mercury-based antibiotics created by alchemists were the only effective tools for the treatment of syphilis, pneumonia, infections, and the plague.

Arnold of Villanova (1240–1311) was a Spanish alchemist who became a leader of medical alchemy in the late thirteenth century. His tonics cured many ailments, and his elixirs were said to rejuvenate body tissue and increase longevity. He treated several national leaders and popes, although he was briefly imprisoned in Paris for his heretical views on the alchemical nature of the Holy Trinity.

Paracelsus, one of the greatest alchemists of all time, is considered the founder of modern medicine. He was the first to begin using chemicals as drugs in the treatment of disease. His hybrid of alchemy and medicine, which he called *iatrochemistry,* became extremely popular in the sixteenth and seventeenth centuries. The word comes from the Greek word for doctor (*iatros*) and literally means "doctor-chemistry." Iatrochemists believed that health was dependent on keeping a specific balance of bodily fluids that could be controlled by understanding the effect of chemicals in the body.

Nicolas Flamel's Powder of Projection

Another alchemist who benefited the infirm and diseased people of the Middle Ages was Nicolas Flamel (1330–1418). Yet he was no doctor, nor did he produce miraculous cures. Instead, the penniless bookseller suddenly became extraordinarily rich and gave huge sums of money and property to hospitals and other charities. He founded several free hospitals, free schools for the blind, and homes for the poor throughout France. His explanation for his newfound wealth was that he had discovered the secret of making gold.

Nicolas Flamel was well educated in the Hermetic arts, had been initiated into alchemy, and had a driving passion to discover the Philosopher's Stone. His bookstore was full of alchemy books, and he was always on the lookout for new manuscripts to add to his library. One day, a young Jewish man came to him with a rare alchemy book to sell, and Flamel gladly paid him the requested price of two florins. This was during a period in history when Jewish people were being expelled from France, and many of them were selling treasured possessions before fleeing to safety in Islamic Spain.

The curious book had an ancient binding of worked copper on which were engraved curious diagrams and certain characters, some of which were Greek and Hebrew and others unknown. The pages of the book were not parchment but were the bark of young trees covered with script written with an iron point. The pages were divided into groups of seven and consisted of three parts separated by a page showing a strange and unintelligible diagram.

The edges of the book were covered in gold leaf, and the title page listed the author as "Abraham the Jew—Prince, Priest, Levite, Astrologer, and Philosopher." There were curses against anyone who read the book who was unworthy of its contents, and every page carried the word *Maranatha!*, which was a Syrian expression used by Jews of the time as a curse on their enemies. It meant literally, "the Lord cometh to execute vengeance on you."

Flamel could not make any sense of the book. He copied pages from the book, displayed them in his store, and sent them to experts hoping someone might understand parts of them. After 21 years of trying to decipher the book, Flamel decided to travel to Spain to seek the help of Jewish scholars who had settled there. Flamel left the book in safekeeping with his wife and only took a handful of pages copied from the book. He hoped to entice someone to make the journey back to Paris with him to help translate the entire book.

In Leon, Flamel met an elderly Jewish scholar who was familiar with the book of Abraham the Jew and wanted very much to see it for himself, but the man died on their return journey. Fortunately, the scholar had recognized the script on the copied pages as ancient Chaldean and translated several pages. That was enough for Flamel and his wife to begin translating the remaining pages, and three years later, they finished the complete translation.

According to his diaries, Flamel followed the instructions of Abraham the Jew and changed a half-pound of mercury first into silver and then into pure gold. Simultaneously, as Flamel put it, he "accomplished the same transmutation in my soul."

After only three transmutations of mercury into gold, Flamel was rich beyond his dreams, yet he kept none for himself. Instead, he gave it away to charity. At nearly all his charities, Flamel commissioned strange stones or plaques containing alchemical symbols. Alchemists still make the pilgrimage to view mysterious symbols at Saint-Jacques-la-Boucherie Church, the Cemetery of the Innocents, and other works commissioned by Flamel.

Flamel continued his lifelong labor of copying manuscripts and studying alchemy, but soon lost interest in making gold. Because he saw his fellow alchemists ruined by the love of gold, he locked away Abraham's book and never shared its contents with anyone. He felt that the physical transmutations in his lab had somehow initiated a greater spiritual gold growing within him and his wife, Pernelle, that was worth more than any material possessions.

Flamel continued to live the quiet life of a scholar and wrote many important books on alchemy. He and his wife lived a long, vigorous life into their 80s. He carefully planned how he wanted his wife and himself to be buried and had his tombstone prepared beforehand. It shows a bright sun above a key with a closed book in the middle of various figures. Many have taken this to mean that Flamel chose not to share the key to alchemy with an impure world.

His tombstone can still be seen at his gravesite in Paris at the Musee de Cluny at the end of the nave of the Saint-Jacques-la-Boucherie Church. After the death of Flamel and his wife, their house, monuments, and even his grave were nearly destroyed by people searching for gold or alchemical secrets.

Flamel bequeathed his library to a nephew named Perrier, who he had initiated into alchemy. Perrier kept the family secrets, and Flamel's library was passed down from generation to generation. One of his grandsons, Dubois Flamel, demonstrated what he called his illustrious ancestor's powder of projection in the presence of Louis XIII and is said to have successfully transmuted leaden balls into gold.

The ruthless Cardinal de Richelieu heard of the demonstrations and imprisoned Dubois for questioning. The cardinal eventually condemned him to death and seized all his property, including the book of Abraham the Jew. He then ordered that Flamel's original home be searched and his coffin be pried open. According to reports from the time, no body was found.

The cardinal built an alchemical laboratory at the Chateau of Rueil, which he often visited to study the manuscript and try to understand the hieroglyphs to discover the secret of creating gold. But the ambitious politician never succeeded in cracking the key of Abraham the Jew. After he died, the book itself was never found, although copies of the drawings and some of the text were made. Flamel's marriage contract to his wife Pernelle, his last will and testament, deeds of properties he gave to charity, financial records of his many monetary gifts, and commissions of monuments to his memory are all recorded in the Paris archives for anyone to view.

Isaac Newton and the Light of Consciousness

Famed scientist Sir Isaac Newton (1643–1727) was a practicing alchemist who wrote more on alchemy than any other subject. Yet most of his alchemical works were never published because after his death, the Royal Society deemed them "not fit to print." Today, most scholars agree that Newton considered himself, first and foremost, an alchemist, and that the inspiration for his laws of light and gravity came from his alchemical work.

Newton beliefs were based on a literal interpretation of the Bible, and he desperately wanted to recapture the state of perfect knowledge that existed before the Fall. He believed alchemy confirmed the Biblical stories and provided a path to return to the perfect state in the Garden of Eden. Newton believed alchemy originated with Thoth, who he associated with Adam, and that angelic visitors to ancient Egypt gave it to humankind. For Newton, alchemists were holy adepts seeking the Philosopher's Stone, which, once achieved, would enable communication with the angels again. He prepared his own personal translation of the Emerald Tablet and kept it safely hidden away in his laboratory as though it was a great secret.

Newton was always fearful that the teachings of the Emerald Tablet and secrets of alchemy would leak out into the world and cause fearful political and social consequences because humankind was not ready for such power. In 1676, after fellow alchemist Robert Boyle announced the discovery of a "special mercury" that became hot and glowed when mixed with gold, Newton was terrified Boyle had revealed too much. He wrote Boyle a letter cautioning him to keep everything about alchemy secret.

"Your discovery may possibly be an inlet to something more noble that is not to be communicated without immense damage to the world if there should be any verity in the Hermetic writings," Newton wrote. "Therefore I question nothing but that the great wisdom of the noble Author will sway him to high silence—there being other things besides the transmutation of metals, which none but the Hermetic philosophers understand."

Newton was a true adept of alchemy who revered the divine pattern spoken of in the Emerald Tablet, while Boyle was one of a new breed of materialistic alchemists who denied the existence of hidden forces, correspondences, synchronicities, and invisible influences of any kind.

Newton's lifelong work in alchemy focused on antimony, a brittle, steel-gray metal that tarnishes to a black finish, which hides its silvery metallic luster. It is known in alchemy as the "Black Dragon." Newton was fascinated by the regulus of antimony, which is a star-shaped crystalline form produced when heating antimony ore to high temperatures. If antimony has been sufficiently purified, it forms long and slender crystals, which, during cooling, form triangular branches around a central point that looks like a bright silver star. Alchemists named this peculiar signature of antimony after Regulus, the brilliant double star at the heart of the constellation Leo. The name is derived from the Latin *regulus*, meaning "lesser king." The regulus of antimony combines readily with gold.

Newton believed that the spirit of the Black Dragon of antimony was purified and elevated during the creation of its regulus. He felt the consciousness of the alchemist played an important role in capturing this powerful presence hidden in the black metal. He noted: "On a clear, uncloudy, and windless day, the regulus will become starred quite easily when you're ready and sufficiently skilled in the process. The clear weather helps considerably, but more so does the bond between the matters and the operator."

In the star signature of antimony, Newton found the possibility of gaining cosmic knowledge from the spirits or "innate intelligence" of the metals. He went on to create the regulus of iron and regulus of silver and used them as reflecting mirrors in a telescope to peer deep into space. Finally, Newton applied thrice-distilled mercury to the silver regulus to obtain the most perfect reflecting mirror ever used in telescopes. Perhaps Newton's belief that the regulus of metals could provide information about the universe was realized. About this time, he began publishing his breakthrough papers on the nature of light and gravity.

In the mid-1670s, Newton composed a long treatise entitled *Clovis* ("The Key"), which was the culmination of years of experimentation with the regulus of antimony. He finally admitted he had transmuted antimony into the long-sought Philosophical Mercury that would make gold multiply and grow.

"I know whereof I write," Newton espoused, "for I have in the fire manifold vessels with gold and this Philosophical Mercury. I have such a vessel in the fire with gold thus dissolved, but extrinsically and intrinsically into a Mercury as living and mobile as any mercury found in the world. For it makes gold begin to swell, to be swollen, and to putrefy, and to spring forth into sprouts and branches, changing colors daily, the appearances of which fascinate me every day. I reckon this is a great secret in alchemy."

In his work with antimony, Newton seemed to have confirmed his belief that the spiritual state of the alchemist was intimately connected to the outcome of the experiment. That is why he was so outspoken against his own corpuscular (particle) theory of light because it "robbed matter of its divine essence." He speculated light might be associated with consciousness and exist as *both* particles of matter and waves of energy. It would be over two centuries before science confirmed this startling idea.

Rise of the Puffers

Despite the high-minded work of alchemical philosophers like Isaac Newton and Giordano Bruno, the fascination with gold during the Middle Ages produced a new class of alchemists known as "puffers." They were called puffers because they constantly sat next to their furnaces vigorously fanning their bellows trying to increase the heat of their fires. They were convinced that extremely hot temperatures alone could transmute the metals.

The gold-making fever peaked in the sixteenth century, and large sections of Paris, Cologne, Vienna, Prague, and other European cities were devoted to alchemical workshops in which alchemists pursued their craft with feverish dedication. When their methods failed, the puffers resorted to trickery to produce gold. They covered pieces of real gold with paint that could be easily removed by dipping them in magical elixirs that were really just acidic solutions. Using such tricks, many puffers were able to convince princes, kings, and popes to finance their endeavors, although not a few went to the gallows when they were unable to produce more gold than they consumed. A few heads of state, such as Frederick of Wurzburg, had special gilded gallows built just for hanging alchemists.

The lure of multiplying gold seduced mercenary puffers, who quickly degenerated into charlatans and criminals and eventually brought alchemy into disrepute. In fact, so many people claimed to be making gold that several nations feared it would upset their economies if even a few of the stories of transmutation were true. Many passed laws making the alchemical production of gold and silver unlawful.

Henry IV of England outlawed alchemy in 1404, but Henry VI started issuing licenses in alchemy in 1440. In fact, laws were passed that a certain percentage of all gold coins had to use alchemical gold. All gold coins minted during the reign of Edward III are said to have been made entirely of gold produced by alchemists. Respected alchemists like Isaac Newton, Raymond Lully, and Jacque le Cor were appointed the heads of national mints for obvious reasons.

During the Renaissance, however, European royalty began to realize they did not need alchemists to magically multiply their coffers. They could do it themselves simply by printing paper money. The idea surfaced in the early 1700s in the court of the French prince of Orleans. Like many rulers of the time, he had employed alchemists to produce gold in hopes of paying off his debts, but he promptly dismissed all his alchemists after meeting Scottish gambler and financier John Law, who suggested the prince print worthless paper money to pay off his debts. The promissory notes, each signed by the prince, became legal tender that were traded publicly and never had to be redeemed. The idea caught on as rulers around the world realized that paper could be transmuted into any value much easier than lead into gold.

Alchemy was torn asunder into the two opposing camps of the true adepts and the pseudo-alchemists. The pseudo-alchemists were the worldly puffers and other uninitiated amateurs who relied on physical methods and trickery to produce material gold. The true adepts were a select fraternity of initiated alchemists to whom the laboratory work was a part of a comprehensive philosophical and spiritual system based on the teachings of Thoth and Hermes. The experiments of the true adepts to transmute metals were carried out as a demonstration of Hermetic principles and not just as a way of accumulating wealth.

In studying alchemy, it is extremely important to understand the difference between the two types of alchemists who worked during the Middle Ages. True adepts and pseudo-alchemists both wrote treatises on alchemy that differ greatly in their objectives and dedication to the spirit of alchemy. Very often modern writers on the subject overlook the distinctions between these two diametrically different groups.

Because of the proliferation of pseudo-alchemists in the Middle Ages, the Hermetic principles and spiritual significance of alchemy were shoved into the background. True adepts suffered along with the puffers in the degeneration of their craft and loss of standing in society.

By the late sixteenth century, alchemy was in philosophic disarray and widely regarded as the most confused and difficult system of thought in history. French historian Albert Poisson summed up the situation in his *History of Alchemy* (1891): "Scholasticism with its infinitely subtle argumentation, theology with its ambiguous phraseology, astrology so vast and so complicated, are only child's play in comparison with the difficulties of alchemy."

The Birth of Chemistry

Modern chemistry arose from the purely physical work of the puffers, an entirely different tradition than the Hermetic teachings passed down from ancient Egypt. Puffers were called "chemists" in popular speech in the Middle Ages, and by the Renaissance, chemistry had become a separate discipline from alchemy. Historians sometimes use the term "chymistry" to refer to the short period in the seventeenth century when alchemy and chemistry were not sharply separated from each other. But by the eighteenth century, alchemy and chemistry had gone their separate ways.

The trend was obvious as early as 1595, when Andreas Libavius published a book called *Alchymia*, a guide for chemists that separated the laboratory aspects of alchemy from its spiritual principles. Then, Jan Bantista van Helmont (1577–1644) began working with gases as separate substances and not the single Element of Air. Johann Glauber (1604–1668) continued the trend by treating metals, acids, and salts as everyday things without spiritual or archetypal properties. These "chymists" shared the alchemist's belief in transmutation but no longer felt bound by the Hermetic principles of their craft. A new system that focused only on physical effects slowly supplanted traditional alchemy.

The final demise of alchemy began in 1661 with the publication of Boyle's practical laboratory guide *The Sceptical Chymist*. Robert Boyle (1627–1691) was both an alchemist and chemist who discovered the mathematical laws that govern the formation of gases. That may not sound earth-shaking to us, but Boyle was completely abandoning alchemy with his idea that mathematical laws and not spiritual principles govern the creation of chemical compounds.

Antoine Lavoisier (1743–1794), who developed the mathematical theory of conservation of mass in chemical reactions in 1783, is considered the father of modern chemistry. In 1787, he published his definitive work *Elements of Chemistry* and, two years later, *Characteristics of Chemicals*. In these books, he abandoned all references to alchemical principles and focused only on the physical properties of substances.

The absolute end to any spiritual component in chemistry came in 1803 with the publication of *Atomic Theory* by John Dalton (1766–1844). His billiard-ball theory of matter ignored the elegant crystallization of energy idea that was part of the alchemical viewpoint. The concept of the equivalency of energy and matter would not return until the rise of relativity and quantum physics in the early twentieth century.

The last gasp of alchemy in Europe came when the puffers' methods became mainstream in the nineteenth century with the commercialization of chemistry. Alchemy had degenerated from a practical path of spiritual perfection into a competitive race for commercial products to put up for sale. New drugs and miraculous chemicals had replaced the lure of gold, but the basic techniques and motivation of puffers and chemists were always the same.

The practice of alchemy could not survive in the new atmosphere of industrialization, where the work was solely on the gross physical level. The key to success in the ancient art had always been the ability to work on all levels of reality—not only on the physical but on the psychological and spiritual levels as well. The alchemist's workshop was "between worlds," and things that took place there could never be reproduced on a production line.

In this chapter, we learned about the fortuitous rebirth of alchemy in Europe after the Dark Ages ended, even though it took hundreds of years for Europeans to decipher exactly what the Alexandria alchemists were talking about. To make matters worse, the medieval Church was quick to persecute alchemists because of their heretical spiritual beliefs and disregard of religious dogma. By the sixteenth century, alchemists had split into two factions: true adepts who followed the ancient Hermetic teachings and the materialistic puffers or pseudo-alchemists. Modern chemistry was born of the practical yet spiritually incomplete laboratory work of the puffers.

This chapter concludes our work tracing the development of alchemical philosophy through the long and unexpected history of alchemy. Our examination of the lives of alchemists provides a much deeper appreciation of alchemy than any cursory description of the principles themselves. Now it is time to actually start doing some alchemy of our own. We begin this journey in the Inner Laboratory in Part 2 of this book.

WORKING IN THE INNER LABORATORY

Changing the base metal lead into the noble metal gold is only a metaphor for a greater process that involves the integration of the personality, rejuvenation of the body, and perfection of the human soul. Though the alchemists spoke of retorts, furnaces, acids, and chemicals, they were really talking about changes taking place in their own minds, bodies, and souls. One of the central ideas in alchemy is that no transformation is complete unless it occurs simultaneously on all levels of reality—the physical, the mental, and the spiritual. This distinction is what makes alchemy a unique and powerful discipline that combines the viewpoints of science, psychology, and religion. Higher alchemy seeks to unite the opposing masculine and feminine ways of knowing in a process known as the Sacred Marriage. The child of this marriage is the Philosopher's Stone, which in spiritual alchemy is the embodiment of a permanent state of perfected awareness.

Inside an Alchemist's Laboratory

The popular image of the crazed and disheveled old alchemist working late at night away from prying eyes in his cluttered laboratory is not really accurate. For one thing, alchemical laboratories during the Middle Ages and Renaissance were very well organized. As we can see from alchemists' workplaces that have survived, there was a place for everything, and everything was in its place. Equipment and chemicals were kept on shelves or bins where they could be easily accessed, and the vast variety of glassware alchemists used were usually sorted by size and conveniently hung on the walls.

Except for the money-hungry puffers, most alchemists were serious experimenters, not eccentric crackpots. They were usually highly educated, intelligent people with a keen interest in discovering the secrets of nature. Alchemists were known for their dedication to scholarly pursuits, and it was necessary to know Latin and Greek to even begin learning the subject. They studied the original treatises religiously, kept careful records of their own work, and traveled extensively to compare their findings with other alchemists.

Alchemists were among the leading philosophers and scientists of their times. Many government leaders and religious authorities were alchemists. In Europe, scores of monks, bishops, and even a few popes practiced alchemy. Nearly every physician in the late Middle Ages used alchemical remedies and was familiar with the basic theories of alchemy. At one time, Hermetic philosophy and alchemy were taught at universities in Europe, and nearly every major university had a practicing alchemist among its faculty members.

Historian Mircea Eliade described the traits needed by an alchemist: "He must be healthy, humble, patient, chaste; his mind must be free and in harmony with his work; he must be intelligent and scholarly, he must work, meditate, and pray."

A Tour of a Medieval Laboratory

Perhaps the best way to get to know the alchemists and how they worked on different levels of body, mind, and spirit is to take an imaginary tour of where they spent their time. Our alchemy laboratory is a composite of several actual labs used by alchemists, and we have incorporated features that were customary in several different time periods and countries.

Let's begin our virtual tour of an alchemical laboratory by politely knocking on the thick wooden door of the lab. While a few alchemists were willing to talk about their theories, almost none allowed outsiders actual access to their laboratories, so this is a rare opportunity. Why did alchemists not encourage visitors? The need for secrecy in their work was the most important reason, though safety was also a factor. Often several experiments were in progress that took weeks to complete, plus potent chemicals and fragile glassware were usually involved. Beyond that, many alchemists believed that other people's impure thoughts and emotions could actually ruin their delicate experiments, so they were careful about who they let in.

But the door to this lab opens, and we are invited into the alchemist's sanctuary. He respectfully greets us with a bow of his head and then cautions us about a few experiments he has going on. Before he even finishes his sentence, however, we are distracted by a powerful odor carried by a draft of air going out the door. It smells like a combination of rotten eggs and strong vinegar. The alchemist explains the repugnant odor is coming from the large digesting tub full of rotting material in the corner behind the door. He uses this digester in the operations of putrefaction and fermentation.

The Athanor

We glance over into the foul, black, gurgling liquid in the digesting tub and wonder if this might be a good time for a quick exit. But before we can turn toward the door, we notice a tall cylindrical brick furnace at the center of the room. Gentle warmth emanates from the furnace, and we move closer.

Called the athanor, this brick or clay oven is where most of the alchemist's transformations take place. The word comes from the Arabic word *attannaur*, meaning "oven." It is also known as the "Philosophical Furnace," the "Furnace of Arcana," or the "Furnace of Secrets." In popular parlance in the Middle Ages, it was known simply as the "tower" because it usually stood over five feet tall.

The sixteenth card of the Tarot often depicts the alchemist's Tower furnace being struck by lightning. The card is associated with sudden unforeseen changes and danger, as well as unexpected liberation. The alchemists nicknamed their tower *Piger Henricus* ("Slow Henry") because of its steady, slow-burning fire. Designed to maintain a constant, even heat over long periods, it had several different compartments suitable for the different stages of the work. Its primary function was to incubate an egg-shaped Hermetic vessel used for the preparation of the elixir.

Philosophically, the athanor was like a womb or fertilized egg, and many experiments required the alchemists to keep it burning for 40 weeks, which was based on the maturation time for the human fetus. It also alludes to the 40 days Jesus spent in the desert undergoing psychological putrefaction.

On the spiritual level, the athanor was a metaphor of the inner fire in the alchemist's mind and body. If the psychic connection between the alchemists and their work was strong enough, corresponding changes were expected to occur in the alchemists themselves as the transformations took place in the athanor. Just as the athanor was the heart of the laboratory with everything built around it, so were the alchemists' lives centered around their sacred furnaces.

The Secret Significance of Alchemical Vessels

On the wall to the right of the athanor hangs a bewildering array of glass vessels on wooden pegs. The opening of each vessel is inserted over an appropriate-sized peg, and the vessel is hung there to dry or for safe storage. It is easy to discern which ones are seldom used because they are covered in dust.

Many alchemists were skilled glassblowers and potters, and each of the glass or earthenware vessels they designed had a specific function. Alchemists used these vessels to carry out the operations of alchemy, and making or finding strong and durable vessels was an important part of their work.

Alchemists viewed their vessels as containers of spiritual energies, and each had esoteric as well as practical uses. Psychologist Carl Jung noted: "Although an instrument, the alchemical vessel nevertheless has peculiar connections with the First Matter and Philosopher's Stone, so it is no mere piece of apparatus. For the alchemists, the vessel is something truly marvelous and miraculous. It is more a mystical idea, a true symbol like all the central ideas of alchemy."

The most popular vessel among alchemists was the retort, a glass sphere with a long neck or spout. It could be tightly sealed with a stopper, and the long spout was handy for pouring or connecting to another vessel. The retort was a versatile vessel that could be used to mix, separate, decompose, heat, or distill solutions.

The standard distillation train had three parts, one of which was the alembic, which was a kind of retort that fit on the upper part of a still to collect and direct the distilled vapors into a condenser. The lower part of the still containing the boiling liquid was called the cucurbit. Alchemists sometimes called it the "gourd" because of its shape. The final part of this apparatus was the receiver, which was the flask attached to the outlet of the condenser that collected the distilled product or distillate.

Other vessels used by alchemists included the matrass, which was a round-bottomed flask with an exceptionally long neck that was also known as a *bolthead*. The aludel was a pear-shaped glass open at both ends. Used in the process of sublimation, it was also called the Hermetic Vase. Other glassware included a wide assortment of different-sized beakers, cylinders, bottles, flasks, and jars.

Crucibles and cupels were used in melting and other high-temperature operations. Crucibles are small clay or porcelain containers made to withstand high temperatures in the oven. When the alchemists made these, they added graphite to increase the heat resistance of native clays. Crucibles were also symbolic of intense personal work, such as the introspective fires of consciousness during self-calcination.

Cupels are porous pots made of bone ash and clay. They were used primarily in a process known as cupellation, a form of fire assaying in which noble metals were separated from base metals. Lead and other impurities were absorbed into the bone ash of the cupel or released as fumes, leaving behind only the noble metals silver and gold.

Noble metals are metallic elements that resist chemical attack and oxidation even at high temperatures. They were valued by alchemists for their ability to stabilize and control rates of chemical reactions. There are nine noble metals known to chemists today, but alchemists knew only of silver and gold. Gold is still the noblest of the noble—the purest, most beautiful, and least reactive of all metals.

Each operation of alchemy had its own special vessel designed to contain the transforming matter as well as preserve the energies at that stage. Many of these were patterned after nature and named for animals. One of the most popular was a circulatory distillation vessel called the "pelican." This impressive glass vessel had two side-arms that fed condensed vapors back into the body and resembled a pelican pecking at its breast. It was a common belief in the Middle Ages that pelicans wounded themselves to feed their hatchlings with their own blood.

Other names the alchemists gave their vessels reflected the spiritual and psychological processes associated with them. Among these intriguing names were Philosopher's Egg, Skull Cup, Brain Pan, Angel Tube, Spirit Holder, Moon Vessel, Mother of the Stone Container, Matrix Vase, Hermes Cup, Cup of Babylon, and Tomb of the Dead.

The Chemicals Used by Alchemists

On the opposite wall of the laboratory are several shelves full of alchemical treasures. The lower shelf holds assorted vials, crocks, and burlap bags containing the salts, powders, colored liquids, and other compounds used by the alchemist. Each container is carefully marked with a unique cipher that signifies its contents. Alchemists had hundreds of compounds, powerful acids, metals, and other chemicals at their disposal.

The colorful names alchemists gave to their compounds were full of hidden meaning. For example, *sal ammoniac* (ammonium chloride) was so named because it was first made with camel dung from the Temple of Ammon in Egypt. Ammonia was also known as Spirit of Hartshorn because it was distilled from an ancient substitute for yeast and baking soda known as hartshorn (ammonium bicarbonate). Another name for ammonia was Salt of Urine because—you guessed it—it was distilled from urine.

Many of the compounds used by alchemists in the Middle Ages dated back to ancient Egypt, and among the ones the Egyptians discovered were four important chemicals that became known as the *arcana* to later alchemists. *Arcana* is Latin for "great secrets," and medieval alchemists held these chemicals in the highest esteem for their practical as well as spiritual value. They called them vitriol, natron, *liquor hepatis*, and *pulvis solaris*.

Vitriol

The earliest alchemists secured both sulfuric acid and iron from an oily substance that appeared naturally from the weathering of sulfur-bearing rocks. This substance was known as green vitriol and in its natural state, it was a powerful disinfectant. When heated, it broke down into a mixture of iron sulfate and sulfuric acid.

The Egyptians used iron sulfate to heal wounds and prepared a therapeutic tonic from it. A relaxing powder known as the Narcotic Salt of Vitriol was also made from it. Iron sulfate had many other uses in alchemy and was known as the Green Lion in the Middle Ages.

The sulfuric acid distilled from green vitriol is brown and stinks like rotten eggs. It is an extremely powerful and corrosive acid that reacts with most metals but not gold. Further distillation produces a heavy, nearly odorless, yellow liquid known as Oil of Vitriol, which has a tremendous thirst for water. If a flask of Oil of Vitriol stands opened for some time, it absorbs water vapor from the air and overflows its container. Alchemists considered sulfuric acid to be liquid fire and the agent of change in most alchemical experiments. It remains an indispensable agent in many modern industries.

Natron

The word natron is from the Arabian name for the white salts that accumulate on dry lake beds. Philosophically, natron symbolized the common principle in all salts to form bodies out of solutions. Chemically, the word refers to either of two sodium compounds. The first of these is *natron carbonicum* (sodium carbonate), which appears on dried lakebeds or is mined out of the earth. The world's oldest known deposits are in Egypt. It can also be prepared by pouring sulfuric acid over common table salt.

The second natron was *natron nitricum* (sodium nitrate). It occurs naturally as cubic-saltpeter and needs only to be filtered to be used medicinally. It can also be obtained by pouring nitric acid over common table salt. The alchemists who made nitric acid by pouring sulfuric acid over common saltpeter (potassium nitrate) called it *aqua fortis* (strong water) and used it to dissolve silver out of gold.

Liquor Hepatis

Ancient alchemists prepared *liquor hepatis* ("Liquid of the Soul") by distilling a solution of sulfur, lime, and *sal ammoniac*. They considered it a permanent solution because they had no methods of breaking it down once it was prepared. Because of its deep reddish-brown color, liquor hepatis was associated with the liver, and the name comes from the Greek word *hepar,* meaning "liver." The alchemists also referred to it as Oil of Sulfur.

The Egyptians were fascinated by the pungent odor of *liquor hepatis.* They believed it originated from a presence hidden in sulfur that was purified by lime and brought to life by ammonia. The Egyptians equated this hidden presence with soul, which they believed resided in the liver. Soul was the ultimate universal essence and, like *liquor hepatis*, could not be broken down into parts. Not only did *liquor hepatis* contain soul, but it suggested the idea of the soul's possible resurrection.

The Egyptians made a balm of *liquor hepatis* by mixing it with wax and fat. This sacred balm, said to incorporate the powers of rejuvenation and healing, became known as the Balsam of the Soul or the Balsam of the Alchemists.

Pulvis Solaris

If *liquor hepatis* represented soul to the ancients, then *pulvis solaris* ("Powder of the Sun") represented spirit. *Pulvis solaris* was actually a mixture of two compounds known as red *pulvis solaris* and black *pulvis solaris.* These red and black powders were created separately by combining highly purified sulfur with either red mercuric oxide or black antimony.

Red mercuric oxide was made by heating mercury in a long-necked flask. The mercury oxidized into a white powder and red crystals. This white powder was a deadly poison, but the red crystals had healing properties. When the red crystals were mixed with pure sulfur, they combined immediately to form the red powder of the sun.

Black antimony is a naturally occurring mineral known as stibnite, which is a sulfide of antimony. The mineral was smelted and ground fine. It also had healing properties and was made into a tonic by mixing the fine powder in distilled water. When the black powder was mixed with pure sulfur, they combined immediately to form the black powder of the sun.

Mixing the red and black powders created *pulvis solaris*, which the alchemists believed had tremendous healing power on all levels of body, mind, and spirit. The way the original two powders immediately clumped with sulfur to form new compounds demonstrated the natural longing or love of these archetypal ingredients for one another.

By combining the red and black powders of the sun, the alchemists felt they had created a mystical third incarnation in which the sum was greater than its parts. The esoteric chemistry here also underscores a fundamental principle. Namely, soul is an indivisible, eternal thing, while spirit is a kind of energy that originates from the tension of polarized forces.

Hidden Energies in the Lab

As we continue our tour of the laboratory, we move our attention from the chemical supply shelf to a middle shelf that contains haphazard piles of tools and utensils that the alchemist uses. We notice assorted tongs, scoops, pincers, stirrers, spoons, ladles, and other items. Most of these are made of brass or copper, although a few are cast iron. Stainless steel was unknown in Europe at the time. We also see a set of balance scales and a small herb press on this shelf. Small and large leather bellows are stacked at the end of the shelf.

But the items on the upper shelf make our jaws drop. The dried carcasses of assorted frogs, birds, rats, rabbits, and other less identifiable creatures adorn this shelf, and a few preservative-filled jars appear to contain large insects. The alchemists were fascinated by all aspects of nature and often had large collections of preserved animals—especially rare or unusual creatures.

Alchemists believed the life force was like a substance that they could separate from living things and preserve in special tinctures. They could then use these living alchemical solutions to impart health to sick people or even give life to inanimate objects. Many famous alchemists claimed to have created little artificial beings (*homunculi*) by infusing the life force into flasks of chemical compounds.

The life force was the Quintessence the alchemists sought in plants and fermented organic matter, and one of the pieces of equipment they used in this endeavor stands next to a cluttered workbench at the back of our laboratory. Known as a serpent condenser, the giant air-cooled apparatus was used for distilling the foul-smelling solution poured off the digester. Towering over the height of man, it is composed of a shaky array of copper tubing that zigzagged upward from a thick, pear-shaped clay vessel on the floor.

Using the serpent condenser, the alchemist hoped to purify and isolate the living essences of substances. The gentle, low-temperature distillation performed by the serpent condenser was thought to safely remove and preserve the purified essences from even the foulest liquid.

The Oratorium

Next to the serpent condenser, a large dark curtain hangs suspended from the ceiling. It is carefully draped completely around a small altar on the floor. This tabernacle forms a private meditation space known as the "oratorium," and as much work is done within this sacred space as is carried out in the laboratory. One of the mottos of alchemy is *Ora et Labora* ("Pray and Work"). Alchemists spent many hours in solitary contemplation, attempting to purify and focus their minds, so they could connect with the divine powers.

The following illustration, which is an engraving of an alchemical laboratory called the "Amphitheater of Eternal Wisdom," shows the typical oratorium. The German spiritual alchemist Heinrich Khunrath designed the lab in 1609. In it, we see the work of the alchemist divided into the oratorium on the left, where the spiritual work was done, and the laboratorium on the right, where they performed the practical work. The doorway at the center of the engraving symbolizes the completion of the Great Work when the alchemist leaves the physical laboratory behind and enters a whole new level of being.

Hidden somewhere in the oratorium could usually be found the alchemist's incubator. This insulated, copper-clad wooden box was the most sacred spot in the lab. The sealed container, kept warm by the fermenting matter within, was where the alchemist directed his thoughts and visualizations.

During the process of fermentation, the First Matter was most exposed and most open to the influence of the alchemist. However, it was a delicate operation. At the beginning of fermentation, the resurrected life force was easily corrupted by another's impure thoughts, which is why the alchemist always kept the incubator hidden—even from other alchemists. He believed that if anyone other than himself touched or even looked upon this box, all would be lost.

This attitude might seem superstitious to us, but we should not judge the alchemists too quickly. They were acting completely in accord with the ancient principles of Hermetic philosophy. As we noted earlier, to alchemists, consciousness is a force of nature that can be purified and directed through prayer and meditation. This esoteric part of the experiment is absolutely necessary for its success.

The alchemical laboratory is a place where meditation, prayer, and physical work come together to achieve transformation.

(From Amphitheatrum Sapientiae Aeternae by Heinrich Khunrath, 1595)

As we come to the end of our tour, we thank the alchemist for allowing us to visit his private workshop and for sharing his work with us. We have learned much about the fundamental tools of alchemy. As we pass by the digester on the way out of the lab, the odors are not nearly so repugnant as when we first encountered them. To our surprise, it now seems like a magical fragrance is in the air.

Alchemists and Chemists

The alchemical principle that the consciousness of the experimenter influences the outcome of the experiment just might explain why many alchemical experiments cannot be duplicated in a chemical laboratory. It is not that the experiments never worked but just that chemists do not know how to perform them.

Chemists fully believe their experiments take place only on the mundane physical level and see no need to purify themselves or meditate prior to beginning work in the lab. Their mindset is that chemistry operates by rearranging atoms like so many billiard balls—a methodology much too crude for the alchemist. From the alchemist's viewpoint, chemistry is a superficial and artificial science that deals only with the external forms in which substances manifest while ignoring the essences of energy and light that created them.

The uncanny identification with the processes in the laboratory was absolutely necessary because the alchemist and their work fed on each other. The alchemist suffered with their work, felt its same temperament, and changed with it. For if the experiment was truly a success, the alchemist also was transformed. The key to this whole process was the conscious connection or correspondence the alchemist was able to forge between his own mind and the "mind of nature" as expressed in the experiment.

In our tour of an alchemist's lab in this chapter, we have seen the fundamental tools of medieval laboratories that made alchemy such a unique blend of science and spirituality. Still, from our modern viewpoint, it's hard to imagine how much a part of their experiments were the alchemists themselves. All matter was alive to them, and they sympathized with the subject of their work every time they exposed it to fire, submerged it in acid, or bathed it in cooling waters. In the next chapter, we will learn some meditations actually used by alchemists to enter the sacred space of the Inner Laboratory.

CHAPTER
6

Entering the Inner Laboratory

The first thing to understand about the Inner Laboratory is that it is a secret sacred space within your own mind. In this inner sanctum, your consciousness is unfettered and free to go where it wants. No subject is taboo, and no social or conventional restrictions apply. Your subconscious mind, rational mind, and higher or mystical mind all work together in the Inner Lab. What goes on in there is private and rarely shared with the outside world unless it is concealed in some form of artistic expression.

Concealment and secrecy are fundamental characteristics of Hermetic practice, of which alchemy is a part. The term "hermetically sealed" means making a container perfectly sealed and airtight. That kind of closed-off, uncontaminated spiritual environment is where Hermetic meditation, rituals, and initiations take place.

The path of Hermetic enlightenment is not in theoretical discussion and argument, but it is in the cultivation of silence. In the *Discourse on the Eighth and Ninth*, Hermes tells his son to become "a pure receptacle, a womb that understands in silence." Hermes instructs him to "sing while you are silent" and let the "cosmic hymn flow through you" by remaining quietly receptive.

The Union of Solar and Lunar Consciousness

Disciples of the Hermetic teachings, still known as "Sons of Hermes," reach the primal presence of the One Mind only by passively receiving—and then actively uniting—with its creative energies. At that point, one's own consciousness becomes divinely inspired. The unique combination of masculine (Solar) consciousness and feminine (Lunar) consciousness proved a powerful tool on the path to enlightenment.

The Solar masculine way of knowing is rational, deductive, argumentative, and intellectual thinking that is the hallmark of science and our patriarchal Western culture. It involves left-brain talkative activity such as linear thought, schematics, formulae, lists, formal arguments, and logic. Among its symbols in alchemy are the blazing Sun, Fire, Sulfur, the King, Spirit, and ultimately, the One Mind of the universe.

The Lunar feminine way of knowing is a nonlinear, image-driven, and intuitive way of thinking that is an accepted tool of the arts and religion. It involves right-brain activity mostly in silence dealing with subjective feelings expressed in meditation, imagination, paintings, mandalas, music, sacred objects, talismans, and jewelry. Among its symbols are the Moon, Water, Mercury, the Queen, the Holy Ghost, Soul, and ultimately, the One Thing of the universe.

The wordless merging of the Lunar and Solar ways of knowing result in a Stellar consciousness, which is a unified state of incorruptible wisdom that Egyptians called "Intelligence of the Heart." Its primary alchemical symbol is the androgenous Philosopher's Child that results from the marriage of the King and Queen. Other symbols include Sophic Mercury, Gold, the Philosopher's Stone, the Astral Body, and of course, the Stars themselves. In the ancient teachings of the alchemists, we have all embarked on a journey through the manifested planets—a journey home to the stars.

The idea of the union of the masculine and feminine powers is reflected in the word "hermaphrodite," and its mystical meaning is best understood by examining its mythic origins. While the mythology here can get a little complicated, try to view the gods as archetypal forces of creation, and focus on their energetic relationships.

*Hermes points to the union of the Solar and Lunar powers,
which are the masculine and feminine ways of knowing.*

(From Symbola Aureae Mensae by Michael Maier, 1617)

The Mythic Son of Hermes

The Greek name of the son of Hermes was "Hermaphroditus" because he was born through the union of Hermes and Aphrodite. Aphrodite is the Greek goddess of beauty and love who became the Roman goddess Venus. Aphrodite represents pure sexuality and was born when Cronus castrated his father Uranus and threw his genitalia into the sea.

Uranus is the primordial first god and father of all who was born of the First Matter that emerged from the original Chaos of creation. Cronus is the Greek god of time (the Roman god Saturn) who personified the sky and heavens and created the Titans. This myth is telling us that Aphrodite is the powerful archetype of libido created from the separated sexuality (or life force) of the first god when it was thrown into the primal sea of manifestation.

Not surprisingly, Hermaphroditus was a boy of exceptional beauty, and he attracted the attention of the naiad Salmacis. A naiad is a female sea nymph, which is an elemental nature deity tied to subconscious energies symbolized by the sea. Naiads are personifications of natural energies, and in the myths, they are usually tied to a certain location or landform. Salmacis fell so deeply in love with Hermaphroditus, that she wanted to be completely absorbed into him. She prayed ardently for a union with him, and as a result, they were united bodily in the dark waters. What emerged was a new body combining both male and female characteristics.

This mythic moment carried tremendous significance for alchemists. They referred to the primal sea of elemental energies as the "Mother of the Stone" and sought to re-create it in their laboratories. From these dark waters would be born the androgenous Child of the Philosophers, who would mature into the Philosopher's Stone. In their work in the Inner Laboratory, the unified or androgynous state of consciousness—the union of Solar and Lunar ways of knowing—would emerge from the swirling slurry of subconscious energies into the conscious mind.

If we dig a little deeper into the mythology, we can see how the son of Hermes was cast as the emerging Philosopher's Stone, which is a fundamental part of the creation of the universe. As a son of Hermes, Hermaphroditus is consequently the great-grandson of Atlas because Hermes's mother Maia is the daughter of Atlas. The god Atlas is a former Titan condemned to hold up the celestial heavens or sky for eternity. In other words, Atlas separates the Above from the Below, thus making the path to enlightenment possible. Our Atlantic Ocean was originally known as the "Sea of Atlas," and the word for the enlightened utopia of Atlantis comes from the Greek words for "Atlas's Island." Hermaphroditus was sometimes called "Atlantiades" to reflect his kinship with Atlas.

Myths are metaphors for what is going on in the deepest parts of human consciousness, and the alchemists recognized that. In their writings and drawings, you will find countless references to the Greek and Roman gods. Pay attention: The authors are invoking a second or deeper level of interpretation. It will be utterly confusing to the uninitiated, but the Sons of Hermes will find the right path.

The Sons of Hermes in Europe

The rising influence of Hermeticism in Europe spread into the Church, which appropriated the teachings for its own purposes. The rational excuse for adopting Hermes into the Church was the Hermetic doctrine of *Prisca Theologia*, which is the idea that a single, true theology exists in all religions, and that this theology was given by angels to mankind in antiquity. This view seemed to authenticate Catholicism as the universal church. Fathers of the Church at the time accepted Hermes Trismegistus as an Egyptian priest-king who was a contemporary of Moses.

To the dismay of the Church fathers, the Hermetic teachings quickly blossomed into several rogue Christian mysticism movements that the Church spent centuries trying to suppress. One of the most popular was the Quietist Movement, born in Spain in the writings of Catholic nun Teresa of Avila (1515–1582) and priest Miguel de Molinos (1640–1696), who, as we noted in Chapter 4, was imprisoned during the Inquisition for teaching that people could reach the divine through meditation and prayer outside the Church.

Like the Sons of Hermes, the Quietists believed it possible to have an inner experience of the divine within the human soul, which can achieve divine union while still on earth. We know from their journals and diaries that many Renaissance alchemists practiced Quietist techniques in the privacy of their chambers. For them, these methods enabled them to enter the sanctum of the Inner Laboratory repeatedly and confidently.

The Quietist Technique

As an example of how alchemists entered an inner sanctuary, follow the four steps [of this] powerful technique given in the following paragraphs. Practice in a private [place] where you will not be disturbed. Do not proceed to the next step until you have [succe]ssfully completed the one you are working on. Then move seamlessly from one [step t]o the next until the whole regimen is mastered.

[Ste]p 1—Quieting the Mind

[To b]egin the Quieting process, sit comfortably with your spine upright and close your [eyes.] Do not perform Quieting while lying down. The best time to practice is early morning, after a nap, on a day off, or other time of solitude without interruptions. This basic process of Quieting takes place through all levels of body, mind, and soul. Beginning on the level of your body, slowly withdraw your attention from physical sensations and sensory inputs. Start "softening" the body by relaxing the muscles and releasing tension.

On the level of mind, Quieting requires stilling the constant chatter of thoughts and the swirling chaos of emotional energy. During this initial stage, the mental faculties are not yet completely purified, and one tends to be distracted by lingering thoughts, emotions, memories, fantasies, planning, worrying, and other lingering impressions in the mind. Simply ignore these without deliberately trying to control them in any way. Try not to invest any energy pushing them away or attempting to bury them. Let them dissolve by not paying attention to them.

Other distractions that arise during this kind of activity are insights, breakthroughs, and self-reflected comments such as "Am I doing this right," "I feel so peaceful," and so on. All these attachments—even the positive ones—will cause the mind to descend into worldly concerns.

The mind should be clear without any ideas or impressions. It might take some time to achieve this state, but it will manifest eventually if you maintain an attitude of dissolution and surrender and keep reducing everything to a state of simple awareness. When mental quieting has been attained, your attention should be rested behind the eyes or forehead.

On the level of soul, the Quieting process is one of release from earthly desires and ambitions. It is a way of soothing your inner being by letting go of nagging feelings of guilt, greed, pride—intrusive desires of any kind. It is also necessary to overcome feelings of deficiency, sinfulness, or inferiority and to realize the Soul is infinite and not tied to this world or to the acts of any temporal ego that emerged from it. Successful quieting of the Soul results in a feeling of loving innocence and transcendent peacefulness.

Once body, mind, and soul are quieted, the work focuses on the Cultivation of Silence. The primary work here is on the individual will, which becomes lost or absorbed into the divine presence within the sacred Stillness. Remember, it is the Stillness itself that dissolves you.

Do not set a time limit or use an alarm to end the Quieting phase. Do it as long as you can, and when you feel it is time, gently withdraw from this Inner Laboratory and end the session. Clarity of intent is what makes this work. Once that is lost, it is time to stop.

Step 2—Reversion

Once Quieting is mastered, move directly from that phase to the second step, which is Reversion. During Reversion, the focus is on surrendering oneself completely to the divine Will and seeking higher guidance to replace your own personal will. Ironically, this occurs most easily when a person is at the end of their rope—frustrated and disappointed in their efforts to change themselves. It can happen to anyone trying to do something extraordinary with their lives and being thwarted by peers, family, careers, social expectations, dogma, politics, or other cultural restrictions.

To really understand Reversion, you need to understand the ways in which you have rejected the divine connections in your life. Some people throw themselves into daily chores, busy work, obligations, and jobs and forget or never acknowledge the spiritual level of their lives. They deny mystical experiences or think accepting such ideas would somehow interfere with their practical goals. Others are consumed by soul-robbing careers that demand all their time and energy, and they do not have the luxury of experimenting with spirituality. Still others are hardened into a materialistic approach to the world through greed, rejection, abuse, or painful experiences, or they just lack love in their lives.

The practice during this stage is to reflect on your failures, put them in perspective, and accept higher spiritual powers. Reflect on how your competitive, materialistic approach has robbed your life of depth and meaning. Acknowledge the ways in which your soul has been damaged because of it. All that should remain is the sincere urge to be healed and made whole again.

Step 3—Recollection

The third step in the Quietist method is Recollection, which is a process of transcending duality and affirming the divine Source of all things. The work of Recollection begins with intense mental focus in which one concentrates on the withdrawal of the Soul from worldly temptations and enters devout contemplation on the power of spiritual passion. The two previous steps must be mastered completely before proceeding to the Recollection stage.

The primary tool of Recollection is deep contemplation, which must be practiced inside the heart and not intellectually. A deep piety will develop in you that is beyond any that can be achieved through religious dogma or ceremonial performances. This innocence or purity in the heart becomes a steadfast guide, as the Soul desires to be led by the divine Will only.

From the Hermetic viewpoint, the emerging spirit here is Thoth/Hermes, the inner guide that is born in the purified heart. In practice, one must agree to the necessity of divine assistance—something totally separate from one's being—that will provide the confidence and actualized faith to proceed to the final stage in this process.

It is important to persevere in a state of deep contemplation and continue residing in the heart until your personal ego dissolves. In terms of spiritual chemistry, the vessel of the soul must be hermetically sealed so nothing from the mundane world contaminates it. Suddenly, you feel "refreshed and renewed" by the unmistakable presence of divine grace.

At that point, *contemplation must cease immediately without discursive thinking of any kind, and the methods by which you achieved this state must be abandoned.* Your soul must allow the divine to work within it—and through it. The Soul must bloom naturally without hindrance and allow the influx of grace to continue if possible. The work is now proceeding only from Above.

Step 4—Infused Contemplation

The final step of the Quietist method might take some time to achieve because the flowering of the Soul depends on maintaining an open gateway to divine grace. Proceeding directly from the previous step, one now enters a state of passive contemplation in which one witnesses the infusion of divine energy. It is experienced as an expansive fascination and profound humbling in the presence of something greater. One feels completely fulfilled, fully alive, and requires nothing else. The frenzied search for truth ends, and one exists in a state of gnostic bliss. It is a rare and wonderful state beyond time and space that human beings can—and have—achieved.

Each soul is also part of the greater Soul of the universe. Therefore, one's soul is also the center of the universe because a person can become one with the divine Mind by cohabiting the same sacred space. To stay in this holy place, continuous self-denial and mortification are required. Pride and self-love on any level must be banished, so that all that remains is the simple and pure desire to remain in the presence of the divine, which is the Soul's desire and true home.

Spiritual Chemicalization

Your role during Infused Contemplation is to become the perfect vessel for divine energy. Thinking you are or trying to visualize it is not enough. You must continue in this final phase in a wholly passive state. Physical sensations will eventually disappear. Memory and imagination will now be absorbed in the divine, and a feeling of ecstasy will permeate one's being as the energy condenses into a new incarnation or body.

Iamblichus named this new body the *Augoeides*, which is from the Greek term meaning "luminous body." It is also known as the "Cloak of Hermes," the tangible body of light or transformed spiritual body worn by the initiate who has overcome the limitations of physical consciousness. In the Golden Dawn tradition, Aleister Crowley taught that the *Augoeides* is born within the initiate as a separate identity—a higher spirit or guardian angel.

But the *Augoeides* is just one form that can be taken by the grounding of divine energy. The work in the Inner Laboratory is all about connecting inner and outer and mind and matter. Theurgic alchemists refer to the conscious projection or manifestation of desires in the physical world as "chemicalization," although it has nothing to do with laboratory chemicals.

The term "chemicalization" refers to the use of certain methods to condense one's spiritual powers into etheric "chemicals" that can react and have an effect in the real world. While the steps in this psychospiritual process vary in different traditions, the basic stages are outlined below. This kind of theurgic work requires relentless willpower and aggressive focus to succeed. Chemicalization can be performed in the mental space of the Inner Laboratory or in an outer ceremonial space using an altar and ritual items.

Stage 1—Sealing

The first step is to get a clear image of what it is you want to accomplish and understand what might be preventing it. Then, try to isolate the relevant essences and primal forces associated with your goal. Next, seal these raw ideas and emotions in the Vessel of Transformation. The vessel could be a ritual space or sacred state in your own mind, but it must be hermetically sealed and purified of outside influences. This work in the Inner Laboratory might take some effort to connect with the archetypal essences of the situation or desire. Each contributing force must be identified as separate "chemicals" with their own inherent properties.

Stage 2—Agitation

This is a process of stirring up the energies or bringing them to life in the sealed vessel. It involves an active imagination—visualizations and guided imagery designed to encourage the trapped essences to express and release their archetypal energies.

Nothing agitates mental contents more than releasing the inner dragon of unconscious energy and images into the mixture. It is a dangerous phase when uncontrollable energies can explode in the Inner Laboratory, but it is clear that alchemists were projecting subconscious material to deepen their connections with the subjects of their work. The approach of theurgists, however, is more objective. They work with random images and energies that emerge from the unconscious, stay with them, and analyze them to bring them into consciousness with the intent of controlling them.

Stage 3—Combustion

Having released the volatile "inner vapors," the combustibles are now set afire with forceful, focused intention. You need to turn up the fire to gain control and direct the energy towards completion of your goal. This begins with a period of purposeful chaos and inflammation. In this tumultuous state, you will find the truth you are looking for not in the mind but in the blood—in your feelings and desires.

Next is a courageous and unrelenting intrusion of your intention into the inner cauldron. It is the aggressive application of your will over the seething powers trapped inside. Finally, as you gain control, the energy changes. It becomes more coalesced and starts flowing on its own—like lava. This feeling is the hallmark of the fact that chemicalization has succeeded. The forces you have channeled are like physical chemicals, each with its own set properties that react in the real-world environment.

Stage 4—Withdrawal

The willful fires are abruptly withdrawn and the aggressive focusing of the flame of consciousness turned off. Total silence—without any thoughts or feelings—must prevail. The essences in the vessel are now cooking in their own heat, digesting in their own juices. There might be a black period of doubt or depression within you, but this is part of the process. To succeed, you must let go without losing interest.

Stage 5—Manifestation

After the ritual ends, you have to release the "chemicals" into the environment to work their transformations. Eventually, the original desire or goal begins to reappear in your life. But you must not rush it or want it too badly. Never talk about it or share the experience with others at this point. Enthusiasm must be contained—let the desire gain power slowly *on its own*. Allow the energy to congeal and flow at its own pace toward the target. The pregnancy of your intention must have time to mature in the darkness. Soon, perhaps unexpectedly, your desire will manifest into reality.

The process of projection and manifestation requires a lot of inner work and discipline. The ritual sacrifice being made is yourself, and you are an ingredient in the process. The purification and concentration of your desire, willpower, and imagination reignite the Secret Fire on a higher level that fuels the continuing transformation as an independent force or entity, which is sometimes referred to as a "servitor."

In this chapter, we examined what happens in the Inner Laboratory, as well as methods on how to enter that inner sanctum. We revealed the mythic roots of the marriage of the Solar King and the Lunar Queen and the birth of the androgenous Philosopher's Child that results. We detailed some actual meditative techniques used by alchemists to enter and work in the Inner Laboratory. In the next chapter, we will see how alchemists applied conscious intent in their practical laboratory work. Using common kitchen materials, we will show you how to become part of the experiment and create potent, alchemically active tinctures and elixirs.

How to Use Signatures in Healing

Alchemy was the first medical discipline that attempted to treat the whole person physically, mentally, and spiritually. But this new holistic approach required the development of medicines that acted on all three levels of healing. Early alchemists searched for plant-based medicines using their physical and esoteric characteristics in what came to be called the Doctrine of Signatures. The great Swiss alchemist Paracelsus (1493–1541) took that ancient practice one step further with his introduction of a new healing modality he called "spagyric."

Paracelsus created the word by combining the Greek words *spao* ("tear apart") and *ageiro* ("gather together"). So, the term "spagyric" literally means to tear apart and bring together again. In spagyric work, a plant is dried, ground up, or pressed to concentrate its essences, which are then separated and brought back together in a more purified and potent form.

The objective of spagyric is to isolate the living essences of a plant and preserve them for later use, while at the same time, getting rid of the useless or impure parts. "Spagyric," said Paracelsus, "teaches you to separate the false from the true."

Understanding the Three Kinds of Medicines

In the modern world, there are three basic options for making medicines: allopathy, homeopathy, and spagyric. Contemporary medicine relies on the *allopathic* approach, which means it uses drugs designed to evoke the opposite symptoms from the disease being treated. The allopathic approach focuses more on acute symptoms and less on preventive care. The guiding principle in allopathy is that the more powerful the medicine and faster the cure the better.

According to Paracelsus, one of the most prevalent afflictions of the Middle Ages was constipation. So, let's take a look at how the three types of medicines would be used to cure constipation. One allopathic solution would be to use the chemical phenolphthalein. It provides fast relief by leaching water from the intestines, and it was the main ingredient in most popular laxatives for more than 50 years. But it later was found to be toxic with continued use and was quietly withdrawn from the market.

While allopathic medicine uses compounds that elicit symptoms directly opposite to those produced by the disease, *homeopathic* medicine uses minuscule doses of a compound to treat a disease in which large doses of the same compound would produce the same symptoms. This is done in the hopes of eliciting a healing response from the body. The German physician Samuel Hahnemann, whose motto was "like cures like," developed the homeopathic approach in the early nineteenth century.

For example, the homeopathic preparation *Nux vomica* is given for constipation. This nut from the strychnine tree contains a powerful poison that causes dehydration, constipation, and binding of the bowels. In extremely small doses, however, it relieves constipation.

In the spagyric approach, the goal is to increase or redirect the life force itself by using living essences with the relevant signatures or properties to cure the disease. Spagyric is careful not to use allopathic chemicals, which are considered dead remedies.

Spagyric is also different from homeopathy, though both systems make use of the essences of plants and treat disease as disturbances of the life force. The primary difference is that plant essences are not diluted; in spagyric preparations, they are concentrated.

In practice, spagyric medicine is a middle approach between the extremes of allopathy and homeopathy. For example, to relieve constipation, a spagyricist might prescribe a few drops a day of a tincture of Oregon grape, *Mahonia aquifolium*. Oregon grape is ruled by Mars and stimulates the liver and gall bladder to increase acid production in the stomach to cure chronic constipation. In other words, the tincture slowly induces the body to cure itself. Paracelsus also recommended making a tincture from the leaves of the senna plant if faster action was needed.

In general, spagyric compounds work on subtle levels, and mixing them with allopathic or homeopathic remedies can have unpredictable results. Alchemists consider spagyrics to be living essences that grow stronger with age and maintain a characteristic ability to adapt to changing conditions. They are reactive spirits that are trapped in a bottle and possess a kind of primitive intelligence that can be influenced by the conscious intent of both the patient and therapist.

The Doctrine of Signatures

By the sixteenth century, most alchemists were using the spagyric process to make healing tinctures and elixirs. Spagyric medicines take much longer to make than chemical preparations, because spagyric preparations must be made during specific alignments of the planets that are determined by the signatures of the plant itself.

It takes a special kind of awareness to see the signatures of plants. Chinese alchemist Lao Tzu said seeing the true signature of something required being able to sense its "inner virtue." This means understanding the hidden relationship between heavenly powers and earthly manifestation.

The Doctrine of Signatures originated in ancient Egypt with the idea that divine correspondences can be found in the manifested world. This concept was inspired by the Emerald Tablet's dictum of "As Above, so Below." According Paracelsus in his book *Archidoxies* (1525), signatures are the hidden archetypal patterns in things that "have the power of transmuting, altering, and restoring us."

"Man is a microcosm, a little world," he wrote, "because his is an extract from all the stars and planets, from the earth and the elements, and so he is their quintessence."

To make applying the Doctrine of Signatures more objective, Alexandrian scholars had begun categorizing plants by their signatures. They defined signatures as the observable characteristics plants and other objects shared with the planetary powers and astrological events in the heavens.

But Paracelsus expanded the Doctrine of Signatures into nearly every aspect of human life. He taught that the inner essence of a plant should be carefully defined from its properties, structure, color, odor, and habitat. These signatures reveal the resonating correlations between plants and human beings. Each human being has its own unique signatures that can be intuitively assessed. In fact, Paracelsus created a whole new system of planetary and astrological correspondences between plants and human organs that allowed physicians to prescribe herbal remedies according to the symptoms of their patients.

Paracelsus the Great

Paracelsus, who was widely considered one of the greatest alchemists of all time, was not a very appealing person and had few friends. With his squat, pear-shaped body, large misshapen head, and protruding lips, he was not a handsome man. But what really repulsed people was his antagonistic, in-your-face demeanor and his relentless air of self-importance.

His real name was Philippus Aureolus Theophrastus Bombastus von Hohenheim, but he took the Latin name "Paracelsus" ("Beyond Celsus") to show that he surpassed the great Aulus Celsus, a revered Roman physician who wrote the first European medical text in 1478. Paracelsus was so confrontational in discussing his ideas that his middle name (Bombastus) became synonymous with the loud and self-reverent speaking style of "bombastic" people.

In 1525, Paracelsus publicly burned the works of the iconic physicians Galen and Avicenna before the assembled citizens and physicians of Basel in Switzerland. Such actions were typical of this stubborn genius, who expounded his ideas with great vigor and seasoned his words with biting sarcasm. Paracelsus's provocative actions certainly did nothing to calm his detractors. Some evidence even suggests that a group of physicians from Vienna murdered him in his home in Salzburg.

Paracelsus also upset the alchemists of his time with his frequent criticism that they should give up trying to make gold and instead should assist physicians by finding new cures. His determined efforts to liberate the incipient science of alchemy from the "narrow and sordid domination by the multipliers and bellows-blowers" gave alchemy a new and nobler direction.

Almost single-handedly, Paracelsus rescued alchemy from the puffers and gave it a new orientation in the service of mankind. As the founder of iatrochemistry, Paracelsus added minerals, metals, and chemical compounds to the physician's arsenal of herbs and plants. Today, Paracelsus is recognized as the father of modern medicine for his revolutionary practical advances in healing.

Despite his contributions to science, Paracelsus always believed that too much reliance on intellect instead of intuition would spell disaster for the world. His mercurial mysticism was rooted in theurgy, the magical tradition of Alexandrian alchemists. "Magic," he explained, "has the power to experience and fathom things which are inaccessible to human reason; for Magic is a great secret wisdom, just as reason is a great public folly."

By using theurgic methods, Paracelsus believed he had discovered the long-sought "Azoth" of the alchemists. The Azoth is the universal solvent (Alkahest) or universal medicine that reveals the hidden essence or soul of anything and thereby enables its perfection. This "Mercury of the Wise" works because it contains the signature of all things within itself, the alpha-omega or A–Z of the universe.

Paracelsus with his prized sword, the pommel of which bears the inscription "Azoth."

(Rosicrucian portrait of Paracelsus, 1567)

Paracelsus held the same beliefs about the origins of alchemy as did Isaac Newton almost two centuries later. In his popular treatise, Aurora of the Philosophers, Paracelsus states the Egyptian god Thoth was, in fact, Adam, and the Pillars of Hermes were actually stone tablets that contained the secrets of nature written in the sacred language of hieroglyphics. He claimed that after the Great Flood, Noah discovered the tablets on Mount Ararat, and the teachings of Thoth were passed down to Abraham to become the common foundation of Judaism, Christianity, and Islam. The Three Magi who brought gifts to the infant Jesus were really Sons of Hermes, enlightened alchemists following the Egyptian path of wisdom.

Planetary Signatures

Paracelsian spagyric remedies work by healing people of systemic blockages or imbalances in their life forces. The spagyricist creates a specific medicine based on its planetary signatures that will cause the body to cure particular ailments. Here are the planetary signatures used by Paracelsus that were first established in Alexandria. Every plant is associated with at least one of these planets:

- The signatures of **Saturn** are associated with fate, structure, and the passage of time. Saturn rules the bones, teeth, spleen, and slow chronic processes, such as aging. The therapeutic effects of Saturn are drying, coagulation, and mineralization of tissues.

- The signatures of **Jupiter** are connected with general well-being and overall health. Jupiter rules growth, the metabolic system, the liver, and the enrichment of the blood from food. Jupiter's therapeutic effects preserve the body and promote healthy growth and organ function.

- The signatures of **Mars** are associated with stimulation and action. Mars rules the blood, adrenal glands, genitals, and the immune system. Mars's therapeutic effects are toning the blood and stimulating the immune system.

- The signatures of **Venus** have to do with refinement of energy in the body and mind. Venus rules the face, skin, and kidneys. Its therapeutic properties are detoxification, improvement of sense organs, and reversing impotency and sexual dysfunction.

- The signatures of **Mercury** are mental clarity and creative energy. Mercury rules the vocal organs, throat, lungs, and lymph glands. Its therapeutic effects are physical and mental adaptability and improved regulation of bodily rhythms.

- The signatures of the **Moon** are growth and fertility. The Moon rules the stomach, womb, and fluids of the body. The therapeutic effects are sedative, cooling, moisturizing, balancing, and breaking of bad habits and physical addictions.

- The signatures of the **Sun** are vitality and improved overall systemic function. The Sun rules the heart and circulation, metabolism, and the distribution of bodily heat. Its therapeutic effects are balancing, heating, and energizing in a steady and controlled way.

The Hidden Star in Plants

Paracelsus often referred to the inner essences or virtues of a plant as its "inner star." By the Doctrine of Signatures, "As Above, So Below," a plant's inner star is closely related to the stars in the heavens. Heavenly bodies rule plants because the plant's inner, microcosmic star corresponds to a universal or macrocosmic star. For Paracelsus, the star in a plant is what gives it its signatures.

In general terms, the inner star is the truest part of anything. It is the divine thought or ideal that gives a thing its form and being. By opening a plant and revealing its inner star, the spagyricist hopes to tap into its incorruptible power to affect similar things in predictable ways. "One must understand," elaborated Paracelsus, "that the medicine must be prepared in the stars and that the stars themselves become the medicine."

Using Planetary Charts

The star, or what Paracelsus sometimes referred to as the "astral energies" of the visible planets, affect plants on Earth in predictable ways. Each planet influences some plants more than others, depending on the inherent astrological and planetary signatures within the individual plant. He described this active connection between plant and planet with the term "sympathy."

Sympathy governs most of the basic characteristics of the living things on our planet, and each of the seven visible planets affects plants, animals, and humans in specific ways because of this underlying sympathy. For instance, each planet rules an organ or organ system in the human body—and by extension, its diseases. Similarly, each planet rules the plants that support the organ or are able to balance it with the corresponding planetary energies.

All aspects of spagyric processing, including harvesting the plant, cutting, and sifting it, drying it, wetting the plant material with alcohol for extraction or distilling it, and adding its salts and other separately extracted materials, should take place during the times ruled by its corresponding planet.

The planetary powers are greatest when the planet is visible in the sky, which is called the planetary hour. Traditionally, the planetary hours are determined by using charts originally developed by Johannes Trithemius (1462–1516), who was Paracelsus's teacher. Three types of planetary charts are used to determine the proper time to work with a spagyric compound. You can download all three planetary charts from links in Recommended Resources (see Appendix A).

The simplest planetary chart is the *Mercury Level Chart*, in which a single planet rules each day, all day. A Mercury-level preparation is directed toward disturbances and depletions of the life force, such as chronic fatigue or lethargy.

To attune a spagyric to the Mercury level, a highly refined alcohol is used for extraction, which is elevated before use in a process called animation. Animation of the Mercury is a method of spiritizing the material, making it volatile so it can open and receive the universal life force and then close again to hold that life force.

To attune a spagyric preparation to the Sulfur level, the essential oils are extracted separately using steam distillation and other alchemical methods. The *Sulfur Level Chart* changes each hour, beginning at sunrise, and each planet rules several periods in a single day. A Sulfur-level preparation is directed toward physical or mental aberrations and deep-seated disturbances of the soul.

To attune a spagyric medicine to the physical or Salt level, a concentrated extract is made with all the mineral components extracted and included in the remedy. To accomplish this, all the plant matter that would have normally been discarded is burned to an ash. From that ash, the Salt essences are extracted in alcohol. These operations must be performed at the time of day indicated in the Salt Level Chart, which divides the day into seven equal planetary periods. A Salt-level preparation is directed toward specific bodily injuries and ailments.

Making a Spiritized Tincture

1. Pick an herb with the properties you wish to capture. The Saturn herb Lemongrass (*Melissa officinalis*) was preferred by alchemists because of its wide range of healing powers. Before you begin tincturing, however, get to know your herb's signatures by physical contact, odor, and meditation. This will help you release the herb's inner

strengths. Major operations on the herb, such as picking, drying, mixing, and tincturing should begin on the planetary day ruling the herb.

2. Begin the **extraction** in the planetary hour of the ruling planet of the herb. Find a clean 100 ml (3–4 oz.) lab jar, jelly jar, or small Mason jar. Meditate for the creation of a sacred space within the vessel.

3. **Crush** the dried herb by hand into small pieces. If available, use a mortar and pestle or coffee grinder to grind to a fine powder. Place about 40 ml (1.5 oz.) of the powder in the jar.

4. With focused intent, pour the **menstruum** over the herb until it is saturated but not over ⅔ full (70 ml or 2.5 oz.). The menstruum can be pure ethyl grain alcohol, vodka, or brandy. The higher the proof the better.

5. **Animate the Mercury** by encouraging the mixture to breath on its own. Warm the open container between your hands or very gently over an alcohol burner. Swirl it gently as you synchronize your breathing with the imagined inhalations of the herb. Visualize the enlivening spirit of Celestial Fire carried by the Air Element entering the solution with each breath you take.

6. **Hermetically seal** the jar. If a metal lid is used, it must be completely covered in plastic wrap because the tincture solution should never come in contact with metal at any time during processing.

7. **Incubate** the jar. Wrap the sealed jar in cloth or foil because it should not be exposed to light during the initial incubation period. Place it in an incubator or other warm location, such as near a radiator, furnace, or water heater. Ideal temperature is 85–98° F (30–36° C).

8. Begin the **distillation** by shaking the jar vigorously once or twice a day. The fluid inside will evaporate as it warms up and condenses again. As this inner distillation repeats, the soul of the herb is regenerated by minute degrees closer to perfection. This circulation and maceration, or "chewing," is responsible for the tincturing process. The fluid will become darker with each passing day. In alchemical terms, the coloration or tincturing is the extraction of the Sulfur (or soul) from the Salt plant matter by Mercury or the spirit alcohol medium.

9. Continue this process for two to three weeks, until the color of the tincture is dark. This is your **Philosopher's Child** and must be treated with a caring attitude. Let no one else handle the jar, and each time you handle it, treat it as a physical representation of your own inner spirit. As the alchemical Sulfur is extracted from the murky herbal mass, so are you separating your own soul from the dregs of everyday life.

10. After the color of the liquid is sufficiently darkened, begin the **separation** process by allowing the jar to cool to room temperature. Open the jar and press out any remaining liquid from the mass of plant matter. Filter the solution (using medium filter paper or paper coffee filters) until it is clear from all physical debris. The resulting liquid (the tincture) contains the Sulfur or soul of the herb (its essential oils and vegetable fats) along with its Mercury or spirit (alcohol). Save all the phlegm and debris removed by filtering for use in making the elixir. These are the dead Salts.

Preparing the Elixir

1. Take the essence-depleted **dead Salts**, the *caput mortum* ("dead head"), which consists of the phlegm and debris left over from the tincturing process. Place the material in a heatproof bowl or metal pot and cover with a wire screen.

2. **Ignite** the material and let it burn. This is best done outside. It may be necessary to put the pot on a flame to boil off any excess liquid. When all the liquid is gone, the mass will begin to roast and finally incinerate. Let the dead plant matter burn itself out and cool.

3. Take the **ashes** from the initial combustion and grind to a fine powder. Place the ashes in a covered crucible or heatproof dish. Heat in an oven, at the highest temperature possible, until the ashes have turned grayish white. Continued heating at extremely high temperatures would turn the ashes white then red. Store the purified Salt ashes in a clearly labeled jar.

4. **Mix** the tincture extract you made previously with the Salt ashes at the correct planetary hour on the planetary day ruling the herb. Pour the entire extract over the purified Salt. If the tincture is still living, there should be a slight fizzing sound. This is the first breath of the resurrected essence. Continue animating the Mercury in the solution as we did during the tincturing process.

5. Shake vigorously, then hermetically seal the flask. Put the flask in an incubator or near a heat source to **digest**. Shake three times daily. During this time, the Salt will completely absorb the extracted essence.

6. After three weeks, pour off any remaining liquid, leaving the Salt residue in the flask. Hermetically seal the flask and let it sit for another few weeks to **incubate** in a warm spot out of direct light.

7. Open the jar and let the material dry up and granulate. Scrape this **regenerated Salt** out of the jar after it has dried, then grind it to a fine powder in a warm mortar. Store it in a clean dark-glass jar. The elixir powder is ready for use; it can either be used dry or mixed with pure ethyl alcohol in dark-glass bottles. The elixir represents the resurrection of the herb on a higher level. The conscious combination of the alchemist's grounding spirit and the Celestial spirit from Above makes the elixir magically healing.

In this chapter, our teacher was the great alchemist Paracelsus. He showed us how to break open a plant to release its fundamental living essences and how to preserve that essence for purposes of healing. Signatures guide us in choosing the correct plant for a specific cure. We do this spagyric work during the planetary hours the powers of the corresponding planet are at their peak. Finally, we applied his teachings to make alchemically active tinctures and elixirs. In the next chapter, we will move on to the mineral work and experience the powerful archetypal energies of the metals, known as the Seven Dragons to alchemists.

Getting to Know the Seven Dragons

Imagine the ancient landscape before civilization. There was only sky and earth, mountains and valleys, and rivers and trees. We survived by nature's bounty and perished by nature's fury. But hidden in this unforgiving environment was a great and powerful secret waiting to be discovered. Concealed in rocks, crevices, and caverns all over the planet was a miraculous gift from the gods—the metals.

Glistening, durable, transformable—each with its own unique characteristics. There was nothing like the metals anywhere in nature. And how to coax that magical essence from bland-looking rocks became the first secret of alchemy.

Maybe the first alchemist was just a tribesman huddled next to a warm fire in the dark of night who happened to notice a shiny liquid oozing out of cracks in one of the rocks around the fire pit. Some ores of lead or mercury will do that at comparatively low temperatures. Then, the next morning, the tribesman looked through the ashes only to discover something more beautiful and amazing than anything he had ever seen. Maybe that person started looking for similar rocks and roasting them over fire to collect the mysterious essence from the rocks.

People today have a hard time understanding the alchemists' obsession with the metals. We take metal for granted and have lost our connection to the intimate powers that each of the metals possesses. But nothing has transformed this planet more than the metals. Just try imagining our world without metals. We would be living in thatch huts and dried mud buildings. There would be no airplanes dotting the sky, no cars clogging the roadways, or no towering steel skyscrapers in our cities. And there would be no refrigerators, televisions, or computers for that matter.

The metals made civilization possible and everything that came with it, too—from weapons and wars to science and space travel. The metals quickened our minds, and the universal operations of alchemy were revealed to us by learning to extract the metals from their ores, refine them, and change their properties. Make no mistake: We did not transform the metals. The metals transformed us.

To alchemists, the seven metals of their world were fierce spirits that carried the fundamental patterns or archetypes that are part of the fabric of creation. The untamed powers of the metals are so furiously expressed in their reactions that alchemists sometimes referred to them as the "Seven Dragons."

While dragons in eastern cultures were four-legged, serpentine creatures associated with water and good fortune, the fearsome alchemical dragons of Europe had wings and horns and breathed fire. Like the metals they represented, the ferocious beasts lived in underground caverns guarding hidden treasures. They gave nothing away and had to be tamed before they would share their secrets.

The lustrous metals are so different from other kinds of natural materials, alchemists thought the first metals originated in heaven and fell to Earth, where they grew to maturity in the darkness underground. The metals reflect their heavenly origins in their signatures. Each of the visible planets in the sky has its expression in a corresponding metal on Earth: Saturn produces lead; Jupiter produces tin; Mars produces iron; Venus produces copper; Mercury produces quicksilver; the Moon produces silver; and the Sun produces gold. Each planet and its metal are so identical in properties and behavior that alchemists assigned them the same symbol.

The Dragon's Breath in the Laboratory

Researchers have documented the uncanny relationship between planets and their metals many times. In the late 1920s, in a series of impressive experiments, Lilly Kolisko of Germany's Biological Institute showed that changes in the relationships between planets are reflected in changes in the chemical behavior of metals on Earth. For example, during a Moon-Mars alignment, mixtures of iron and silver compounds tend to be more active.

More recently, researcher Rudolf Hauschka demonstrated that the relative speed of a planet in the sky is directly proportional to how electrically conductive its corresponding metal is. For instance, Saturn has the slowest apparent speed across the heavens, and lead has the lowest conductivity of the metals; the Moon has the fastest speed, and silver has the highest conductivity.

Statistical studies of the fluctuations of the prices of the metals also show a connection between the planets and their metals. For instance, during conjunctions of the Moon and a planet, the value of the corresponding metal falls, while during a conjunction of the Sun and a planet, the value of the corresponding metal rises. Other planetary events have also been shown to influence the value of their corresponding metals.

To understand the mystery of the archetypal planet-metal relationships, we will look at each of the seven metals of alchemy to discover their deepest signatures. We will also learn how alchemists used the signatures of the metals to transform them.

Remember, these signatures are part of you, too. They are expressed in your personality and physiology. The planetary archetypes are expressed in our relationships, careers, and creative work. Learning to transform the metals within from base metals to noble metals is the basis of the alchemical psychology that was rediscovered in the twentieth century by Herbert Silberer and Carl Jung.

The work we do in this chapter getting to know the properties or signatures of the Seven Dragons is essential to our continued psychological and spiritual work in later chapters. These universal archetypes are at the heart of alchemy. In reviewing the characteristics of the metals in the following paragraphs, try to imagine how their signatures are expressed in people. The planetary powers effect all of us and create our personalities or temperaments.

Saturn's Metal: Lead

While alchemists considered lead to be the lowest of the base metals, they treated it with a great deal of respect because lead was said to carry all the energy necessary for its complete transformation into gold. To the alchemists, the ancient metal was a powerful "sleeping giant" with a dark and secret nature.

Lead is indeed an ancient metal, a stubborn metal known for its durability and resistance to change. Lead products dating from 7000 B.C.E. are still intact, and lead water pipes installed by the Romans 1,500 years ago are still in use today.

Lead is the heaviest metal and a boundary of heaviness for all matter. All the metals beyond lead (of greater atomic weight) disintegrate over time by radioactive decay and transform back into lead. Geologists measure the age of radioactive rocks by how much lead they contain. So, radioactive decay is really a process of Saturn that introduces a new characteristic in the metals—that of time. No natural process is more unalterably exact than radioactive decay, and atomic clocks are based on this leaden process. In many ways, lead carries the signature of Saturn's Father Time.

Lead is an incredibly stubborn metal. There is comparatively little of it in the earth's crust, but once you make the metal, it never goes away. More than half the lead in the world today has been around for centuries and is being recycled over and over.

Lead ores lack the slightest water content, and lead does not react with water in any way. Lead also resists many acids, including the traditional "liquid fire" of the alchemists—sulfuric acid. In fact, lead bottles are still used to store the highly corrosive acid.

Lead and Silver

Lead has a strange relationship with the noble metals. In the periodic table, lead is in the same group as gold, and when it occurs in nature, it is always found with gold and silver. In fact, the chemical symbol for lead (Pb) is from the Latin word plumbum, which refers to liquid silver. We derive our words plumbing and plumb bob from the use of lead in those applications.

The most common ore of lead is galena (lead sulfide), which also contains the noble metals of silver and gold. The amount of galena processed for lead produces enough silver as a byproduct to make galena the leading ore of silver as well.

In the smelting of silver, lead plays an important role by forming a layer over the emerging molten silver and protecting it from combining with air and splattering out. The volatile molten lead covering is gradually burned away until only the pure silver metal "peeks out from the veil of lead" (in the smelter's terminology) in a stabilized form. Thus, lead protects and even sacrifices itself for the nobler metal.

Saturn Signatures in Lead

Fresh-cut lead looks just like silver, but the silvery luster quickly fades as if the metal were dying before our eyes. Lead metal is incredibly soft and can be easily gouged with a fingernail. Lead is a sluggish metal that alchemists often described as lethargic. It is the slowest conductor of electricity and heat, the least lustrous, and the least resonant of the planetary metals.

Lead's saturnic signature of lethargy is expressed both in the fact that it is the heaviest metal and in its tendency to form inert and insoluble compounds. No other metal forms as many inert and insoluble compounds. Lead reacts with more chemicals than any other metal; however, instead of producing something new and useful, lead "kills" the combining substance by making it inert, insoluble, and unable to enter further chemical reactions.

Another of Saturn's signatures of lead is its ability to "dampen" or absorb energy. Unlike other metals, when lead is struck, the vibrations are immediately absorbed, and any tone is smothered in dullness. Lead is an effective sound-proofing medium, and thin lead sheets are used extensively in the walls of high-rise buildings to block the transmission of sound. Thick pads of lead are also used in the foundations to absorb the vibrations of street traffic and even minor earthquakes.

Lead is truly a destroyer of light and is known for its ability to absorb all types of radiation. Lead sheets are widely used in roofing to block solar rays, and lead foil is used to form lightproof enclosures in laboratory work. Added to high-quality glassware, lead crystal, it absorbs light reflections and makes the glass clearer. Sheets of lead are impermeable to all forms of radiation, including high-energy X-rays and gamma rays. Lead is the perfect shield against radioactivity, which is why it is used to transport and store radioactive waste.

Lead Poisoning

Lead is poisonous to all forms of life. Young growing plants are adversely affected by even the smallest trace amount of lead in the soil because it accumulates in the roots of plants and slows down the breathing process.

Lead poisoning in humans is known as saturnism, and symptoms include lack of energy, depression, blindness, dizziness, severe headaches at the back of the head, brain damage, attention deficit disorder, antisocial behavior and anger, atrophy of muscular tissue, excess growth of connective tissue resulting in rigidity, rapid aging, and early death. Lead accumulates over time in the bones of the human body where it can never be flushed out.

Children are especially vulnerable to lead poisoning, and it is believed to be an important factor in stillborn fetuses. Children with more than just 0.3 parts per million of lead in their blood suffer a significant slowing of brain function. Lead in paint has caused mental retardation and premature aging in thousands of children.

Many research studies link lead exposure to anger and violence, especially in adolescents. One recent study conducted by Colorado State University of all counties in the United States revealed that the murder rate in counties with the highest lead levels was four times higher than in counties with the lowest levels of lead.

The Hidden Promise of Lead

To the alchemists, however, lead was still the metal of redemption and transformation. They knew that fire ruled lead, for the metal had an extremely low melting point and was easily separated from its ore by roasting in an open flame. The metal itself melts in a candle flame. Lead is extremely sensitive to heat, expanding on heating and contracting on cooling more than any other heavy metal.

Lead has an amazing property that few people know about. When made into a fine powder, lead erupts spontaneously into flames. Powdered lead metal must be kept in a vacuum to keep it from catching fire. Otherwise, it ignites all by itself and burns down to a bright yellow ash. The alchemists were right; lead truly does carry the fire of its own transformation.

The wonder of lead is that hidden deep inside the gray, dead metal is a tiny, eternal spark that is the seed of its own resurrection. In the eyes of alchemists, this made lead the most important metal, despite its unattractive darkness. This is because dull lead and gleaming gold are really the same thing—only at different stages of growth or maturity.

Jupiter's Metal: Tin

To the casual observer, tin seems like a more perfected form of lead. In fact, the Romans called tin *plumbum album,* or white lead. Like lead, tin resists weathering and corrosion. Tin utensils buried underground or lost at sea in sunken ships shine like new when unearthed after hundreds of years. Like lead, tin is endlessly recyclable. Tinkers were gypsy craftsmen who wandered from neighborhood to neighborhood in Europe melting down old tin kettles and utensils and recasting them.

Natural tin metal is known as *stannum,* which is the Latin word for tin and also gives the metal its chemical symbol (Sn). Natural tin is extremely rare and is found with gold and copper deposits. Most tin comes from its sparkling ore cassiterite (tin oxide), which has been an important source of tin for thousands of years. In ancient times, the metal was considered semi-noble and was used for jewelry in Babylonia and Egypt.

But unlike lead, tin has pleasing acoustic effects and is used in the making of bells. It has a highly crystalline structure, and because of the breaking of these crystals, a "cry" is heard when a tin bar is bent. For many years, large tin sheets were used in theaters to simulate the sounds of thunder, which is very appropriate because Jupiter is the god of thunder.

Tin metal has only a few practical uses, and most tin is used in a variety of useful alloys. The development of bronze, an alloy of 5 percent tin and 95 percent copper, marked a new age of advancement known as the Bronze Age. Most solder is a combination of tin and lead; pewter is also an alloy of tin and lead. Other tin alloys are used to make tin cans and tin roofs, and a thin layer of tin applied to other metals provides protection from corrosion.

Jupiter Signatures in Tin

Oddly, the distribution of tin on Earth follows an ecliptic angle to the equator that is the exact track of the orbit of Jupiter slicing through the Earth. Even stranger, these jupiterian forces seem to form tin veins that follow a distinctive zigzag pattern through the rocks that resembles a lightning bolt. This is no haphazard effect; instead, it is an astonishing confirmation of Jupiter's energy expressed in the distribution of its metal on Earth.

The German philosopher Goethe was fascinated by the distribution of tin and suspected it might explain how all the metals were arranged in the crust of the Earth through the distant effects of their corresponding planets. "A remarkable influence proceeds from the metal tin," he wrote. "This metal has a differentiating influence and opens the door [to a mechanism through which a way is provided for different metals to be formed in primeval rocks."

The Tin Plague

In the late Middle Ages, a curious "tin plague" began as growths on organ pipes in European cathedrals, where it was thought to be the work of the devil trying to disfigure God's work. This tin plague started as white blisters that spread until all the tin metal "sickened" and disintegrated. The plague spread to tin roofs and became a serious problem during Europe's frigid winters.

We now know that the impurities of aluminum and zinc found in tin made in the Middle Ages caused its crystalline structure to change when it was heated or frozen. This caused the tin metal to break down into a white powder that appeared to eat away the metal and had the ability to "infect" other tin surfaces it came in contact with.

Mars' Metal: Iron

Iron is an abundant element in the universe and is even found in the stars in considerable quantity because iron nuclei are very stable. Iron is the most prevalent metal on Earth and the second oldest metal used by man, after lead. Known in prehistoric times, it was smelted by the Egyptians at least as far back as 1500 B.C.E., and iron artifacts from Asia have been found that are 5,000 years old.

Our word iron comes from the Anglo-Saxon word *iren,* which is derived from an earlier word meaning holy metal because it was used to make the swords used in the Crusades. The chemical symbol for iron is Fe, from the Latin word for iron, *ferrum,* which means to create, form, or bear forth.

Iron is very reactive and forms compounds immediately, so pure iron does not occur in nature. The purest iron on our planet comes from outer space in the form of meteorites, which are usually alloys of nickel and iron.

One of the many ores of iron is iron sulfide, also known as pyrite or Fool's Gold. Its beautiful golden luster has often been mistaken for the gleam of gold nuggets, and it has been frequently found in genuine gold deposits. Like gold, iron pyrite carries the golden signature of the Sun, and a flattened round variety called the "Pyrite Sun" is prized for its esoteric properties.

Remarkably, the iron sulfide structure of Fool's Gold is the same as the lead ore galena (lead sulfide). The only difference is that a pair of sulfur atoms in pyrite replace a single sulfur atom in galena. This pair of sulfur atoms disrupts the stubborn four-fold symmetry of the more ancient galena ore and produces a stunning transformation into Fool's Gold. In esoteric terms, in the evolution of the metals, the appearance of the sulfur compound of iron (Fool's Gold) has freed the lead archetype of its stubborn materiality and set form, and this notable transmutation is marked by the signature of gold.

Iron's Love for Carbon

European alchemists noticed that when they dropped bits of charcoal into molten iron, the iron hungrily "devoured" the charcoal to produce what we now call cast iron. While pure iron was soft and malleable, the new metal was hard and brittle. By controlling the amount of charcoal introduced, it was possible to produce steel, whose characteristics lie between the extremes of pure iron and cast iron.

The alchemists deduced that iron had a profound love for carbon, with which it could form the nobler and stronger metal—steel. Our modern attitude toward iron is much less romantic. Nearly all iron produced today is used in the steel industry, which transforms iron into steel in carbon-based, forced-air blast furnaces. This process is one of the most significant industrial processes in history and has resulted in iron (as steel) becoming the most common metal on the planet.

Iron also has a passion for other metals, each of which adds different qualities to the iron to produce unique forms of steel. The alchemists viewed these other metals as spiritual brothers of iron and named them accordingly. Cobalt was associated with the "kobolds" or mischievous gnomes who lived deep in the earth and were said to harass miners. Alchemists considered cobalt an earthier and more primitive form of iron.

Nickel was associated with the "nixies" or underwater spirits. Alchemists viewed nickel as the watery brother of iron, which expressed its watery nature in its shiny liquid surface and in the sea-green compounds it produced. Manganese was the fiery brother of iron because it produced fiery red salts. Added to iron, manganese produces extremely hard and dry steel. Shiny chromium was considered iron's sister. Chromium restores the shiny liquid look of pure iron to steel. Later alchemists found they could produce steel almost as hard as diamonds by adding tungsten and vanadium to iron.

Mars Signatures in Iron

The influences of the planet Mars in its metal iron are obvious. Throughout its history, iron has always served man's will in his weaponry or in the industrial conquest of nature. In classical mythology, the Iron Age is the final epoch of the world, marked by war and degenerate selfishness.

The expression of Mars in our world seems to be in the struggle for material possessions in which only the fittest—or perhaps richest—survive. If the predominance of the iron archetype in our culture continues, we can only expect a further distancing from nature and mechanization of life. Some nature-oriented civilizations, such as the Druids, were aware of the spiritual dangers of iron and forbid its use in their culture.

Alchemists were careful in working with the signatures of iron on the personal level. While an iron will and aggressive tactics are often required to succeed in our culture, over the long run the energies of iron tend to make you brittle, suspicious, and unforgiving. Martian energies must always be balanced with the compassion and understanding of Venus.

In the Hermetic teachings, the incarnating function of iron was meant to assist cosmic or spiritual elements to enter the sphere of gravity and matter. But when iron becomes too predominate, it becomes destructive to life and tends to rigidify and mechanize living systems. "The Mars impulses at work in iron," noted researcher Rudolf Hauschka, "are the carriers of the forces of embodiment, but these forces lead to mummification if they become too active and overwhelm the system."

The alchemists were certainly aware of the hidden signatures of iron and the social implications of the Iron Age. Some alchemists have warned of the spiritual dangers of iron, even though they recognized it was a necessary stage in the Great Work and that the iron phase eventually led to the "transformation of the body into the Spirit-Become-Form." In *Alchemy*, Titus Burkhardt quoted several alchemists who warned of the dangers of the Iron Age. One described it as "an active descent of the Spirit into the lowest levels of human consciousness, so at this stage of the Work, the Spirit appears submerged in the body and as if extinguished in it."

Venus' Metal: Copper

The discovery of copper dates from prehistoric times, and copper beads dating back to 9000 B.C.E. have been found in Iraq. Copper pottery dating from 4900 B.C.E. has been unearthed in Egypt. Copper is found in its metallic state in nature and has been mined for thousands of years. The name and chemical symbol (Cu) for copper comes from the Latin word *cuprum*, meaning "the island of Cyprus," which was one of the main copper mining areas in the ancient world. The island took its name from the Assyrian word for copper, *kipar*.

Copper was used so early partly because it was so easy to shape. Methods for refining copper from its ores were discovered around 5000 B.C.E., and the Phoenicians and Sumerians made all their tools and weapons from copper. Then, around 3100 B.C.E., Egyptian alchemists discovered that when they mixed copper with other metals, the resulting alloys were harder than copper itself. For example, both brass (a mixture of copper and zinc) and bronze (a mixture of copper and tin) are harder than copper. The discovery of bronze changed the evolution of humankind, and the Bronze Age began around 2100 B.C.E.

Copper is a reddish-brown metal with a bright metallic luster. In the periodic table, it is in the same group as gold, and like gold, it is remarkably ductile and can be pressed into extremely thin sheets and strands. Copper is an excellent conductor of both heat and electricity.

Venus Signatures in Copper

The alchemists described Venus, copper's planetary source, as dressed in a blue cloak over a red gown. This is a reference to the observation that copper burns with a blue-green flame with sporadic flashes of red. Molten copper is a sea-green color, and copper tarnishes with a green color.

Copper has always been associated with beauty and harmony. Egyptian women used the powdered copper ore malachite to beautify their eyes. Copper pigments make wonderfully colorful paints and ink, and much of the color in birds comes from the presence of copper in feathers. Some birds, such as the alchemically symbolic peacock, contain as much as 6 percent copper in their feathers.

The Love Affairs of Copper

Copper combines readily with most other elements to form alloys or complex salts. In fact, copper is so ready to form unions with other substances that alchemists called the metal *Meretrix Metallorum*, "Harlot of the Metals."

Copper shows a special love for sulfur, and geologists agree that copper and sulfur have been locked in an embrace in the bowels of the earth since primordial times. Copper sulfate, known as "Blue Vitriol" to alchemists, is one of the most beautiful and useful compounds formed by copper. It dries into a white powder when exposed to air but rapidly returns to its beautiful blue crystals when exposed to water. Unlike lead and iron ore, copper ore has a great affinity for water, and copper salts, such as copper sulfate, contain as much as 35 percent water.

Veins of copper run extensively throughout the planet like veins of blood in the human body, and the metal has many applications in the modern world as wiring, electrical components, and tubing. Nearly all coins in the world contain copper. In addition to copper pennies, our dimes and quarters are about 85 percent copper. Even the nickel is 75 percent copper. Most modern copper production is from sulfide ores containing little copper but quite a bit of iron, which is another element copper likes to spend time with.

The signatures of copper are especially important in working with all the metals, especially iron. Copper tends to balance and elevate the energy of metals, and it symbolizes the importance of the feminine influence in the Great Work. As shown in the following illustration, the work requires a cooperative effort between the male and female energies both in the lab and at the spiritual level shown in the upper half of the drawing. The male and female alchemists in the drawing represent masculine and feminine ways of working with the substance at hand. The union of these two ways of being in the world is necessary to success in alchemical transformations.

The Dragon of Transmutation of Metals embodies the Tria Prima of Salt, Sulfur, and Mercury.
(Della Transmutation Metallica by Giovanni Battista Nazari, 1589)

Mercury's Metal: Quicksilver

The silvery liquid metal mercury was known as quicksilver to alchemists. Mercury is the only metal that is liquid at room temperature, and it is the heaviest natural liquid on the planet. According to alchemical theory, all the metals began in the liquid state on our planet, but only mercury was able to remain true to its original innocence and resist taking on a final form.

Mercury can be found in its natural state pooled in caves and rock formations. It was known to ancient Chinese and Hindus before 2000 B.C.E. and has been found in Egyptian tombs dating from 1500 B.C.E. Mercury was first used to form alloys with other metals in about 500 B.C.E. and became the object of much speculation and experimentation among the Alexandrian alchemists.

Mercury the metal is named after Mercury the planet. The chemical abbreviation for mercury is "Hg" from the Latin word *hydrargyrum*, meaning "watery silver." In Indian and Taoist alchemy, the cipher for mercury is an eight-spoke wheel. Today, mercury is used in thermometers, barometers, diffusion pumps, and many other laboratory instruments. It is also used for mercury switches and other electrical apparatus, for making batteries (mercury cells), in pesticides, and in antifouling paint.

Cinnabar (mercury sulfide) is the primary ore of mercury. The word cinnabar comes from the Persian word for "dragon's blood." The mineral is a beautiful scarlet-red, is semi-precious, and is used as a high-grade paint pigment known as vermillion. Early metal workers and alchemists considered the affinity between mercury and sulfur in cinnabar to be a fundamental and magical principle.

The Romans mined cinnabar for its mercury content, and it has been the main ore of mercury throughout the centuries. Some of those ancient Roman mines are still being mined today. Cinnabar is often found with deposits of quartz, stibnite (antimony), and pyrite (Fool's Gold).

Mercury is a relatively poor conductor of heat, though it is extremely sensitive to it. Mercury expands and contracts in a direct linear relationship to temperature, which is why it is used in thermometers. It is an average conductor of electricity in its liquid state but becomes one of the best conductors known (between copper and gold) when frozen.

In its chemical reactions, mercury acts as a harmonizer because it serves as a catalyst that combines chemicals with opposing properties and speeds up reactions. The power of mercury to balance diverse substances makes it useful as a mediator in explosive devices, and a mixture of mercury and nitric acid (mercury fulminate) makes a reliable detonator for explosives. Mercury is also used in the making of nuclear bombs as a mediator in the detonation process.

Mercury Signatures in Quicksilver

Mercury moistens and dissolves other metals the way water dissolves salt, and for this reason, the alchemists believed it was the key to the transformation of the metals. The dissolved alloys of mercury are called amalgams, and the ease and speed with which mercury amalgamates with gold makes it of primary importance in the recovery of gold from its ores.

Mercury dissolves gold, silver, copper, tin, lead, zinc, cadmium, and all the alkaline metals, but it does not affect iron or any members of the iron family, such as nickel and aluminum. The alchemists thought this antipathy between iron and mercury stemmed from the two metals' diametrically opposed signatures. Iron represents the mechanical processes of structuring and control, while mercury represents the living processes of growth and mobility.

Since ancient times, mercury has stood for the life force and the light of awareness in matter. In the writings of alchemists, it is often referred to as *Mercurius Vivens* ("living mercury"). Because of its signatures of life and growth, mercury has long been associated with twisted serpents, such as in the Staff of Hermes, the medical caduceus, Asian fighting dragons, shamanic serpents, and even the structure of DNA. All these symbols allude to the fact that the metal mercury somehow carries the principle of life.

Strangely, mercury exhibits a "breathing" pattern when heated almost to its boiling point; at that point, it starts sucking in oxygen and produces a yellow-red oxide. Upon further heating, the process reverses, and the mercury expels the oxygen like a metallic lung. This odd characteristic of mercury led chemist James Priestley to discover the element of oxygen.

The Dual Nature of Mercury

One of the signatures of mercury is that it has a dual nature and can exhibit opposing qualities. Mercury is often referred to as the *rebis* ("double thing") by alchemists. The *rebis* was depicted as an androgenous body with two heads—one male and the other female.

During the Renaissance, mercury became a symbol for consciousness to alchemistic philosophers. The liquid metal is amorphous and takes on the shape of its container (or thoughts), and it reflects whatever object or light put in front of it. Mercury's dual androgenous nature (the *rebis*) suggests that pure consciousness is unitary at its source, consisting of both Solar (masculine) and Lunar (feminine) ways of knowing.

Mercury's dual nature is also evident in other ways. While mercury is a symbol of the life force, it is also intimately connected with the forces of death and decay. While some mercury compounds are therapeutic (red compounds), others are extremely poisonous (white compounds).

Organic mercury compounds are especially dangerous because they can be readily absorbed into the human body. Methyl mercury is a lethal pollutant from industrial waste dumped in rivers and lakes. Mining applications and the use of mercury in commercial products have increased the organic mercury content of our environment to ten times its natural level. High concentrations have been detected in shellfish and tuna and other aquatic species, and mercury compounds from soil are detectable in nearly every kind of food.

In the body, mercury follows the blood and nerves and goes right for the brain. In a demonstration of mercury's affinity for gold, one eighteenth-century English alchemist put a gold coin in his mouth and then stuck his big toe into a saucer of mercury. Within thirty minutes, the liquid metal had traveled to his mouth and coated the gold coin in a swath of silvery mercury. Unfortunately, he was able to perform his stunt only a few times before he died of mercury poisoning.

Mercury poisoning attacks the consciousness and spirit of a person. Symptoms begin with problems in concentration and attention and progress to anxiety, agitation, excessive emotions, impaired motor function, impaired memory, depression, hallucinations, tremors, slurred speech, and mental retardation. The mental deterioration caused by mercury is known as erythism and was first diagnosed among nineteenth-century hat makers who used a mercury compound to kill bacteria in felt and fur hats. The syndrome became known popularly as "mad hatter's disease."

Do not be seduced by the lure of mercury into handling mercury metal. Open containers of mercury emit poisonous yet completely odorless fumes at room temperature. The threat increases significantly under warmer conditions. If mercury is spilled, it breaks up into scores of tiny balls which dramatically increase the surface area and the amount of vapors released. Sulphur clumps together with mercury instantly and is sometimes used to clean up mercury spills. Health authorities consider even small amounts of mercury metal toxic because it is so volatile.

The Moon's Metal: Silver

Silver has been known since ancient times and is mentioned in Genesis. People knew how to separate silver from lead ore as early as 3000 B.C.E. It has always been popular in jewelry and for coinage, but in the past 150 years, the demand has skyrocketed because of photographic and industrial uses.

Our word "silver" comes from the Anglo-Saxon word *siolfur*, which was their name for the metal silver. The origin of the chemical symbol for silver (Ag) comes from the Latin word *argentums*, meaning silver. Alchemists associated silver with the Moon, which they called Luna and designated it the Queen of alchemy. They used the name *Luna Philosophorum* to refer to the planetary spirit of silver. Pure silver has a brilliant white metallic luster similar to that of the full Moon. Contrary to popular belief, silver does not tarnish when exposed to pure air or water vapor; it only tarnishes in the presence of sulfur compounds in the air or to ozone. Silver has the highest electrical and heat conductivity of all metals but also has the peculiar property of reflecting electricity and heat without being affected by it. In other words, heat and electricity pass directly through silver without leaving much behind in the metal.

Silver is usually found with deposits of lead and copper. And silver forms the most organic or living crystals of all the metals, which is to say that silver crystals tend to grow into structures that resemble living plants and animals rather than the more mechanical mineral crystals formed by lead and iron.

Lunar Signatures in Silver

Like the Moon, silver comes to life in reflected light. Used in the making of mirrors, the lunar metal is the best reflector of visible light known. Silver nitrate, silver bromide, and many other silver salts are photosensitive. In photographic film, the crystals of the silver nitrate are rearranged through the action of light.

Silver has other lunar signatures. When melted and hardened again, trapped oxygen is expelled in gas eruptions that leave behind a lunar surface pocked with craters. The Moon is associated with the tides and water, and its influence over the oceans draws silver to it. Most of the silver metal on our planet is now dissolved in sea water.

It has also been shown that the behavior of silver nitrate in filter media varies with the phases of the Moon. Researchers have even documented disturbances in the behavior of silver nitrate caused by lunar eclipses.

In alchemy, the Moon and its metal were always associated with the soul. On the psychological level, the lunar powers represent the subconscious self, of which the conscious self is a reflection. Hermeticist Titus Burckhardt said: "The Moon and silver were considered to be analogous to the soul in its state of pure receptivity, whereas the soul transmuted and illumined by the spirit was analogous to the Sun and the metal gold."

The Sun's Metal: Gold

Gold was known and considered sacred from the earliest times, and Egyptian inscriptions dating back to 2600 B.C.E. describe gold. Around the world, nearly every culture associated its supreme god or goddess with gold. For many centuries, only the images of gods graced gold coins, until 330 B.C.E when Alexander the Great began the trend of rulers' images appearing on gold coins.

The chemical symbol for gold (Au) comes from the Latin word *aurum,* meaning gold. The alchemical cipher for gold is a rendition of the Sun, and gold was considered a kind of congealed solar light. Sol is the King of alchemy, and his royal purple color is the indicator of gold particles in solution.

Pure gold metal found in nature seems to like the company of the purest white quartz and is also found mixed with deposits of pyrite (Fool's Gold) and a few other sulfur minerals. Gold rarely unites with any other substance, although it does form compounds with tellurium sulfides and a few other sulfur compounds.

Still highly valued, gold is used as coinage and is a standard for monetary systems in many countries. Gold is extremely ductile, malleable, and relatively easy for artisans to work with, so it is used in making jewelry and artwork and in dentistry, electronics, and plating. Because it is an excellent reflector of infrared energy (such as what emerges from the Sun), gold is used to coat Earth satellites, interstellar probes, and windows of modern skyscrapers.

Solar Signatures in Gold

Gold is an aloof and stubbornly pure metal when it comes to reacting or even associating with lesser elements. That signature explains many of the chemical characteristics of gold. Unlike other metals, no plants contain even trace amounts of metallic gold, and there are very few gold ores because the noblest metal never alloys with baser metals. It only alloys with silver, although it makes an amalgam with mercury.

Gold embodies an inner equilibrium of forces that make it pretty much indestructible. Gold never tarnishes, and whether found buried in the ground, at the bottom of the ocean, in an ancient tomb, or in the ring on your finger, it always looks the same. It is the most flexible, enduring, and beautiful of all metals. One ounce of gold can be stretched into a single wire 35 miles long or beaten flat to just a few atoms thick.

The immortal metal is endlessly recycled, and all the gold known today is very nearly equal to all the gold that has ever been mined.

Sol Philosophorum was the name alchemists gave to the archetypal principle of the Sun, the refined essence of heat and fire expressed in the metal gold. According to the medieval alchemists, Nature continually seeks to recreate the perfection it achieved in gold, and every metal yearns to become gold. Gold is at the head of the metals, and alchemists paired it with what in their minds was the strongest and purest planet, the Sun.

The Sun's Influence Over Gold

Chemist Lilly Kolisko performed experiments with gold chloride and showed that its chemical behavior coincided with events that altered the strength of the Sun, such as the weakening in solar forces during solar eclipses or their increase during the summer solstice.

Moreover, she found that both silver compounds and gold compounds seemed to be equally influenced by the Sun. In the case of silver, the structure or patterns changed, whereas with gold, the colors changed. Silver shapes moved from jagged spikes to smooth rolling forms, but the colors remained hues of gray; however, the basic shape of gold patterns remained the same, but the colors changed from brilliant yellows to violet and reddish-purple hues.

This work, which others have duplicated, presents an amazing confirmation of how the king and queen of alchemy, the archetypal Sol and Luna, work together. The female lunar principle represents soul and form, and the male Solar principle represents spirit, energy, and light.

In this chapter, you have learned as much about the seven metals of alchemy as you would have in many weeks of handling them in the lab. These draconic metals express their archetypal presence stronger than any other materials, and their powerful signatures should be easy for you to sense. These fundamental planetary energies are present everywhere in the universe, and we will work with them on a deeper personal level as we continue our initiation into alchemy in Part 3.

APPLYING THE PRINCIPLES OF ALCHEMY IN YOUR LIFE

Alchemy is based on the precepts of the Emerald Tablet, an ancient artifact attributed to Hermes Trismegistus ("Thrice Greatest Hermes"). The Hermetic teachings describe a dynamic living universe that arose from a primordial soup known as the One Thing or First Matter. Hermetic concepts permeated ancient philosophy, religion, and science and have been passed down to us in an "Underground River" of secret teachings. These teachings were kept hidden because of their great power to tap into universal patterns and transform reality in accordance with the deeper laws of nature. The actual methods and operations used by alchemists were concealed in unique ciphers, glyphs, symbols, and coded words that they used to communicate with one another in what became known as the "Language of the Birds."

The Secret Language of Alchemists

Alchemists communicated with each other in a special language of metaphors, symbols, and unique ciphers. Many alchemists even invented their own alphabets and secret scripts to keep their work private.

The tradition of secrecy in alchemy goes back to its origins in Egypt, where priests believed the universal principles contained in the writings of Thoth were so powerful that they must not be shared with those who might abuse them. So, they discussed the secrets in riddles, symbols, and images that only the initiated would understand.

To pass the Hermetic teachings down through the ages, the ancients encoded them in sacred writings and symbolic images carved into public monuments and buildings. This tradition of hiding secrets in plain sight in the architecture of buildings was carried on in the Middle Ages in the sacred architecture of cathedrals and the symbolic sculptures and monuments at the center of cities.

Language of the Birds

Alchemists used an oblique writing style to communicate with one another publicly while concealing their true subject matter. This method of symbolic transmission of knowledge appears unintelligible unless you have the necessary key to the symbolism to be able to interpret it.

A few alchemists referred to their way of speaking as the "Green Language" or "Living Language" to indicate that it carried more than just static words. Before long, however, the alchemists' style of symbolic communication became known as the "Language of the Birds," which was considered a higher or more perfect language for discussing intuitive insights. This idea arose from the haunting suspicion that the high-pitched chirping of birds was a superior language beyond our comprehension. It was believed certain holy men and sorcerers could converse with birds and thereby learn mystical secrets of nature. King Solomon, the Nordic warrior Siegfried, and St. Francis of Assisi are some of the historical figures who are said to have understood the Language of the Birds.

The alchemists' Language of the Birds was like a higher-frequency coded language that was out of the normal "hearing" range of everyday people. The alchemists' secret communication was driven by symbols, surreal images, and secret ciphers that were silent to the uninitiated.

Alchemical teachings have been associated with birds since the beginning of recorded history. Thoth, the inventor of writing and language, was depicted with the head of the long-beaked ibis bird. Some Egyptologists believe the hieroglyphic language originated by tracing the movements of birds in the sky and on the ground. And scholars believe the first known style of writing (cuneiform) may have originated from bird tracks.

The Birds of Alchemy

The alchemists spoke in the Language of Birds in the most literal sense, too. They used images of birds to stand for some of their most important concepts, especially those dealing with volatile or spiritual processes.

The movements of birds are highly significant in alchemical drawings. Ascending birds indicate the volatilization or evaporation of compounds, while descending birds indicate the fixation, condensation, or precipitation of compounds. Birds that are shown both ascending and descending specify the operation of distillation.

A standing bird usually designates the kind of alchemical operation that is underway. The crow or raven indicates Black Phase operations such as calcination or putrefaction, which involve the breaking down of structures by fire or decay. The white goose, white swan, or albatross stand for the White Phase operations of separation and purification. The rooster or cockerel means the operation of conjunction or union is underway, and the peacock announces the beginning of the fermentation operation.

The pelican stands for the distillation operation at the beginning of the Red Phase of alchemy. The eagle also suggests distillation, as well as the operation of sublimation. The color of the eagle sometimes indicates the color of the vapors being released during distillation. For instance, a white eagle represents steam. The Egyptian *Bennu* bird or Phoenix, the mythical bird that was reborn in the fire, stands for the final operation of coagulation and the creation of the Philosopher's Stone.

Other bird symbolism in alchemy includes the double-headed eagle, which indicates the *rebis* or androgynous state of mercury. Sometimes, the bat also signifies dual-natured substances and androgyny. The dove is a symbol of renewed spirit or infusion of divine energy. Chemically, the dove heralds the purifying transformation from the Black Phase to the White Phase of alchemy.

The basilisk is a symbolic mythological creature with the head of a bird and the body of a dragon. According to legend, the wingless creature was hatched from a hermaphroditic cock's egg and nursed by a serpent. Chemically, the basilisk stands for the union of mercury (the bird) and sulfur (the dragon) in the mineral cinnabar. Spiritually, it symbolizes the melding of our higher and lower natures of spirit (the bird) and soul (the dragon) to create a new incarnation called the "Child of the Philosophers."

In alchemy, eggs, in general, are highly symbolic. They stand for any kind of sealed vessel, which includes closed glass vessels, as well as unexpected items as coffins, tombs, and sepulchers. References to eggs and the hatching of birds and serpents abound. For instance, the alchemist's insulated fermenting box was referred to as the "House of the Chick," and the whole cosmos itself was sometimes depicted as a serpent hatching from or entwined around an egg.

Another egg symbol, the Griffin's Egg, is an allusion to the Vessel of Hermes in which the conjunction (alchemical marriage) of volatile and fixed substances takes place. The Griffin is a mythical beast that has the body of a lion and the head and wings of an eagle. Because the lion is considered the king of the beasts and the eagle is considered the king of the birds, their union in the Griffin makes it the most powerful and majestic animal imaginable.

Animal Symbolism in Alchemy

While birds and flying animals generally indicate spiritual or volatile principles, terrestrial animals usually stand for physical or fixed principles. Whenever two animals are found, they usually signify sulfur and mercury or some relationship between fixed and volatile principles.

Animals also symbolize basic principles of alchemy. For example, they might be associated with the Four Elements in drawings. The Earth Element is often symbolized by an ox or lion, the Water Element by fish or whales, the Air Element by doves or eagles, and the Fire Element by salamanders or dragons.

Serpents represent the life force, or the energies being exchanged in transformations. Two entwined serpents represent the opposing masculine and feminine energies that make up the vital force (such as depicted in the caduceus) or the union of opposing substances in the lab. Winged serpents represent volatile substances; wingless serpents represent fixed substances. A crucified serpent represents the fixation of a volatile substance or the manifestation of spiritual energy in physical reality. Three-headed serpents or three serpents in a group stand for the three principles of Sulfur, Mercury, and Salt, which we go deeper into in Chapter 11.

In alchemical drawings, frogs and toads indicate the First Matter and the energies of materialization. The black toad symbolizes the First Matter being released by the putrefaction of a substance. The chaining or tying together of a toad on the ground and an eagle in the sky represents the union of fixed and volatile components, such as silver and mercury or soul and spirit.

Other animal symbols include two fish swimming in opposite directions, which designate the essences of spirit and soul during the operation of dissolution. Bees, beetles, and butterflies are symbols of purification and the rebirth of soul or inner essence. The mythical unicorn is a symbol of sublimation and is associated with the white tincture and white powder of purity. The noble stag with large antlers is associated with the red tincture and red powder of projection. Scenes of the stag and unicorn meeting in the middle of a forest indicate the completion of the work and the successful creation of the Philosopher's Stone.

Wolves symbolize the wild, untamed spirit in humans or the chaotic forces of nature. Dogs represent the domesticated spirit or natural forces working to assist the alchemist. Chemically, the dog is Philosophical Mercury, which is the purified or benevolent spirit of the metal mercury.

The Gray Wolf stands for the metal antimony. The Gray Wolf is a fearsome beast. When molten, antimony mercilessly devours other metals such as lead, tin, and copper. Drawings showing dogs fighting with wolves represent the process of purifying gold with antimony, a grayish metal that fuses with other metals to remove them from molten gold.

The Lions of Alchemy

Lions are important symbols, and they are usually associated with the properties of sulfur or the application of heat or acids to the metals. Chemically, the lion is any salt or fixed substance obtained from the metals.

The Lion is black, green, or red according to its state of transformation. The first of the lions is the Black Lion, which represents a black salt, lead ore, or, in general, the darkest part of a substance that must be purified and transformed by fire.

When working with minerals and metals, the Green Lion is the root of the essence of a metal or its soul. The Green Lion was known for devouring the metals; the chemical signature that gave it its green color was iron sulfate, and acids made with iron sulfate were called the Green Lion. These included vitriol or sulfuric acid (which dissolved most common metals such as iron and copper) and nitric acid. When nitric acid was mixed with hydrochloric acid, it produced the greenish acid *aqua regia*, which could even dissolve gold. Images of the Green Lion devouring the Sun refer to this ability. The Green Lion is also associated with green copper sulfate or the green acetate of lead in its oily or unredeemed form.

When working with plant essences and vegetable matter, the Green Lion signifies the vital force in the leaves of plants. In this case, the Green Lion eating the Sun is the process of photosynthesis that creates the greenness of nature from the pigment chlorophyll. Alchemists understood this process and tried to isolate the life force in plants to use in their experiments and even create artificial life forms.

At the next level of the work—the work with animals—the Red Lion is the vital force in blood. In the work with minerals and metals, the Red Lion is the red acetate of lead in its crystallized form. Generally, with the Red Lion, we gain control over untamed or unredeemed forces by feeding the Green Lion a seed of gold or purifying it with a catalyst or transmuting agent.

Philosophically, the Green Lion symbolizes the raw forces of nature or the subconscious mind that we are seeking to tame, and the Red Lion is the successful assimilation or control of those forces. In the final stages of the work, the Red Lion grows wings. The Winged Lion is the volatile or spiritual aspect of a substance, which, in the lab, is the sublimated salt needed to make the Philosopher's Stone.

The Dragons of Alchemy

As we learned in the previous chapter, dragons are another group of important symbols and often represent the properties of the metals, especially Mercury as the *élan vital* or animating force. Chemically, the dragon is the mercury acid obtained from the metals. Dragons also symbolize the actions of any acid in general. Like lions, the alchemical dragon is black, green, or red according to its level of transformation.

The Black Dragon is the blackened metallic compound undergoing putrefaction, death, and decay. The Green Dragon is the indwelling spirit or life of the metal, the thing that gives metals their active properties. Philosophically, the Green Dragon is a formerly ferocious and unforgiving dragon that is now tamed. Its energy is contained by having been crystallized, or psychologically, the formerly threatening unconscious elements have now been assimilated into consciousness.

The Red Dragon appears at both the beginning and end of the work. It is the chaotic energy of the First Matter at the beginning of the work that becomes the Philosopher's Stone at the end of the work. Chemically, the Red Dragon signifies the pure red oil of lead in its initial state and the red powder of projection in its perfected or tamed state.

A fire-breathing dragon or a dragon in flames indicates a metal melting or a substance undergoing calcination. Several dragons fighting amongst themselves depict metals undergoing the process of putrefaction. Dragons with wings represent the volatile (spirit or energetic) principle, and wingless dragons represent the fixed (soul or material) principle. The cyclic interplay of volatile and fixed, light and darkness, spirit and soul, energy and matter, and creation and destruction, is rendered in drawings showing two dragons, one winged and the other with feet, each eating the other's tail.

A dragon or serpent eating its own tail is known as an ouroboros (or uroboros). It symbolizes the union of opposing energies and is one of the primary symbols for the Philosopher's Stone. The caption "All Is One" is usually included with drawings of the ouroboros. Alchemists sometimes referred to the ouroboros as the *Agathos Daimon* ("Good Spirit"), which was another name for Thoth, the father of alchemy.

Silent Secrets of the Rose

No symbol inspired alchemists of the Renaissance more than the rose. The flower is one of the fundamental symbols of alchemy and became the philosophical basis of the Rosicrucians, an alchemical movement that flourished in the seventeenth century. So important was it to alchemists that dozens of manuscripts were named *Rosarium* (Latin for "Rose Garden"), and they all deal with the alchemical relationship between the King and Queen.

The rose garden is a symbol of sacred space and could mean a meditation chamber (Oratorium) in a lab, a sacred tabernacle, a sacred location in nature, the Inner Laboratory of mind, or paradise itself. In all these instances, the rose garden is the mystical bridal chamber, the place of the sacred marriage. "Mystery glows in the rose bed and the secret is hidden in the rose," wrote the twelfth-century Persian alchemist Farid Attar.

The rose is much more meaningful, much older, and more deeply embedded in the human subconscious than most people realize. In Europe, rose fossils 35 million years old have been found, and archeologists have unearthed petrified rose wreaths from the oldest Egyptian tombs. To understand the alchemists' fascination with the rose, let's take a deeper look into its complicated symbolism.

The rose is a paradoxical symbol of both purity and passion, both heavenly perfection and earthly desire. Originally a symbol of joy, it was associated with the mystical center of a person, our hidden heart of hearts. In the nineteenth century, the rose signified the secrecy and silence of forbidden love, but today, the rose is commonly associated with open romantic love. In general, the color of the rose denotes its meaning:

- Red roses are symbols of passion, soulful love, deep creativity, and deep personal energy.
- White roses symbolize purity, innocence, acceptance, and unconditional love.
- Black or withered roses indicate that love is gone or is over, as well as impending disaster, depression, or death.
- Pink roses stand for gentleness, thankfulness, and loving or supportive friendship.
- Yellow roses signify compassion, charity, sociability, free-flowing conversations, confidence, and security.
- Orange roses carry feelings of enthusiasm, fascination, and optimism.

- Blue or purple roses indicate deep spiritual longing, meditation, and the promise of a perfect world.
- Gilded or golden roses convey the idea of personal perfection, a successful marriage of opposites, completion of the Great Work, or birth of the Golden Child.

In general, the rose is a symbol of the alchemical operation of conjunction, the sacred marriage of opposites. It represents the regeneration of purified essences and their resurrection in a new compound or body.

The marriage of the White Rose and the Red Rose is one of the most significant events in alchemy. It represents the mystical marriage of opposites, the union of spirit and soul, and Solar and Lunar consciousness into an integrated immortal whole.

The white rose is associated with the White Queen of alchemy and represents the feminine, receptive, contractive principle of the lunar soul. White roses were also linked to the White Phase of the work and the White Stone of Multiplication.

In spiritual alchemy, the white rose represents a special kind of love in which one melts away into the beauty of another, and the old identity is sacrificed for that of the beloved or for a higher identity discovered within oneself. Sufi spiritual alchemist Rumi had this idea in mind when he wrote: "In the driest, whitest stretch of pain's infinite desert, I lost my sanity and found this rose." In this sense, the rose is a symbol of complete surrender and permanent transmutation.

The red rose is associated with the Red King and is regarded as a masculine, active, expansive principle of the solar spirit. The red rose was also associated with the Red Phase and the Red Stone of Projection. "The rose red color," said psychologist Carl Jung, "is related to the *aqua permanens*, an eternal water or blood of the soul, which are extracted from the First Matter."

German alchemist Michael Maier (1568–1622) discussed the symbolism of the red and white roses in his *Septimana Philosophica* ("the Philosophical Week"): "The rose is the first and most perfect of flowers. The Gardens of Philosophy are planted with many roses, both red and white, whose colors correspond to those displayed by gold and silver. The center of the rose is green and is emblematical of the Green Lion or First Matter. Just as the natural rose turns to the Sun and is refreshed by rain, so is the Philosophical Matter prepared in blood and grown in light. In and by these, it is made perfect."

In Christian alchemy, the rose and the rosary became symbols of union between God and human beings. This idea is reinforced by scenes of Mary in a rose garden, under a rose arbor, or before a tapestry of roses. In the art of the Middle Ages, Mary is almost always shown holding a rose, which indicates her power comes from divine love.

Because of its association with the deepest workings of the human heart, the rose has come to symbolize inner secrets and things that cannot be spoken. The Latin phrase *sub rosa* ("under the rose") is used to indicate discussions or writings that should be kept secret. The concept originated in the medieval tradition of hanging red roses from the ceiling of meetings of Hermetic organizations (such as the Rosicrucians, Freemasons, or alchemy guilds) to indicate that the discussions were not to be shared with outsiders. For instance, in Sebastian Brant's fifteenth-century alchemical treatise *Ship of Fools*, the author warns: "What here we do say, shall under roses stay."

Secret Ciphers of the Alchemists

Ciphers are symbolic glyphs used by alchemists to indicate chemicals, metals, and the basic principles and operations of their craft. These silent symbols were also part of the Language of the Birds and embodied some of the most esoteric secrets of the alchemists.

In the process of alchemical initiation, ciphers were used as coded teaching tools, and meditation on ciphers was thought to convey unspoken wisdom. The alchemists' ciphers have much to say about the hidden meanings and archetypal power of their materials and operations.

Symbol	Meaning	Symbol	Meaning
△	Air	♄	Lead, Saturn
	Albedo (White Phase)		Life Force, Health
	Alembic	☿	Mercury, Quicksilver
	Amalgam		Mixture, to Mix
	Antimony		Multiplication (Aquarius)
♏	Autumn Work		Nigredo (Black Phase)
	Boiling, to Ferment	∴	Oil
♀	Copper, Venus		Precipitation
	Combine	♓	Projection (Pisces)
	Composed of	♌	Purification
♉	Conjunction (Taurus)	☆	Quintessence
	Crucible		Receiver
	Crystal, Crystallization		Retort
	Day and Night		Rubedo (Red Phase)
	Decompose		Salt (General)
♌	Digestion (Leo)		Salt (Magnesia, Clay)
♋	Dissolution (Cancer)	♏	Separation (Scorpio)
♍	Distillation (Virgo)	☽	Silver, Moon
▽	Earth		Silver (Spirit of)
	Electrum, Platinum		Spirit
	Essence		Spring Work
	Essence (Plant)		Stone (Elemental)
♑	Fermentation (Capricorn)		Stone (Philosopher's)
	Filter	Ω	Sublimation (Libra)
⊕	First Matter (rectified)		Sulfur
⊗	First Matter (unrectified)		Sulfuric Acid
△	Fire		Summer Work
♊	Fixation (Gemini)	♃	Tin, Jupiter
	Fuse, Meld		Vitriol
☉	Gold, Sun	▽	Water
♐	Incineration (Sagittarius)		White Lead
♂	Iron, Mars		Zinc

Chart of Alchemical Ciphers

The Precious New Pearl Engraving

As an exercise in deciphering ciphers, let's investigate a Renaissance drawing intended to help initiates penetrate the deeper relationships of the fundamental ciphers of alchemy. In the engraving titled "Precious New Pearl" (shown below), we see an esoteric schematic drawing that is imbued with archetypal influences. The Sun, Moon, and 15 stars look down over symbols centered on a tree trunk with a massive root system in the ground.

The Quintessence

To the right is a five-petal flower indicating the presence of the Quintessence, and on the left is a seven-branched plant indicating the steps or operations of perfection. On top of the tree is an eagle representing the operation of distillation, which in this case, is the mental operation of distilling these symbols. It is a sign that we need to reflect or meditate on this drawing.

The "Precious New Pearl" engraving shows the relationship of the basic ciphers in the creation of the Philosopher's Stone.
(From Pretiosa Margarita by Giovanni Lacinio, 1714)

Two Lions Support the Work

Supporting the tree trunk are two lions, one with wings and one without, representing the union of the volatile and fixed faculties of spirit and soul, which we must use together to understand these symbols. In other words, we must combine the masculine, logical, and argumentative way of knowing of spirit with the feminine, intuitive, and reflective way of knowing of soul. This union of opposites is the key needed to decipher the coded material being presented. In fact, without knowledge of this key principle, alchemy remains an obscure puzzle.

Cipher for the First Matter

In the engraving, we see two ciphers buried in the ground at the foot of the tree. These are the basic raw materials with which the alchemist works. On the left is the symbol for salt, which represents the physical or incarnated energy at the beginning of the work. On the right is the cipher for the First Matter, which is the spirit matter of the work, that is the elusive ether that exists between worlds.

The cipher for the First Matter can be shown in two orientations. Shown in the figure as a plus sign (+) in a circle, it signifies the purified or rectified First Matter. If it were shown as an "X" in a circle, it would have signified the chaotic or unrefined First Matter.

The other ciphers in the figure are arranged in the shape of a cross with horizontal and vertical components. In Hermetic geometry, horizontal lines and earthly orientation stand for material reality or things fixed in time and space. Vertical lines and heavenly orientation stand for energetic or spiritual forces that are not fixed in time and space.

Ciphers for the Elements

On the horizontal component of the cross are the ciphers for the Four Elements that make up our material reality. On the left side of the tree trunk, the first cipher is Fire, which is a triangle pointing upward. Fire seeks to ascend because of its hot and dry qualities.

On the right side of the tree trunk, the first cipher is Water, a triangle pointing downward. Water seeks to descend and condense because of its cold and moist qualities. Fire and Water are the purest Elements, and if allowed full expression of their urges, Fire would disappear into the Above, and Water would be absorbed into the Below.

Next to Fire on the left is the cipher for Earth, which is the downward-pointing triangle cipher of Water with a horizontal line through it. Next to Water on the right is the cipher for Air, the upward-pointing triangle of Fire with a horizontal line through it. In other words, Earth is cold and dry and seeks to descend, but its dry component blocks its full descent, and the horizontal line in the triangle of Water indicates this. Air is hot and moist and seeks to ascend, but its moist component blocks its full ascent, as is indicated by the horizontal line in the triangle of Fire.

The elements Earth and Air are suspended in time and space, caught between and connecting the extremes of Above and Below. In the Hermetic teachings, Earth and Air are considered to be more manifested and stable versions of the Elements Water and Fire.

Ciphers for the Three Essentials

The triangular shape of the ciphers for the Elements is not without significance. It indicates that the Elements of creation are made up of three primordial forces present in the First Matter and expressed in all created things. The alchemists called these three essential ingredients Sulfur, Mercury, and Salt, and for now, we are concerned only with the ciphers alchemists chose to represent them.

In the drawing, the ciphers for the Three Essentials are arranged vertically on the trunk of the tree. This orientation indicates these are archetypal forces from Above that are not fixed in time and space. At the bottom of the tree nearest the ground is the cipher of heavenly Salt, which is the universal principle of materialization. This is the same cipher as the one for terrestrial or physical salt. Alchemists usually capitalized the "heavenly" or spiritual words or called them "sophic" to differentiate them from their mundane meanings. For instance. Sophic Salt is the philosophic or deeper principle of salt.

While vertical orientation indicates spiritual processes, horizontal orientation indicates physical processes. Thus, the horizontal line through the salt cipher suggests its materiality or tendency to form bodies.

The next cipher up the tree trunk is for Sulfur. It consists of the cipher for Fire with a cross attached beneath it. The cross indicates the Fire Element is being expressed along both the horizontal (material) and the vertical (spiritual) axis of reality. Common sulfur is known as brimstone (literally the "burning stone") and carries the signatures of the Fire Element.

Above the cipher for Sulfur and at the same level as the horizontal line of elements is the cipher for Mercury. Mercury's position on the cross of ciphers is significant, as it is the transforming medium that exists in both material and spiritual realms. This is also indicated by the cross at the base of the cipher.

The circle in the middle of the Mercury cipher stands for the Sun and is sometimes shown with a point or dot at its center, which is the cipher for the Sun as well as for gold. The curved line or semicircle at the top of the cipher stands for the Moon. The semicircle or crescent is the cipher for the Moon as well as for silver. Therefore, the cipher for Mercury results from a union of the Sun and Moon, which in alchemy means just one thing. It is the sacred marriage, the union of the King and Queen within, the merging of masculine and feminine ways of knowing, and the creation of the Philosopher's Stone.

The symbol for the Philosopher's Stone is shown above Mercury at the top of the tree. It is represented by the cipher for rectified antimony, which is a circle with a cross above it. It means that Above and Below have been reversed to create paradise on the earthly plane. The material elements (the cross) have been elevated, and the divine realm (the circle) is now manifested Below.

We have seen in this chapter how alchemists spoke in the Language of Birds to conceal their secret teachings in public view. They realized the rigid mindset of the Church fathers and other authorities would never be able to penetrate the esoteric and often heretical topics they were discussing. In the following chapters, we will dig deeper into the alchemists' coded language to learn exactly what they were talking about.

CHAPTER 10

Prima Materia:
The Elusive First Matter

The First Matter (*Prima Materia* in Latin) is one of the most important yet confusing concepts in alchemy. Even alchemists had a hard time defining it. The 1612 edition of the *Lexicon of Alchemy* lists more than 80 different definitions for First Matter, and at least 200 different descriptions of it are found in the writings of medieval alchemists.

Among the popular synonyms for the First Matter were such alchemical concepts as Fire, Water, Air, Earth, Sulfur, Mercury, Salt, Quintessence, the Sun, the Moon, and the Stone. Also included were philosophical ideals like imagination, love, light, consciousness, thought, spirit, soul, and God. Even such terms as blood, urine, menses, manure, and dirt were considered fitting definitions by alchemists.

The reason the First Matter is so hard to pin down is that it is everything and nothing at once. It is the primal One Thing that existed before time; it's also the chaotic plethora that contains all possibilities—the infinite cornucopia from which all created things in the universe emerge. It is the formless ether that is the fabric of the universe and carries the germ or seeds of all things that ever existed and ever will.

Yet this unbelievably elusive and potent cosmic force was the subject of the alchemists' practical work as they tried to accumulate it in its pristine form from natural sources and expose it in metals and other compounds through their chemical manipulations. They sought it deep in underground mines and in the black virgin soil in the middle of forests. They carefully spread out burlap bags to collect the morning dew, which they believed held traces of the First Matter. They even distilled hundreds of gallons of children's urine seeking the magical essence. They looked for it everywhere, including in their own bodies, minds, and souls.

What Is the First Matter?

The Emerald Tablet refers to the First Matter as the "One Thing," the primordial chaos of the universe that is fashioned into material reality by the thought or Word of the One Mind. This idea of a divine presence seeking expression in the material universe seems to have originated with the ancient Egyptians and has become a basic tenet of Hermetic philosophy.

The Egyptians denoted the First Matter with the hieroglyph known as *kh,* which looks like a circle with two wide horizontal black bands running through it. This cipher for the First Matter is the first hieroglyphic letter that makes up the Egyptian word *khem,* which is the root of our word "alchemy." It is also the only hieroglyph for which no traditional Egyptologist is certain of the meaning. Other hieroglyphs are associated with a common item, such as a basket, stool, owl, vulture, and so on. But this particular symbol has both tangible and intangible nuances. The easiest definition is "black matter that is alive," but what exactly is that? Most language experts have translated it as "placenta," but others think it might mean "fertile dirt" or "living black soil." In fact, it is the sacred script for the First Matter, the basic dark matter of the universe from which all things have sprung.

The ancients thought of the First Matter as a spiritual substance of which external visible nature is an expression and manifestation. This etheric matter contains the powers that form minerals and metals, vegetables and animals, and everything that breathes; all forms are hidden within its depths, and it is, therefore, the first principle or beginning of all things.

In ancient China, philosophers referred to the First Matter as the "Tao," which is an equally difficult term to describe. The Chinese spiritual alchemist Lao Tzu (circa 500 B.C.E.) considered the Tao as plural in manifestation but singular in essence; totally real, yet totally unknowable; and a nonpersonal, amoral, and primordial chaos.

Lao Tzu described it in the *Tao te Ching*: "There is a thing confusedly formed, born between heaven and earth. Silent and void, it stands alone and does not age, goes round and does not weary. It is capable of being the mother of the world." The Tao is the unborn origin of the universe and the chaotic source of all that exists between Heaven and Earth.

Western alchemists depicted the First Matter as the ouroboros (or uroboros), which is a serpent or dragon eating its own tail. In alchemical drawings, sometimes two serpents or dragons were shown, with a lighter, winged serpent above and a darker, walking serpent below. The interplay between these two primordial principles is the engine that drives reality. The spinning ouroboros creates the singular force behind the evolutionary perfection of the universe.

Psychologist Carl Jung commented on the psychological meaning of the ouroboros in his *Mysterium Conjunctionis*: "In the age-old image of the ouroboros lies the thought of devouring oneself and turning oneself into a circulatory process, for it was clear to the more astute alchemists the *Prima Materia* of the art was the alchemist himself. The ouroboros is a dramatic symbol for the integration and assimilation of the opposite, i.e., the shadow. This feedback process is at the same time a symbol of immortality, since it is said of the ouroboros that it slays itself and brings itself to life, fertilizes itself, and gives birth to itself."

To alchemists, the First Matter is a primordial, unorganized state of energy or protomatter that is the same for all substances and exists in an unmanifested state between energy and matter. The chaotic energy of the First Matter is organized or directed by the light of consciousness. Hermetic philosophers believe the whole universe came into being because of an image, thought, or word projected by the divine mind into the fabric of the universe, the First Matter.

Unfortunately, our Western culture has rejected the concept of the First Matter. For us, things are either real or not real. We have no room in our thinking for the gray area of reality between manifested and unmanifested, where the First Matter exists. For this reason, alchemists often referred to the First Matter as the "cornerstone the builders forgot." That is why rejected things like feces, manure, urine, and even the shadowy dark desires and beliefs we shove into our unconscious are symbols of the First Matter.

Properties of the First Matter

Down through the ages, alchemists have written about the characteristics of the First Matter to help identify, accumulate, and transform the mysterious substance. From their writings, we can discern five characteristics of the First Matter on which they all seem to agree.

The First Matter Is Eternal.

Like our concept of energy, the First Matter cannot be created or destroyed; it can only be transformed. The amount of First Matter in the universe is fixed, permanent, and unaffected by time. Modern alchemists associate it with dark matter, which the equations of physics say makes up most of the universe but cannot be detected. Physicists believe dark matter is responsible for the basic structure of the universe and have theorized that billions of bits of the invisible matter stream through our bodies every second.

The First Matter Is Everywhere to Be Found.

Because the First Matter is the source of all things, it is present everywhere and in all things—including our own minds. To find your personal First Matter, you must search in the twilight area between manifested and unmanifested reality and between the unconscious and the conscious. Scholars call the kind of space in which the First Matter appears a "liminal" location, which means anything at the edge, crossroads, or threshold where normal boundaries fade away.

The First Matter Is Cyclic.

Both Eastern and Western alchemists understood the cyclic nature of the First Matter and believed it changed into all things manifested and unmanifested in a grand pattern of continuous transformation. In the West, the ouroboros symbolized this idea. The Eastern symbol for this process is the Tai Chi or Yin-Yang diagram, which depicts the spinning forces of darkness (Yin/matter) and light (Yang/mind), each containing the seed of the other and constantly changing into one another. Yin is seen as feminine, passive, and satisfied in its existence, while Yang is seen as masculine, active, and hungry.

The First Matter Contains All the Elements.

The First Matter contains all the components of creation, including the Four Elements and the Quintessence. The alchemists believed that the actual form the First Matter takes when it manifests into a material substance depends on the proportions of the Four Elements being expressed. The Elements can be changed into each other, and this manipulation of a substance's First Matter is what transforms it.

The First Matter Is the Source of the Philosopher's Stone.

The First Matter was believed to be the only thing from which the Philosopher's Stone could be prepared, and as far back as the Alexandrian alchemist Zosimos, alchemists stated that once the First Matter was known and purified, it became the much-sought-after Stone. The German alchemist Heinrich Khunrath described the First Matter as the true Light of nature, which guides and illuminates all seekers after divine truth. "It is in the world," he wrote, "and the whole edifice of the world is beautifully adorned and will be naturally preserved by it. But the world knows it not. Above all, it is the subject of the great Stone of the philosophers which the world has before its eyes and yet knows it not."

Working with the First Matter

No alchemical process of transformation—whether in the laboratory, in the body, or in the soul—can succeed without the participation of the elusive ingredient of the First Matter. Certainly, nothing was more important to an alchemist's work than this spiritized essence. The alchemists made it clear in their writings that by applying the grades of fire with which they worked, they could extricate the First Matter from any substance and render it tangible and visible.

Alchemists, in their attempts to change base metals into gold, developed most of the laboratory methods of working with the First Matter. The idea behind their work is simple. If you strip a metal of the gross qualities and physical properties that identify it, it will yield the one "primitive matter" that is the same for all metals. Next, if you impose the appropriate new qualities upon the primitive matter, the desired new substance is attained.

So, the metals all originate from the same matrix, which is their First Matter. "The metals are similar in their essence, and differ only in their form," wrote Albertus Magnus in *De Mineralibus* ("The Minerals"). "One may pass easily from one metal to another, following a circle." The modern atomic theory of matter expresses a strikingly similar conclusion.

Trying to extract the First Matter from a substance represented months of hard work roasting, pulverizing, dissolving, and breaking down materials said to contain large amounts of the transcendent essence. Alchemists also referred to the First Matter as the "Mercury of the Philosophers," because they believed the essence or soul of all metals was mercury, and therefore, they spent much effort trying to extract the First Matter from mercury.

The alchemists often referred to the hidden essence of First Matter in a substance as its inner "star," and appearances of the First Matter are often accompanied by displays of light. In this sense, the First Matter is the *Anima Mundi* ("Soul of the World") and is present in all things. Alchemists believed the First Matter also existed in the human body as the eternal star that we call the soul. The spiritual work in alchemy focused on purifying or rectifying the First Matter within, thereby, perfecting the very soul of the alchemist.

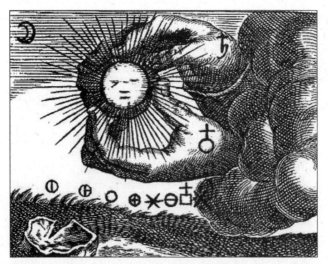

"Here is the Shining Perfection held by the hands of the Absolute. To possess it, you must know the Subject of our work and how to prepare it, then you must apply the Secret of Saturn, or the way to dissolve and putrefy it."

(From De Groene Leeuw by Goossen van Vreeswijk, 1674)

The *Tria Prima* (Three Essentials)

Alchemists believed the First Matter was a real substance that could be extracted from matter and made visible, and they even listed it as an ingredient in their experiments. The primary tool for manipulating it was the spiritual connection they made with the First Matter, in which their consciousness identified with it and changed it. Meditation, prayer, and ritual were tools used by both alchemists and magicians in their pursuit of the First Matter.

The work with the First Matter is clearly demonstrated in the alchemists' work with the metals. It was thought the metals matured naturally underground, slowly changing from base metals like lead into noble metals like silver and gold. This process could be sped up by accessing the First Matter responsible for it, which, in the case of the metals, was mercury.

Mercury was considered the First Matter of the metals because it has the power to dissolve and balance the other metals. To transform metals, it is necessary to melt them in fire, but mercury is naturally in a liquid state. As quicksilver, it seemed alive and always changing. As a heavenly body, it was always closest to the sun and appeared to follow its own independent path in the heavens—sometimes even going backward.

Paracelsus (1493–1541) elevated Mercury to a universal power in a triad of primordial forces known as the *Tria Prima* or "Three Essentials." Fiery Sulfur (brimstone) was equated with energy; Salt (cubic sodium compounds) represented matter; and shiny, reflective Mercury was associated with light. The *Tria Prima* became the prevalent working theory of medieval alchemists and is still represented in modern scientific theory as energy, matter, and light ($E = mc^2$).

The First Matter in Alchemy and Magic

The concept of the First Matter (*Prima Materia*) was central to both alchemy and the Egyptian magic tradition (theurgy) and united their practitioners in the Great Work. For alchemists, Mercury is the force of conscious will or transforming agent identical to the theurgical idea of the Universal Magical Agent.

In magical work, Sulfur is the *anima* or the transformative soul that burns through time. Salt is the *corpus* or physical effect to be manifested. Mercury is the *spiritus* or transformative power of consciousness. In terms of application, Sulfur is the expansive force or binding agent between the spiritual realm above and the manifested world below. Salt is the contractive force or substantiating agent.

The Hermetic teaching that the First Matter was part of the Three Essentials became a doctrine in many esoteric groups, including the Freemasons, Theosophists, Ordo Templi Orientis, Aurum Solis, Golden Dawn, and various Rosicrucian orders and Templar groups. As noted earlier, Eliphas Levi (1810–1875) said the doctrines in many Hermetic organizations are a Perennial Philosophy that keeps resurfacing in different forms through the ages:

"Behind the veil of all the hieratic and mystical allegories of ancient doctrines," Levi observed, "behind the darkness and strange ordeals of all initiations, under the seal of all sacred writings, in the ruins of Thebes, on the crumbling stones of old temples and on the blackened visage of the Sphinx, in the marvelous paintings of the Vedas, in the cryptic emblems of old books on alchemy, in the ceremonies practiced by all secret societies, there are found indications of a Hermetic doctrine which is everywhere the same and everywhere carefully concealed."

The First Matter in You

Alchemical psychologists consider the unconscious mind to be a kind of First Matter and seek to access it using the operations of alchemy. According to Sigmund Freud (1856–1939), the unconscious mind is the primal cause of most of our behavior. For him, this part of the mind is not available to introspection awareness. Its contents include instincts, sexuality, habitual thought processes, buried memories, latent interests, automatic responses, and unknown motivations.

Our motives, feelings, decisions, and relationships are greatly influenced by instinctual responses and past experiences, and this "programming" is stored in the unconscious mind. Unconscious beliefs and suppressed feelings can be the cause of neurotic behavior and mental unrest. The unconscious is the hidden source of sudden anger, self-defeating thoughts, relationship problems, sexual promiscuousness, gambling, spending sprees, and other forms of compulsive behavior. The unconscious is like a knee-jerk reaction over which we have no control. Environmental cues in the media and the behavior of others trigger responses unconsciously, without us realizing it.

But the matrix of the unconscious mind is also the transition of unknown to known and from potential to manifestation in consciousness. It is the source of imagination, creative energy, and deep connection to the substratum of reality. The unconscious is the gateway to unlimited possibilities and new energy, too. The unconscious is the fabric of our mind, just like the hidden First Matter is the fabric of the universe. Many of the most perplexing alchemical drawings are about unconscious content rising to the surface in alchemists exploring the contents of the unconscious mind.

That fabric of mind can be refashioned using the principles of alchemical transformation. We can transmute addictive habits and reactions into good habits and useful traits in the same way the alchemists hoped to transform the dark, stubborn, caustic properties of lead into the shining light of wholeness and a purified mind that gold represents.

To create positive habits of behavior in the unconscious mind, we have to train the dragon and tie our new behaviors to regular times and locations with clear connections to a higher frequency—a higher spiritual instinct that exists in all of us. We must raise the frequency of our environment and replace negative cues and examples of leaden behavior with positive examples of what it means to be golden. We will learn more about the transformation of unconscious content in the operation of Fermentation in Part 4.

We have devoted this entire chapter to the First Matter because of its importance in both spiritual and practical work. Renaissance Hermeticists pointed to a new permutation of First Matter in individuals—a third "transcendent function" that arises from the tension between the unconscious and conscious minds and supports their union. We will explore this unifying function further in Chapter 13. But next, in the following two chapters, we will investigate how the First Matter unfolded around us to create the world as we know it.

The Three Essentials of Creation

The Three Essentials are the trinity of forces that are part of the act of creation itself. They emerged from the darkness of First Matter in the very first act of creation—the tremendous burst of energy and light that we know as the Big Bang.

The Three Essentials were the first organizing principles to emerge from the primal chaos, and they continue to be present in any act of creation or transformation. Conversely, all created things consist of the Three Essentials, and alchemical procedures can break everything back down into these same three principles.

The Three Essentials became a central doctrine in alchemy, and eventually, in modern physics as the fundamental forces of energy, light, and matter. In the writings of alchemists, the Three Essentials were also referred to as the "Three Supernals," "Supreme Trinity," "Three *Principia,*" "Three Universals," "Three Treasures," "Three Magisteriums," or the "*Tria Prima.*" Once created, the three primal forces are indistinguishable from the First Matter in their powers of transformation, and their hidden interaction is responsible for the myriad manifested things in the world.

At the end of the Great Work, the Three Essentials are reunited and integrally fused into the Philosopher's Stone. An alchemists' motto conveyed this idea: "The Stone is single in essence but triple in form." We see this same idea in one of the symbols for the Philosopher's Stone–the three-headed serpent or dragon. When compared to the similar beast of the First Matter, there are some distinct differences in coloring and attitude, but the point is that the First Matter itself has been transformed somehow.

The Two Contraries of Sulfur and Mercury

The roots of the alchemists' Three Essentials theory lie in an ancient doctrine known as the "Two Contraries." The Two Contraries were seen as reciprocal principles of nature, which are usually described as male and female or active and passive. Symbolized by the Sun and Moon, they were an expression of the fundamental natural law of energy exchange and reproduction.

Originating in Egypt in the myths of Isis and Osiris, the doctrine of the Two Contraries eventually spread to Babylonia and China. Although the two opposing principles took on a variety of names, they always shared the same characteristics of the original myth. Isis was the Moon goddess—the feminine, receptive, reflective, productive principle of nature. Osiris was the Sun god—the masculine, aggressive, penetrating source of energy and identity. Their child was Horus, who became the symbol for all new birth, growth, the green Earth, manifestation, and transformation in general.

Among Alexandrian alchemists, the principle of the Sun or Osiris became linked with Sulfur, and the principle of the Moon or Isis became linked with Mercury. Their child Horus would eventually become identified with the alchemical substance of Salt. The archetypal principles of the Sun and Moon represented by Osiris and Isis were thought to give rise to all things.

The concept that all things are engendered through the union of two opposing forces took root among alchemists around the world. Alchemists in ancient India believed the metals were born of the union of the gods Hara and Parvati through the powers of Agni, the god of Fire. Sulfur was Agni; Mercury was the glistening semen of Hara; and the crucible of Earth in which their union occurred was Parvati.

In China, the doctrine of the Two Contraries arose from the Taoist concept of First Matter they called the Tao. Around 300 B.C.E., the concept of the Tao changed to include the two opposing qualities of Yang and Yin. As we noted earlier, Yang is sulfuric, masculine, positive, expansive, solar, and fiery; and Yin is mercurial, feminine, negative, contractive, lunar, and watery. Yang is light and tends to rise into the sky; Yin is heavy and tends to descend into the Earth. Yin is the unperfected soul and the only thing that can quench the yearnings of Yang, which is the perfect spirit. The interaction between these two contrary principles is what creates the material universe.

The Arabian alchemist Jabir expanded the doctrine of the Two Contraries by combining his philosophical readings with his experimental observations. Jabir believed the First Matter deep at the heart of the Earth gave off two opposing "exhalations" or spirits that became Sulfur and Mercury.

According to Jabir, metals were formed by differing impurities and concentrations in the union of Sulfur and Mercury. Gold was the purest and most balanced or perfect combination of this primal pair. To transform base metals into gold, it was necessary to purify and balance their Sulfur and Mercury. Jabir also believed there existed a Philosopher's Stone that would instantly transform base metals into gold by permanently joining the Two Contraries of Sulfur and Mercury.

The *Tria Prima* of Paracelsus

For nearly 700 years, Jabir's version of the Two Contraries dominated alchemy. Then in the sixteenth century, Paracelsus clarified and corrected what other alchemists had been saying about these basic ideas for so many years. He reorganized the Sulfur-Mercury theory to include a third component called "Salt."

The result was his *Tria Prima* ("First Three") theory, which turned Sulfur, Mercury, and Salt into powerful universal principles that gave alchemists greater insight into the nature of reality. Philosophically, the *Tria Prima* were viewed as universal forces present on all levels of reality. Their relationship and interaction determine how substances come into being and are transformed.

Paracelsus defined the *Tria Prima* by how they behave in fire. Sulfur is seen as what fuels the fire or what is changed in the fire. Thus oil, fat, wood, and coal are all forms of Sulfur. Mercury is the volatile watery essence of the fire that Paracelsus called the "phlegma" and is represented by the flames, light, heat, and smoke issuing from the fire. The new principle of Salt exhibits the fixed essence of the substance burning that resists the fire and is found in the ashes. "The three principles from which all things are born and generated," said Paracelsus, "are fat, phlegm, and ash."

In the burning of wood, for example, Sulfur is the wood fuel that is consumed in the fire; Mercury is the smoke, heat, and light that radiate from the fire; and Salt is the wood ashes created by the fire. As Paracelsus put it: "The fire is Mercury; what is burnt is Sulfur; and all ash is Salt."

Sulfur, Mercury, and Salt

In their writings, alchemists often speak of Sulfur, Mercury, and Salt as if they were tangible ingredients in their experiments, but it is important to remember that these are not the common substances of the same name; rather, they are esoteric metaphors that embody many layers of meaning.

Fiery Sulfur

Sulfur is the fiery, active, masculine fuel that gives a substance its aggressive properties and identity in relationship to other substances. In the laboratory, Sulfur is brimstone and also the flammable oily material extracted from substances, such as the essential oils of plants. For alchemists, Sulfur embodied all those characteristics that we now associate with the idea of active or kinetic energy.

Esoterically, Sulfur is the Solar or expansive masculine force associated with the Fire Element, aggressive spirit, personal energy, argumentative intelligence, and logic. Paracelsus thought of it as a kind of soulful fuel hidden throughout the universe like an ether or dark energy connecting the spiritual forces Above and the physical forces Below.

Mystical Mercury

Mercury is the watery, passive, feminine principle that represents the hidden essence or creative source of life within things. In the laboratory, Mercury is usually extracted from substances by the process of distillation, such as the alcohol distilled from fermented grains and fruits. The alchemists thought of Mercury as the "Mother of the Stone" and felt it was the mediator between Sulfur and Salt in the creation of new compounds.

Esoterically, Mercury is the Lunar or transcendent feminine archetype and is associated with soul, intuition, reflective intelligence, the elements of Air and Water, subtle matter, and the life force. In Hermetic philosophy, Mercury is like the mutable blueprint of a thing, the carrier of its image or ideal form that guides the interaction of Sulfur and Salt. Mercury embodied those characteristics that we now associate with the concept of light and mind.

Paracelsus thought of Mercury as a kind of dark or unmanifested matter, which can be seen as etheric or astral protomatter. Mercury is an omnipresent archetype that exists on all levels of reality and transcends the Above and the Below, beyond time and space and life and death.

Tangible Salt

Salt is the contracting force, the static result or resolving force created by the interplay of Sulfur and Mercury. Salt is associated with physical matter, sensation and feeling, and the element Earth, as well as the formation of chemical compounds, condensation of vapors, crystallization, and precipitation. Salt represents fixity, materialization, and the formation of bodies in general. It embodies those characteristics that we associate with the idea of mass or matter.

Esoterically, Salt is the archetype of form and structure, and the principle is active anywhere a new body is created. The alchemists saw Salt at work in the growth of plants, the formation of fetuses and childbirth, and even in the birth of spiritual bodies such as the Philosopher's Child. In their writings, alchemists sometimes referred to Salt as "Magnesia," which is actually a mystical term referring to the transformative principle concealed in Salt.

Like the First Matter, Salt shows up at both the beginning and the end of the Great Work. It is the imperfect and corrupted matter at the beginning of the experiment that must be destroyed and dissolved to release its essences, so they can be purified and reconstituted into the perfected new Salt at the end of the experiment.

The Three Essentials expressed in the three phases of the Work, depicted here as black, white, and red birds in a glass retort.

(From Splendor Solis by Salomon Trismosin, 1582).

The Dance of Sulfur and Mercury

In laboratory work, it is necessary to have a static interpretation of which ingredients are Sulfur and which are Mercury. But philosophically, early alchemists had a hard time defining the deeper characteristics of these two principles. For example, in their writings, sometimes Sulfur is soul and Mercury spirit, while other times it is just the reverse. Today, most alchemists follow the definitions set down by Paracelsus.

"Know then," declared Paracelsus, "that all the seven metals are born from a threefold matter, namely, Mercury, Sulfur, and Salt, although each metal has its own distinct and peculiar colorings. Mercury is the spirit, Sulfur is the soul, and Salt is the body. The soul, which indeed is Sulfur, unites those two contraries, the body and the spirit, and changes them into one essence."

Philosophically, the archetypes of Sulfur and Mercury have a much more dynamic relationship. Sulfur and Mercury—as energy and matter—are like two dancers who morph into one another as they spin around the dance floor. This idea is most clearly depicted in the Taoist symbol of Yang and Yin known as the *Taijitu*. The opposing forces of Yang (Sulfur) and Yin (Mercury) are shown inside a circle that is divided into a white Yang section with a small black circle within it and a black Yin section with a small white circle within it. The smaller circles represent the seeds of its opposite that both Yang and Yin carry. In other words, each carries the seed of its opposite and eventually transforms into it.

The unique relationship of Sulfur and Mercury is also suggested in drawings of the ouroboros showing two dragons or serpents eating each other's tails. One is dark and one is light, or one has wings and the other has feet. As the ouroboros spins through time and space, the two parts change into one another. The alchemists viewed this dance of opposing dragons as the engine that drives reality.

These two fundamental principles are sometimes so hard to distinguish from one another that alchemists believed they were actually two faces of the same thing. This truth is reflected in modern physics in the idea that energy and matter are equivalent aspects of the same thing. Alchemists associated this concept with the Rebis ("double thing") and pictured it as a two-headed hermaphrodite.

The mystical love affair between Sulfur and Mercury is what makes transformation possible, but it is not always easy to label the individual lovers. The true identities of Sulfur and Mercury depend on the time and context in which we observe them. It all depends on where we stop them in their whirling dance. Quantum physicists have rediscovered this uncertainty principle in their work with subatomic particles.

Salt is the resultant force that gives expression and purpose to the dance of Sulfur and Mercury. Salt is like the child of their marriage. Its birth freezes the dance of opposites, grounds them, and condenses their light and energy into form and matter.

The Fundamental Forces of the *Tria Prima*

It should be noted that the *Tria Prima* are truly the first three identifiable forces that emerge from the First Matter in the creation of the universe. The Four Elements, the fundamental properties of matter, have their origin in the *Tria Prima*. The archetypal force of Sulfur gives rise to the Fire Element. Mercury, in keeping with its dual nature, produces both the Air and Water Elements. And finally, the Salt principle is the source of the Earth Element.

Although alchemists and modern physicists use different terminology, they agree about the three fundamental forces of nature. In fact, Einstein's equation of the universe ($E = mc2$) is as valid in alchemy as it is in modern science. Sulfur is energy (E); Salt is matter (m); and Mercury is light (c). For both alchemists and physicists, energy and matter are really the same thing whose final expression is determined by the intermediary of light. In alchemical philosophy, matter is like condensed energy whose form is projected by the light of mind. So, if that lowercase "c" in Einstein's equation stood for consciousness instead of the speed of light, there would be no difference between alchemy and modern physics.

The *Tria Prima* in You

Psychologically, the principles of Sulfur, Mercury, and Salt form a triad of transformative powers that are available to us if we can learn to purify and control them. In people, the *Tria Prima* are represented by the concepts of body, mind (or spirit), and soul. Salt is the body, Mercury is spirit, and Sulfur is soul.

"In the Body," reads the *Book of Lambspring* (1625), "there is Soul and Spirit. He that knows how to tame and master them by Art, to couple them together and to lead them, may justly be called a Master, for we rightly judge that he has attained the golden flesh."

In general, when talking about people, the easily ignited Sulfur of soul stands for our inner passion, anger, and willpower, while the fluid force of the Mercury in spirit represents our ever-changing thoughts and powers of visualization and imagination. The hermaphroditic Salt of their union is the Philosopher's Stone, which is a perfected state of consciousness that fuses passion and feeling with thought and imagination.

In the Golden Dawn and other theurgic traditions, Mercury is associated with spirit and the mental faculty of imagination. Sulfur is associated with willpower and its connection to the deep reservoir of transformative energy in the soul.

"Both the Imagination of Mercury and the Will of Sulfur must be called into action," said one nineteenth-century Golden Dawn member. "They are co-equal in the Work. When the two are conjoined and the Imagination creates an image and the Will directs and uses that image, then marvelous magical effects can be obtained."

The Three Treasures of Taoist Alchemy

In Taoist alchemy, the *Tria Prima* are known as the "Three Treasures" of Shen, Chi, and Ching. These concepts translate roughly as Spirit, Vitality, and Essence, respectively. In general, Shen represents Mercury; Chi represents Sulfur; and Ching is Salt. However, because Taoist alchemy focuses so much on working in the body and not in the laboratory, subtle differences exist between the Eastern and Western viewpoints.

In Taoist teachings, the characteristics of the Three Treasures can be found in the burning of a candle. Shen (Mercury) is the radiant light given off by the flame. Chi (Sulfur) is the heat given off by the candle, and Ching (Salt) is the wax and wick of the candle, which are both its structure and the potential energy of its fuel.

Shen (Mercury) is considered the guiding spirit or mind that directs the energy of Chi (Sulfur). Like Mercury in the Western tradition, Shen is the most important of the Three Treasures in the art of transformation. Shen is experienced as a presence or spirit within that produces an all-embracing sense of compassion that resides in the heart. It gives people their spiritual radiance and is the source of our innate knowledge that everything is one. Shen resides in both Heaven and Earth and gives us the ability to rise above the mundane world.

Chi (Sulfur) is the energy that moves in our bodies and gives us vitality. It is the universal energy created by the constant interaction of Yin and Yang, the two "moving powers" in the world. Chi embodies these Two Contraries of Yang and Yin. Fast-moving Chi is considered to be Yang, while slow-moving Chi is Yin. All movement and all functioning are the result of Chi, and the nature of Chi is to keep moving.

In esoteric anatomy, Chi is carried in the blood and in the air we constantly breathe in and out. Blood is produced from the fires of metabolism, and Chi is extracted from ingested food through the action of the spleen. Red blood cells are nourishing and are considered Yin, while white blood cells are protective and are considered Yang. Chi also enters through the lungs, where it circulates through energetic pathways, called "meridians," throughout the body. The strength of Chi is affected by personal integrity. Lying and immorality weaken Chi, while speaking truth and having honor strengthen it.

Ching (Salt) is a mysterious substance called the "superior ultimate" of the Three Treasures. The word Ching means "regenerative essence" and is considered to be a concentrated energy that manifests physically in the body. Ching is seen as a perfect blend of Yang and Yin energy, and it is, therefore, not moving energy but static or "heavy" energy. It is the source of our sexuality and the applied life force that operates the body's cells and organs.

Ching exists before the body comes into being and becomes the "root" of our bodies when we are born. We cannot live without Ching. It is a fundamental heavy essence that accumulates in the body. If we can learn to conserve Ching, we can live vigorous and long lives. Ching is burned up by chronic stress and excessive behavior such as overwork, overeating, sexual excess, emotionalism, and substance abuse.

Shen is intimately related to Chi and Ching, and only when all Three Treasures are in balance does the whole system thrive. Chi condenses into Ching, and when we develop and accumulate Ching, we also increase Chi automatically. And when Chi is accumulated and purified, it strengthens Shen. "When the Three become One," said the alchemist Lu Dongbin (ca. 900 C.E.) in his treatise *Complete Reality,* "the Great Elixir is made."

In this chapter, we examined the Three Essentials of alchemical philosophy. These are the *Tria Prima* or first three forces that emerged from the First Matter at the beginning of creation. Paracelsus named them Sulfur, Mercury, and Salt, and we explored in some detail how the manifesting Salt principle is born from the mysterious courtship and marriage of Sulfur and Mercury. In the next chapter, we will see how this marriage of energy and light works through the elements to produce the perfected Salt that is the Philosopher's Stone.

CHAPTER 12

The Four Elements of Manifestation

The theory of Four Elements arose out of early philosophers' fascination with the concept of the First Matter. If the First Matter exists in a state of chaos and pure potential, for the universe to exist at all, the First Matter has to become organized into matter at some point.

According to the Emerald Tablet, the organizing principle is the One Mind, which projects the vibration of the Word into the chaos of the One Thing (First Matter) to bring about the creation of the world. The Tablet is quite clear on how this happens: "Its father is the Sun; its mother is the Moon. The Wind carries it in its belly; its nurse is the Earth." In other words, the elements of creation are the Sun (Fire), the Moon (Water), Wind (Air), and the Earth (Earth).

In order for the First Matter to take on form or manifest into space, early Greek philosophers believed that it had to take on a fourfold structure. This idea originated in the teachings of Pythagoras, in that the quaternity (or sacred Tetrad) was the root of all things and the source of nature and every created thing.

Western alchemists used the Greek system of Four Elements (Earth, Water, Air, and Fire). The Greek word for element, *stoicheion,* literally means "letter of the alphabet" and reflects the idea that the elements are the building blocks of the words or thoughts of the creator. In the Hermetic teachings, the Four Elements result from the materialization of light or imagery within the divine One Mind of the universe. Therefore, that quaternity of forces is part of consciousness itself and is embedded into the fabric of reality.

"The quaternity of elements can best be understood as a universal archetype," explained Carl Jung. "It is a logical prerequisite of any holistic [three-dimensional] orientation. To make such a judgment, you must have four dimensions. The Four Elements we find in all traditions are really the four primary properties of manifestation."

According to Jung, the Four Elements are universal archetypes of orientation that are part of consciousness and have their counterparts in the four aspects of personal orientation in human psychology. "For self-determination," Jung noted, "we need a function that states that there is something (feeling-Water) in the other, which establishes what is this thing (thinking-Fire) in the third, which shows us that something fits or not, whether we accept it (sense-Earth), and, finally, determining the source of something and its direction (intuition-Air)."

Development of the Concept of Elements

Several pre-Socratic Greek philosophers proposed the classical Four Elements independently. Thales of Miletus (ca. 624–548 B.C.E.) first proposed that Water was the root of creation; then Anaximenes of Miletus (585–526 B.C.E.) added Air. Xenophanes of Colophon (ca. 595–475 B.C.E.) added Earth to the list, and finally, the Byzantine emperor Heraclitus (ca. 535–575 B.C.E.) declared that Fire was among the fundamental building blocks of nature. Not until Empedocles (494–434 B.C.E.) proposed that all the elements existed together in fixed quantities since the beginning of time did the theory came together as we know it.

In his book *Doctrine of the Four Roots,* Empedocles stated that all matter emerges from the four "roots" of Earth, Water, Air, and Fire. In his view, Fire and Air are expansive and "outwardly reaching" constants of nature that reach up and out, whereas Earth and Water are contractive and turn inward and downward.

To show their archetypal power, Empedocles associated each essence with a Greek god. "Hera rules the fruitful Earth," he wrote. "Hades rules the central Fire, Zeus the luminescent Air, and Persephone the mollifying Water." Empedocles believed these four parts of creation were animated through the interaction of two great dueling energies he called Love and Strife. He associated love with the goddess Aphrodite (Roman god Venus) and Strife with the god of war, Ares (Roman Mars). This idea is similar to the Eastern idea of Yin and Yang, with Yin being the passive, feminine energy of Love and Yang the aggressive, masculine energy of Strife. In alchemy, these two contrary principles became known as the Queen and King.

Plato (427–347 B.C.E.) reiterated the archetypal nature of the Four Elements by describing them as "idea-forms" that had a separate and real existence. He also discovered that the elements were not static but could transform or "go over" into one another. For instance, Water freezes to ice, being solid like a stone or Earth, though it evaporates to vapor to become Air.

Aristotle (384–322 B.C.E.) first used the word "element," and the Alexandrian alchemists popularized it. Aristotle further developed the theories of Empedocles and Plato by explaining the Four Elements as combinations of two sets of opposing qualities of hot and cold and wet and dry. Water is cold and wet; Earth is cold and dry; Air is hot and wet; and Fire is hot and dry. This concept became the foundation upon which Western alchemists based their theories and practices.

Aristotle postulated that wet and dry are the primary qualities of matter. Wet, or moistness, is the quality of fluidity or flexibility, which enables a thing to adapt to its external conditions. Dry, or dryness, is the quality of rigidity, which enables a thing to define its own shape and bounds. As a consequence, wet things tend to be volatile and expansive because they can fill spaces in their surroundings. Dry things are fixed and structured because they define their own forms.

In Aristotle's view, each of the Four Elements has its natural place. He placed the Earth Element at the center of the physical universe and then arranged Water, Air, and Fire in increasing "subtlety" around it. When an Element is out of its natural place, it has an innate tendency to return to its level. Thus, bodies sink in water, air bubbles up, rain falls, and flames rise.

Aristotle added a Fifth Element to his philosophical system to explain the actions of the planets and stars. He called it the Ether Element and said it was what the heavens were made of. Alchemists refer to this Fifth Element as the *Quintessence*, which comes from a Latin phrase meaning "fifth essence." By adding the Fifth Element, Aristotle brought Western alchemy into agreement with Chinese and Indian versions of the elements.

Aristotle also predicted that one substance could be transformed into another by altering the mix of its archetypal elements and their qualities. Aristotle's elegant view was the accepted philosophy of matter throughout the Middle Ages.

The Four Humors

The Greek physician and "Father of Medicine" Hippocrates (460–370 B.C.E.) further developed the theory of the Four Elements. He posited that the archetypal elements are expressed in the body as circulating fluids he called "humors." The idea was a precursor to the discovery of hormones in 1905.

The Choleric (Fire) Humor

Hippocrates associated Fire with the Choleric humor of yellow bile, which is carried in cholesterol as a biproduct of the metabolic fire of digestion in the body. Choleric people tend to be energetic, enthusiastic, and constantly moving. In Aristotle's view, such people are hot and dry.

The Phlegmatic (Water) Humor

Hippocrates associated Water with the Phlegmatic humor of phlegm, which represents the clear fluids of the body carried by the lymphatic system and secreted by the mucus membranes. Phlegmatic people are cold and wet in Aristotle's terms and tend to be in touch with their feelings, though they can be moody and brooding. People in whom the Phlegmatic humor is dominant tend to be flowing and flexible and oriented toward emotional harmony, and they let their feelings guide them.

The Sanguine (Air) Humor

Hippocrates associated Air with the Sanguine humor of the blood, which distributes oxygen throughout the tissues of the body. The word sanguine refers to a ruddy complexion in which the blood flows close to the skin. Sanguine people tend to be very changeable and even flighty; they tend to be a little irritable, though basically optimistic and full of personal integrity. According to Aristotle, such people are hot and wet in their elemental qualities, which produces a melding of intellect and emotions.

The Melancholic (Earth) Humor

Hippocrates associated Earth with the Melancholic humor of black bile, which probably refers to waste products associated with digestion, such as stool, from which useful energy has been removed, leaving only the dregs or ashes of matter behind. Melancholic people tend to be apathetic, passive, stubborn, and sluggish, though they are practical. Because Earth is the principle of structure and materialization, the Melancholic humor is dominant in the person who focuses on physical reality and tends to exhibit the qualities of perseverance, inflexibility, realism, and pragmatism. In Aristotle's terms, such people are cool and dry.

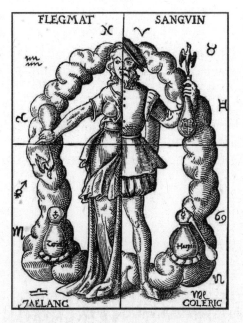

The Four Humors: Phlegmatic (Phlegm), Sanguine (Blood),
Melancholic (Black Bile), and Choleric (Yellow Bile).
(From Quinta Essentia by L Thurneisser, 1574)

Balancing the Elements

Empedocles noted that people who had near equal expressions of the Four Elements in their personalities were more intelligent and had the truest perceptions of reality. Carl Jung noted the same thing in his patients and called the balancing of the elements in a person "integration."

Aristotle's theory of the elements implied a scheme of transformation in which one Element could be changed into another. Because the Four Elements came into being by impressing their opposing qualities of hot and cold and dry and wet on the First Matter, it follows that one Element can change into another by altering these basic qualities.

For instance, when we impose the qualities of wet and cold on the First Matter, the Water Element results. But if we change the quality of cold for that of hot, such as what happens when we boil Water, it transforms into Air (steam). By manipulating this simple relationship between a substance's inherent qualities, we can change one thing into another.

We can visualize this scheme of transformation in Aristotle's Square of Opposition, which depicts all the relationships between the qualities and the elements. Opposing elements form a cross within the square, and each element is composed of two qualities shown in the corners of the square. Thus, Earth is dry and cold; Water is cold and wet; Air is wet and hot; and Fire is hot and dry. The qualities form a diagonal cross of opposition within the square.

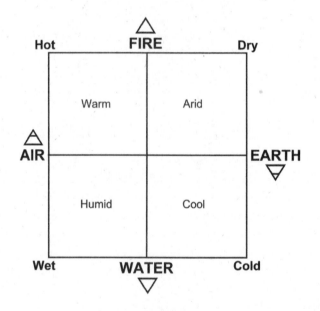

The Square of Opposition

The alchemists considered the Square of Opposition a dynamic rotating machine that was in constant motion. In other words, changes in the qualities of the elements cause movement through the square. Or we could say that the "strife between opposites" is the motor of rotation. This is the tendency for the elements to change over time. Cold warms to become hot; hot cools to become cold; wet evaporates to become dry; and dry moistens to become wet. We call this movement the "Rotation of the Elements." Aristotle explained: "It is clear that the generation of the elements will be circular, and this mode of change is quite easy because corresponding qualities are present in adjacent elements."

This natural circulation of the elements in the Square of Opposition begins with the process of adaptation (Water) and continues through expansion (Air), production (Fire), and retraction (Earth). We can see the same pattern of movement through the elements in many elemental rotations, including the seasons (winter, spring, summer, fall), the ages of man (childhood, youth, maturity, old age), and the cyclic rise and fall of nations and ideas (gestation, expansion, conflict, decay).

Hot (or heat) in the upper left-hand corner of the Square of Opposition is the primary quality, and Fire at the top of the square is the most active element. The alchemists saw Fire as the most important agent of transformation. So important was Fire to alchemists that they often referred to themselves as Philosophers of Fire.

Water, at the bottom of the Square of Opposition, is the most passive element and represents the agent of coagulation or materialization. Air and Earth were considered secondary elements made up of different qualities of Fire and Water. The Greeks believed Air was a combination of the hot quality of Fire and the wet quality of Water and that Earth was a combination of the cold quality of Water and the dry quality of Fire.

Four rules determine movement within the Square of Opposition:

1. Movement progresses in a clockwise rotation starting at Fire, which is where the work of transformation begins. As one moves through the square, each Element follows its dominant quality. Therefore, Fire is predominantly hot; Earth is predominantly dry; Water is predominantly cold; and Air is predominantly wet (or humid). The qualities drive the elemental rotation of the turning square: hot on the top, dry on the descending side, cold on the bottom, and wet on the rising side.

2. Because we can only move around and not across the Square of Opposition, direct transformation of opposing elements into one another is not possible. Thus, Water cannot be transformed directly into Fire because Water and Fire have no common quality; however, Water can be transformed by first changing it into one of the secondary elements of Air or Earth. Then, Air or Earth can be transformed into Fire.

3. The qualities are inversely proportional to each other. That means that the higher the intensity of an earlier quality in the rotation, the greater the rate of increase in the following opposite quality. Or the higher the intensity of a later quality in the rotation, the more the preceding complementary quality decreases. For instance, increasing the hot quality increases dryness and decreases wetness. To illustrate this concept, let's work through one complete cycle, starting at Earth. An increase in heat causes Earth to melt and take on the characteristics of Water. Further heating, however, decreases the cold of the Water component and increases its hot quality, which makes it boil and turn into steam or Air. When Air is heated, its moisture is reduced, and it rises higher into Fire. When Fire becomes cold, it loses its heat and becomes ashes or Earth again.

4. Whenever two elements share a common quality, the Element in which the quality is not dominant is overcome by the one in which it is dominant. This property is known as the "Cycle of Triumphs" and was first noticed by Spanish alchemist Raymond Lully (1229–1315). For example, when Water combines with Earth, Earth is overcome because both are cold. However, cold dominates in Water, therefore Water overcomes Earth, and the result will be predominantly cold. According to this scheme, Fire overcomes Air; Air overcomes Water; Water overcomes Earth; and Earth overcomes Fire.

Using the Square of Opposition to transform things is really quite simple when you work through it a few times. The archetypal relationships between the elements are so plainly depicted in the Square of Opposition that it is an amazingly versatile tool for all kinds of transformations. The alchemists used these same relationships and progressed through the Square of Opposition, regardless of whether they were doing laboratory experiments, producing medicines, or working on their own personal transformations.

To use the Square of Opposition in your own transformation, you must first meditate on the qualities of the elements to know how they are expressed in your personality or temperament. To balance your dominant element, find its opposite on the cross within the square. You want to increase the presence of this neglected element to balance your temperament; however, because they are opposite and cannot be changed directly into one another, you must work through one of the adjacent elements.

For example, if Water is the dominate Element in your personality and you need to balance it with Fire, begin by working with the adjacent element (Air or Earth) with which you are the most comfortable or that is more dominant in you. If you choose the more spiritual path of Air, you need to work to increase the quality of wetness, which means becoming more flowing and allowing emotional energy to surface. If you choose the more material path of Earth, you need to do the opposite and try to become less flowing, more grounded, and more controlling of emotional energy. The choice of which path to follow obviously requires some insight about the true nature of your inner self.

One of the dark secrets about the Square of Opposition is that it is possible to work with the reverse (counterclockwise) rotation. This is known as the "Death Rotation." Heraclitus described the process thus: "Fire lives in the death of Earth, and Air lives the death of Fire; Water lives the death of Air, and Earth lives the death of Water."

So, the Death Rotation is a process of sacrificing one Element to give life to another, and it requires the use of negative imagery and negative energies in its applications. In his book *Purifications*, Empedocles used this reverse rotation as a kind of personal crucifixion to cleanse the soul of broken promises, crimes against humanity, and other bad karma. This tortuous personal alchemy demanded extreme awareness and brutal honesty and it required the alchemist to direct negative energies like anger and disgust inward. Empedocles warned that this process was so cosmic that it might last through numerous rebirths and go on for "thrice ten thousand years" in the soul of the alchemist.

The Quintessence

The mysterious Quintessence of the alchemists is not called the Fifth Element because it was considered one of the elements; we call it the Fifth Element because it lies beyond the elements in both form and function. The Quintessence was viewed as something new and unexpected in creation that transcended the limitations imposed by the Four Elements. As Isaac Newton put it: "The Quintessence is a thing that is spiritual, penetrating, tingeing, and incorruptible, which emerges anew from the Four Elements when they are bound together."

The Quintessence partakes of both material and spiritual realities, and it is described as a luminous light that is invisible to ordinary sight. Like Pythagoras before him, Paracelsus believed the Quintessence is what the stars are made of and that within everything, there exists a hidden star that is that thing's Quintessence.

The idea of the Quintessence is part of the Perennial Philosophy and is present in every spiritual tradition. In Chinese alchemy, the Fifth Element is Wood, which is a product of the plant kingdom and is associated with the life force. In Taoist alchemy, the Quintessence is known as Chi, which is an unseen energy that flows through the body and can be accumulated and directed in moving meditations such as Tai Chi and Chi Kung. In Tantric alchemy, the Quintessence is the kundalini or sexual energy that is coiled like a sleeping serpent at the base of the spine. In Hindu alchemy, the Quintessence is the spirit of breath known in Sanskrit as *prana*. This is remarkably similar to the Western concepts of the spirit of air known as *pneuma* in Greek and *rauch* in Hebrew.

Alchemist Benedictus Figulus described the Quintessence in his book *The Golden Casket* (1608) as a hidden spirit that "fertilizes or brings to life all subjects natural and artificial." In other words, this quintessential life force exists dormant in all substances, whether we are talking about rocks, metals, or the human body. If the alchemist is able to release or re-animate this subtle force, the substance is reborn on a higher level of perfection and health. "In this way," Figulus promised, "may be the cherished renewal of lost youth and serene health be found."

Philosophers of Fire

To alchemists, Fire was the most important element, and they considered it to be the universal agent of transformation that made alchemy possible. "Alchemy is only that which makes the impure pure by means of Fire," said Paracelsus. "Though not all fires do burn, it is however only Fire and continues to be Fire that interests us."

Alchemists recognize four grades or types of fire with which they perform their transformations. Let's take a closer look at each:

Elementary Fire

The lowest grade of fire is known as the Elementary Fire, which is the common fire we are all familiar with. "The Elementary Fire, which is the fire of our stoves," wrote the French alchemist Antoine Joseph Pernety in 1758, "is impure, thick and burning. This fire is sharp and corrosive, often ill-smelling, and is known through the senses. It has for its abode the surface of the Earth and our atmosphere and is destructive; it wounds the senses, it burns, it digests, concocts, and produces nothing other than heat. It is external to the alchemist and separating."

Celestial Fire

The highest grade of fire is the Celestial Fire, which is the brilliant white fire that issues forth from the mind of God and represents the power of divine will. "The Celestial Fire is very pure, simple and not burning in itself," said Pernety . "It has for its sphere the ethereal region, whence it makes itself known even to us. Celestial Fire shines without burning and is without color and odor. It is gentle and known only by its operations."

Central Fire

Between the lowest and highest grades of fire are two more kinds of fire. The first is the Central Fire hidden within matter at its very center. Central Fire is the fire of creation, the embedded Word of God in all manifested objects. According to Pernety: "The Celestial Fire passes into the nature of the Central Fire; it becomes internal, engendering in matter. It is invisible and therefore known only by its qualities. The Central Fire is lodged in the center of matter; it is tenacious and innate in matter; it is digesting, maturing, neither warm nor burning to the touch."

Secret Fire

Alchemists rarely speak of the fourth grade of fire, even though they consider it the primary fire with which the true alchemist works. They refer to it only as their Secret Fire. "The fire of the Sun could not be this Secret Fire," hints Pernety. "It is unequal and does not penetrate. The fire of our stoves, which consumes the constituent parts of matter, could not be the one. The Central Fire, which is innate in matter, cannot be that Secret Fire so much praised, because this heat is very different within the three kingdoms; the animal possesses it in a much higher degree than the plant."

The true nature of the Secret Fire has been concealed in myths and legends down through the ages. "In allegories and fables," Pernety confirms, "the philosophers have given to this Secret Fire the names sword, lance, arrows, javelin, etc. It is the fire which Prometheus stole from heaven, which Vulcan employed to form the thunderbolts of Jupiter and the golden throne of Zeus."

From Pernety's clues, maybe we can figure out the truth about the Secret Fire. It seems the Secret Fire has a direction or evolution and behaves with purpose like a sword or arrow. We also know that animals possess more of it than plants and that it is an ancient secret passed down from alchemist to alchemist in myths and legends.

Let's look for more clues. Dr. Franz Hartmann, a nineteenth-century German physician, was another alchemist who wrote openly about the Secret Fire. In his book *Alchemy and Astrology* (1880), he admitted: "The Secret Fire of the alchemists is sometimes described as a serpentine working power in the body of the acetic. It is an electric, fiery, hidden power, an electro-spiritual force and creative power."

Any alchemist worth his salt knows what the code word "serpentine" means. Since the days of Thoth and Hermes, the serpent has symbolized the life force, the basic animating energy that finds expression in our sexuality and state of health. The life force is the Quintessence of matter, the hidden Fifth Element, the inner divine spark that makes all things come alive. We have just cracked one of the greatest secrets of alchemy—the Secret Fire of the alchemists is the life force itself, and it is an important ingredient in their work. It is something alchemists try to accumulate, control, and add to their experiments.

In this chapter, we have tapped into the power of the elements, which are fundamental archetypes expressed in the manifested world as Earth, Water, Air, and Fire. Respectively, they are expressed in human psychological functions as sensing and touching; feeling and emotions; thinking and logic; and intuition and inspiration. We also saw how the elements surface in the personality as the psychic hormones of Melancholic (Earth), Phlegmatic (Water), Sanguine (Air), and Choleric (Fire). The remaining work in this chapter focused on balancing or integrating the elements using the Square of Opposition and on deeper work with inner Fire, the primary agent of change in alchemy. We continue applying the principles of alchemy in the following chapter on the Philosopher's Stone, the crowning achievement in alchemical transformation.

Chapter
13

Ultima Materia: The Philosopher's Stone

The concept of the Philosopher's Stone originated with Alexandrian alchemists, and it soon captured the imagination of people around the world. By the Middle Ages, the Philosopher's Stone became the Holy Grail of alchemy. Not only was it the key to transforming base metals into gold, but it also held the secret to eternal life and spiritual perfection. Just as the Philosopher's Stone could turn a corruptible base metal into incorruptible gold, it would similarly transform human beings from mortal (corruptible) beings into immortal (incorruptible) beings.

The origins of the concept of the Philosopher's Stone can be seen in the theory of the Four Elements and the possibility of transforming one Element into another. There was also an ancient belief that metals could be transformed into one another, which probably originated with the observation that some precious metals could be obtained from the ores of base metals. For instance, silver is often obtained from galena, the mineral ore of lead. The preparation of metal alloys that imparted the characteristics of gold also suggested a single agent might exist that would transmute the metals.

The spiritual significance of the Philosopher's Stone originated in the Egyptian belief in the perfection of the soul and the creation of an immortal golden or astral body. The mystical doctrine of the regeneration of humankind was part of the spiritual traditions of many early civilizations, and the Philosopher's Stone was the physical manifestation of that fundamental desire for perfection.

The Magical Touchstone

In Latin, the Philosopher's Stone was called the *Lapis Philosophorum* or ("Stone of the Philosophers"), but the Greeks knew it as the *Chrysopoeia* ("Heart of Gold"). It was also referred to as the Magisterium, the Magistry, *Spiritus Mundi* ("Spirit of the World"), Stone of the Wise, Diamond of Perfection, Universal Medicine, Elixir, and *Ultima Materia* ("Ultimate Matter").

The eighth-century Arabian alchemist Jabir did much to popularize the notion of the Philosopher's Stone. He reasoned that one could accomplish the transmutation of one metal into another by the rearrangement of its basic qualities, and that a magical substance would expedite the transformation. He believed that substance could be found in the ashes of burnt metallic compounds, which is the source of the magical elixir sought by alchemists.

Many religious scholars believe the Philosopher's Stone is synonymous with the sacred symbol of the stone found in numerous spiritual traditions, such as the Old Testament stone Jacob rested his head upon; the New Testament rock Christ laid as the foundation of the temple; the Holy Grail or carved-stone cup of Christ; the Yesodic foundation stone of the Kabbalah; and the Cubic Stone of Freemasonry. In some ways, the Philosopher's Stone also resembles the forbidden fruit of Genesis and symbolizes knowledge that human beings are not meant to possess.

No doubt the Philosopher's Stone was the key to success in many aspects of alchemy. Not only could it instantly transmute any metal into gold, but it was also the Azoth that had power over everything—the alpha-omega (or A–Z) of existence. It was also known as the Alkahest ("Universal Solvent"), which dissolved every substance immersed in it and immediately extracted its Quintessence or active essence. The Stone was used in the preparation of the *Aurum Potabile* ("drinkable gold"), a remedy that would perfect the human body. It was also used to restore a plant or animal from its ashes in a process called palingenesis. Because the Philosopher's Stone carried the Quintessence or life force, it could even be used to create artificial living beings called *homunculi*.

What the Philosopher's Stone Looked Like

Much has been written about the Philosopher's Stone, and there are scores of recipes for its preparation. In fact, whole books have been devoted to its creation. One example is the seventeenth century *Mutus Liber* ("Silent Book"), which is a symbolic instruction manual of fifteen illustrations showing how to concoct the Stone.

Surprisingly, we know quite a bit about what the Philosopher's Stone was supposed to look like. It was dark red in color and resembled a common irregular stone or crystal. The material of which the Stone was made was the same red powder of projection so prized by the alchemists.

The Philosopher's Stone is said to exhibit the peculiar property of having a variable weight. Sometimes, it was as heavy as a piece of gold, and other times, it was as light as a feather. Its primary ingredient was an equally mysterious element known as "carmot." Carmot might have been a mythological substance because no mention of it exists outside alchemy, nor does it appear in any list of modern chemical compounds.

Although many reports of the creation of the Philosopher's Stone exist among Arabian and European alchemists, one of the most credible is from the revered alchemist Albertus Magnus, who reported he had successfully created gold by transmutation in the later years of his life. When Magnus died in 1280, he passed the miraculous object on to his student Thomas Aquinas, who is also said to have made many successful transmutations using it.

Another credible report of the creation of the Philosopher's Stone comes from Paracelsus. He was the one who discovered the Alkahest, the single substance that rendered all the elements (Fire, Water, Air, and Earth) visible and tangible. He said the Alkahest was his chief ingredient in creating the Philosopher's Stone.

How to Prepare the Philosopher's Stone

According to alchemical literature, there are two ways to create the Philosopher's Stone: The Wet Way and the Dry Way. The Wet Way, or Humid Way, uses natural processes and is more gradual and safer than the Dry Way, which relies on intense heat and powerful chemicals to achieve the Stone in a shorter time.

Even in spiritual alchemy, there is a Wet Way, in which natural inspiration builds gradually in the initiate to reach the fervor necessary for personal transformation. Also, there is a Dry Way, in which the initiate attempts to ascend on a direct path to divine knowledge by confronting their inner dragons. The Wet Way works with the slow fires of nature, while the Dry Way works with the raging fires of our lower nature.

The rapid spiritual ascent of the Dry Way is extremely dangerous for unprepared initiates and could result in a loss of personal identity or even madness. Tantric alchemists of India follow the direct path by trying to release and control sexual energies, while the path of shamanic alchemy consists of the use of powerful psychoactive plants. There seems little doubt some medieval alchemists made use of such preparations. Alchemists, the first chemists, were very much aware of the psychological and spiritual effects of the compounds they created.

In the laboratory, the Wet Way begins with the slow digestion and putrefaction of the matter, which could go on for many months. The Dry Way begins with roasting and heating of the matter in an intense fire and might only last a few hours. In both methods, these processes are part of what is known as the Black Phase in which the matter is blackened as it is reduced to its most basic essences.

The Black Phase gives way to the White Phase in which a purification of the matter takes place, and the essences are separated from any contamination. In the Dry Way, this appears as a white crust formed by dried matter carried by gases bursting in bubbles on the surface of the material. Sometimes, the crust puffs up and releases a cloud of white vapor into the flask, which is called the "White Eagle." In the Wet Way, a white layer of digesting bacteria called the "White Swan" forms on top of the putrefied material.

During the final Red Phase, the energies released in the previous operations are captured in a solution or powder. In the Dry Way, this is the appearance of a red coloring on the surface of the molten material or in the ashes, which is caused by high-temperature oxidation-reduction reactions. This event is symbolized by the fabled Phoenix rising from the ashes. In the Wet Way, the final phase is sometimes signaled by the appearance of a reddish swirl of oil or pink globules on the surface of the matter. This is associated with the Pelican, which sometimes regurgitated a meal of freshly killed fish for its young and stained its white breast plumage with red blood.

We will go into greater detail about the practical and spiritual work of the Black, White, and Red phases of transformation in the next section of this book (Part 4).

Magical Symbol of the Philosopher's Stone

The most powerful cipher in all of alchemy is a rather odd-looking glyph known as the "Hieroglyphic Monad." It is a depiction of the Philosopher's Stone, and it is said to incorporate some of the powers of the Stone whenever it is drawn. In other words, the cipher is believed to carry its own spirit or intelligence, which is evoked every time it is written down or constructed.

The magical cipher was created by Dr. John Dee (1527–1608), a British alchemist who achieved world renown as a mathematician, mapmaker, cryptographer, magician, philosopher, and astrologer. His library was once the largest in England with more than 4,000 rare texts and manuscripts, and his alchemical laboratory rivaled any in the world at the time.

Having entered Cambridge College at the age of fifteen, Dee began a five-year regimen of sleeping only four hours a day so he could devote more time to studying Hermetic philosophy and alchemy books. Dee said of his time at Cambridge: "I was so vehemently bent to study that for those years, I did inviolably keep this order: only to sleep four hours every night; to allow to meet, eat, and drink two hours every day; and of the other eighteen hours all was spent in my studies and learning."

Dee grew into an imposing figure with a commanding presence. John Aubrey described him in his book *Brief Lives* (1675): "He had a very fair, clear, rosy complexion and a long beard as white as milk. He was tall and slender, a very handsome man. He wore a gown like an artist's frock, with loose, hanging sleeves. A mighty good man was he."

Dee was a close confidant of Queen Elizabeth, who gave him a license to practice alchemy and make gold. As a favor to the Queen, it is said, he "controlled the Elements" and cast a spell on the Spanish Armada by causing bad weather to thwart the invasion of England. Shakespeare used him as the model for Prospero in *The Tempest*, and he is also said to have been the inspiration for Goethe's *Faust*.

With an intense purity of motive and intention, Dee embarked on a systematic plan to discover the Philosopher's Stone. He viewed the Stone as more of a higher state of consciousness than as a physical object. In his view, it was "the force behind the evolution of life and the universal binding power which unites minds and souls in a human oneness." While most alchemists of his time sought the Stone for its alleged ability to transmute base metals into gold, Dee wanted to possess it as a source for spiritual transmutation as well.

The Meaning of the Hieroglyphic Monad

Dr. Dee realized that he could represent all the powers and characteristics of the Philosopher's Stone in one magical symbol. After seven years of intense meditation on alchemical symbols, he found what he was looking for. In just thirteen days in January 1564, Dee entered a state of deep concentration and completed a step-by-step mathematical proof called the *Monas Hieroglyphica* ("The Hieroglyphic Monad").

According to the Greek philosopher Pythagoras, the Monad was the first thing that came into existence in the universe. It can be described as the spiritual atom or egg that gave birth to the whole cosmos. To the Gnostic philosophers, the Monad was the single higher spiritual being (the One Mind) that created all the lesser gods and elemental powers. In Jungian terms, it is the first archetype that contains all the other archetypes. Today, we might look at it as a mega-matrix program code that contains all the possibilities of the universe.

When alchemists depicted Dee's Monad, they often added the Latin caption *In Hoc Signo Vinces* ("In this sign, you will conquer"). All the coded ciphers of the alchemists were thought to be pieces of the Hieroglyphic Monad, and as we shall see, this is geometrically quite true.

In describing the power of Dee's cipher, Hermetic scholar Tobias Churton wrote in *The Gnostics:* "If one can imagine a great ocean of First Matter, then we are seeing the beginning of the universe. If a hand were to, as it were, drop the cipher of the Hieroglyphic Monad into that ocean of infinite potentials, the First Matter would immediately start forming itself into the universe we know today."

In his proof, Dee used the ancient ciphers of alchemy as geometric figures and applied Euclidean geometry to show their deeper meaning and relationships. Dee believed his proof would "revolutionize astronomy, alchemy, mathematics, linguistics, mechanics, music, optics, magic, and adeptship." He even urged astronomers to stop peering through their telescopes and trying to understand the heavens and instead spend their time meditating on his Monad.

Dee believed his Monad carried the secret of transformation of everything in the universe, but he never spoke of its meaning publicly because he felt the Monad was much too powerful to share with the uninitiated. He privately told other alchemists that his symbol not only described the precise interrelationship of the planetary energies, but it also showed the way to transmutation of the metals, as well as the spiritual transformation of the alchemist.

Dee wrote a private unpublished book that explained in detail the workings of the Monad. In the inventory of his massive library was a description of that book, which he intended only for his fellow alchemists. But Dee's secret key was destroyed when a mob of Anglican fundamentalists broke into his home and burned his entire library.

Dee had the final say, however: "He who devotes himself sincerely to these mysteries will see clearly that nothing is able to exist without the virtue of our Hieroglyphic Monad. Whoever does not understand should either learn or be silent."

The Cipher of the Stone

Dee believed his cipher was the true Philosopher's Stone because it provided perfect knowledge of everything. The frontispiece of his treatise *Hieroglyphic Monad* is a succinct explanation of the cipher itself, and it was considered so important in Elizabethan times that it became known around the world as the Greater Seal of London.

Frontispiece of John Dee's Monas Hieroglyphica

At the center of the frontispiece is the Monad cipher within an inverted egg filled with embryonic fluid and known as the Hermetic Egg. The fluid represents the First Matter; the yolk is represented as a circle and point at the center of the figure. The circle with the center point is the cipher for gold and the Sun.

The lunar crescent symbol of the Moon intersects the upper part of the yellow yolk of the Sun. Thus, the Sun and Moon are united in gold at this level, which represents perfection or the end of the Great Work. Within the frame surrounding the Monad are found the Four Elements and the Three Essentials of Sulfur (the Sun on the left pillar), Salt (the Moon on the right pillar), and Mercury (the center symbol).

Two rounded lunar crescents or waves representing the Water Element are at the bottom of the Monad. They also come together to form the ram horns of the sign of Aries, which signifies Fire. So, at this point, the principles of Water and Fire join forces. Aries, the first sign of the zodiac, is associated with the burst of life force in the Spring, at which time the Great Work begins. "To begin the Work of this Monad," noted Dee, "the aid of Fire is required."

Sections of the Monad

There are four sections to Dee's Monad. At the top is the conjuncted Moon and Sun. Next is the Cross of the Elements that connects the bottom and the top of the cipher. At its base is the sign for Aries, which is symbolic of the Secret Fire of alchemists.

By tracing the connecting lines and arcs in the cipher in different ways, one can locate all the symbols of the planets and their metals and thereby reveal the invisible forces behind Nature. All the glyphs of the five visible planets along with the symbols for the Sun and Moon can be found, and the metals are also indicated, since the ciphers for the planet and its metal are the same.

Dr. John Dee's Monad Cipher

Cipher for Venus/copper

Cipher for Mars/iron

The merged planetary ciphers are arranged left to right and top to bottom around the Cross of the Elements. On the vertical axis, the congruent ciphers for Venus and Mars are shown.

Ciphers for Jupiter/tin

On the horizontal axis, the ciphers for Jupiter and Saturn are shown in their reflected duality. The cipher for Saturn/lead is oriented correctly with the standard symbol on the left and the reflected symbol on the right. However, the ciphers for Jupiter/tin have been twisted 90o, so that you must turn your head to see them. Unless you look at them from the right angle, the ciphers for Jupiter and Saturn look identical.

Ciphers for Saturn/lead

According to Dee, by placing the planetary ciphers in their proper relationship, the astronomical symbols are imbued with an "immortal life," allowing their coded meaning to be expressed "most eloquently in any tongue and to any nation." In this arrangement, the Sun is the only symbol that is always the same, and in that sense, incorruptible like gold. No matter which way the Monad is turned—upside down, left to right, right to left, or its mirror image—the cipher of the Sun and gold is always the same.

Cipher for Mercury/quicksilver

The heart of the Monad and the one cipher that encompasses all the others is the cipher for Mercury. In alchemy, Mercury stands for the principle of transformation itself. Just as depicted in the Monad, Mercury is part of all the metals and Elements of alchemy and melds them together as one. Dee embedded the spirit of Mercury at the heart of his master symbol and believed he had successfully captured the essences of all the archetypal Elements and metals.

A Geometric Meditation on the Monad

The following geometric construction uses only a square and compass—the traditional tools of sacred geometry used in Freemasonry. With these simple tools, you can make a point, line, right angle, circle, and semi-circles. This is all it takes to build a universe.

1. At the center of a white piece of unlined paper, make a single dot. This is the Monad, the dimensionless One Point that modern science views as the inexplicable singularity of the Big Bang.

2. Using the Monad point as center, draw a circle with a 1-inch (2.5 cm) radius. The circle delineates the manifested universe. Now look at what you have drawn: it is the cipher for the Sun, and what is about to unfold is the Operation of the Sun. It is also the cipher for the incorruptible metal gold.

3. Now draw a semicircle of the same radius intersecting the top of the cipher for the Sun. This crescent represents the Moon facing the Sun and reflecting its light. This union of Fire (Sun) and Water (Moon) is the Sacred Marriage of the King and Queen in alchemy. The overall figure you have created also represents the Horns of Taurus and the creation of life.

4. At the very bottom of the circle, draw a vertical line downward for 3 inches (7.5 cm). This is the vertical axis of reality or Axis Mundi that connects the spiritual or energetic realm above with the material or manifested world below.

5. At 1 inch (2.5 cm) down the vertical axis, draw a horizontal line 2 inches (5 cm) wide centered at right angles to the vertical line. This is the horizontal axis of reality, and it symbolizes the fundamental duality of creation. It represents the polarities of male-female, King-Queen, light-darkness, good-evil, right-left, and positive-negative that make the world go 'round.

6. The cross we constructed provides deep insight into reality. Known as the Cross of the Elements, it is where the soul is crucified, torn between opposing forces. Dee calls the point where the lines meet the "Copulative Center", meaning a fertile inner point of balance and repose. It represents human consciousness, just as the center point above in the Sun represents the divine Mind.

7. The two lines and their crossing point make up a Tria Prima of forces representing Body or Salt (the horizontal line), Soul or Sulfur (the vertical line), and Spirit or Mercury (the crossing point). The Tria Prima plus the Four Elements constitute the Septenary or sevenfold pattern of creation.

8. A Quaternary or Cubic Space is created by the four intersecting lines, which stand for the Four Elements. The Quintessence or Fifth Element is indicated by their shared crossing point that represents mind or consciousness. This overall construction we have just completed is the cipher for Mercury.

9. At this point, Dee gets rather mystical about the deeper relationship of vertical and horizontal realities. He intuits a hidden Octad, which is concealed "in a most secret manner" in the geometric relationship of the four lines plus the four right angles. He advises the initiate to study this relationship "with great attention." If you are a member of a Hermetic fraternity, you know the importance of right-angles in ceremonies to "rectify" sacred space. Dee's hidden Octad refers to an unseen etheric reality all around us. In his "Discourse of the Eighth and Ninth," Hermes Trismegistus describes it as "the hidden realm beyond words."

10. At the bottom of the vertical line, draw two 1-inch (2.5 cm) radius semicircles—one touching the bottom of the line on the left side and the other on the right side. The two semicircles form the astrological sign of Aries, which is associated with the Fire Element and the burst of life in the Spring. "To begin the work of this Monad," notes Dee, "the aid of Fire is required." The single point at the bottom where the two semicircles meet represents another kind of fiery consciousness—the instinctive lifeforce or sexuality that is part of the Mind of Nature. The sacred construction of the Hieroglyphic Monad is now complete.

In this chapter we explored one of the most powerful concepts in alchemy—the Philosopher's Stone. While some alchemists pursued the Stone as a physical object, a kind of magical touchstone they could use to instantly produce gold, most alchemical philosophers and theurgists saw it as a state of integrated or perfected consciousness. That golden state of mind has more power and application that any goldmaking talisman of the puffers. In fact, in the alchemists' search for the Philosopher's Stone, we see a whole new Science of Consciousness being born. We will explore the alchemical nature of consciousness in the final section of this book (Part 5).

PERFORMING THE OPERATIONS OF ALCHEMY

The secret processes by which alchemists achieved their transformations were organized in an ancient pattern known as the Ladder of the Planets. Following the Emerald Tablet's dictum of "As Above, so Below," the operations corresponded to the order and characteristics of the seven visible planets. The archetypal energies of the planets were reflected on Earth in the evolution of the metals, as well as in the planetary archetypes found in plants, minerals, animals, and human beings. The overall work in alchemy progresses through specific operations that occur in three phases. The initial work of breaking down previous structures takes place during the putrefaction of the Black Phase. Next, the separation of impure materials results in the release of the living essences of the substance during the White Phase. Finally, the purified essences are brought together in a new perfected and empowered body at the end of the Red Phase.

CHAPTER 14

Climbing the Ladder of the Planets

The idea that heavenly bodies influence our daily lives originated in ancient Egypt and Babylonia. This concept was part of the microcosm idea that humans contained within themselves all the parts of the universe. The Doctrine of Correspondences expressed in the Emerald Tablet's dictum of "As Above, so Below" echoes this concept.

Thanks in part to the work of psychologist Carl Jung, we tend to think of these "correspondences" today as universal archetypes, which are inherent patterns or prototypes into which new creations or behaviors merge or emulate. Alchemists believed that once they became aware of these embedded patterns or signatures, they could use that knowledge to make lasting transformations.

As we discussed in Chapter 8, alchemists discovered the archetypal correspondences between the slowly moving planets seen in the sky and the metals buried in the Earth. Experiments by Lilly Kolisko and Rudolf Hauschka showed that the changes in the behavior of the planets are reflected in the chemical behavior of the corresponding metal on Earth. Also, the colors of the planets resemble the hue and brilliance of the corresponding metals. For instance, Mars's reddish-orange color is the same color shown by iron compounds; Jupiter's blue, Venus's greenish white, and Mercury's gray is exhibited in the ores and reactions of tin, copper, and quicksilver, respectively. There are many other similarities that led alchemists to believe the metals are associated with the planets.

At one time, it was believed that as the planets orbited Earth, they spun off their corresponding metals into the ground where they could be extracted. Eventually, each of the planets and its corresponding metal became associated with an alchemical operation. Each metal had its own characteristics that required specific processes to expose and transform it. The operations seemed to progress through the same general stages for all metals.

Alexandrian scholars coupled these practical observations with the Egyptian stages of spiritual perfection in a scheme that became known as the Ladder of the Planets. The Ladder consists of seven steps corresponding to the five visible planets with the Sun and the Moon. The basic tenet holds that the planets represent powerful primordial forces that express themselves on all levels of reality. These powers are arranged in a pattern of transformation that ranges from the most material and base level (Saturn-lead) to the most spiritual and noble level (Sun-gold).

The Operation of the Sun

The Great Work of alchemy is to climb the Ladder of the Planets and reach both material and spiritual perfection. Our spiritual return to the stars—the regaining of our cosmic consciousness—is accomplished by climbing the philosophical ladder of the visible planets from Saturn through Jupiter, Mars, Venus, Mercury, and finally to the Moon and Sun.

The Sun makes the same galactic journey through the Ladder of the Planets that alchemists try to duplicate in their work. In the sky, the Sun appears to travel through the planetary ladder, depending on the time of year. The time it takes the Sun to travel between astrological signs is about one lunar month (28 days).

At the beginning of the year in the Northern hemisphere, the winter Sun is in the signs of Saturn (Capricorn and Aquarius). In the spring, the Sun passes through the signs of Aquarius and Pisces to enter the signs of Mars (Aries and Scorpio), which is when the Great Work traditionally begins. Then it moves on into the influences of Venus (Taurus) and Mercury (Gemini). In summer, the Sun is immersed in the conjunctive signs of the Moon (Cancer) and Sun (Leo). In autumn, the Sun moves through Virgo and Libra into the influence of Jupiter (Scorpio and Sagittarius).

The Astrological Signatures

Babylonian astrologers arranged the archetypes of the stars into 12 regions of the sky known as the Houses of the Zodiac. Each one is associated with the dominant constellation within it. The houses act like archetypal filters that add their own signatures to the expression of planetary energy as a particular planet passes through that House. Any kind of human effort—not just the laboratory work of alchemists—is influenced by the behavior of the stars and planets above us. The chart below summarizes the signatures of each house.

CONSTELLATION	HOUSE	SIGNATURES
Aries "The Ram"	1) House of Self	Ego, personal characteristics and traits, life force, new beginnings, and resourcefulness
Taurus "The Bull"	2) House of Value	Self-worth, material and immaterial things of value, possessions, and gain
Gemini "The Twins"	3) House of Sharing	Intelligence, order, communication, achievements, and distribution of wealth
Cancer "The Crab"	4) House of Home and Family	Foundation, family, household, neighborhood, comfort, security, caretaking, and tidiness
Leo "The Lion"	5) House of Pleasure	Leisure, recreation, enjoyment, entertainment, games and sports, and creative self-expression
Virgo "The Virgin"	6) House of Health	Service for others, tasks and duties, wellness, strength, charity, and inner vitality
Libra "The Scales"	7) House of Balance	Justice, equilibrium, partnerships and matrimony, agreements, and diplomacy
Scorpio "The Scorpion"	8) House of Transformation	Cycles of death and rebirth, karma, sexuality, regeneration, and self-transformation
Sagittarius "The Archer"	9) House of Philosophy	Ethics, culture, belief systems, learning through travel, and exploration

(continues)

CONSTELLATION	HOUSE	SIGNATURES
Capricorn "The Goat"	10) House of Enterprise	Ambitions, career interests, government, authority, business, and politics
Aquarius "The Water Bearer"	11) House of Blessings	Need to belong to a community, friends, connectiveness, volunteering, and loving attention
Pisces "The Two Fishes"	12) House of Sacrifice	Urge for privacy, seclusion, retreat, healing, intuition, secrecy, surrender, and completion

Signatures of the Days of the Week

The psychological feelings and events of the individual days of the week also seem to be ruled by planetary forces. As we learned in Chapter 7, alchemists followed these signatures when performing all phases of their laboratory work. But if you are setting goals or planning special activities, meetings, or events, it is wise to pay attention to the expression of archetypal energies throughout the week. The following chart summarizes the planetary energies of the days of the week.

DAY OF WEEK	PLANET-METAL	SIGNATURES
1) Sunday	Sun—Gold	Warm, bright, and steady
2) Monday	Moon—Silver	Moody and mysterious
3) Tuesday	Mars—Iron	Aggressive and strategic
4) Wednesday	Mercury—Quicksilver	Communicative and enterprising
5) Thursday	Jupiter—Tin	Ambitious and bossy
6) Friday	Venus—Copper	Loving and caring
7) Saturday	Saturn—Lead	Lethargic and relaxed

Planetary Energies in the Body

Another interesting correspondence exists between the Ladder of the Planets and the human body. Each of the planets rules an energy center in the body and the corresponding organs. These seven centers and their relationships to the planetary ladder were known by Pythagorean philosophers, and there is some evidence that the energy centers were also known to the ancient Egyptians. In Indian alchemy, the planetary energy centers in the body are called "chakras" ("spinning wheels"). The following chart summarizes this system.

PLANET-METAL	CHAKRA	LOCATION
Saturn—Lead	1) Muladhara	Base of spine
Jupiter—Tin	2) Svadhisthana	Genitals
Mars—Iron	3) Manipura	Solar plexus (navel)
Venus—Copper	4) Anahata	Heart
Mercury—Quicksilver	5) Vishudda	Throat (vocal cords)
Moon—Silver	6) Ajna	Forehead (Third Eye)
Sun—Gold	7) Sahasrara	Crown (top of head)

Paracelsus popularized the Western system in which each of seven vital organs in the body is influenced by planetary forces. He borrowed the idea from the Hermetic Qabalah, a syncretic esoteric tradition that combined the Jewish Kabbalah with Hermetic teachings. In his system, the heart was ruled by the Sun-gold, the brain by Moon-silver, the lungs by Mercury-quicksilver, the kidneys by Venus-copper, the gallbladder by Mars-iron, the liver by Jupiter-tin, and the spleen by Saturn-lead. The Four Elements were also included in his scheme. The Fire Element ruled the heart, Water ruled the liver, Air ruled the breath, and Earth ruled the lungs. This system is depicted in Figure 1.

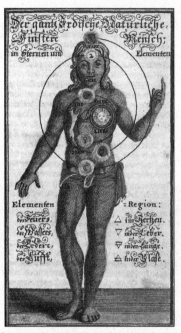

All the natural planetary forces inside man and in the stars and elements."

(From Theosophia Practica by Johann Georg Gichtel, 1638)

The Dark Powers of Saturn

In the remainder of this chapter, we steadily climb up each rung of the Ladder of the Planets to grasp the universal pattern of transformation discovered by alchemists. We start with the darkest, coldest environment of Saturn and the base metal lead.

Saturn, the farthest planet from the Sun, is the first rung on the Ladder of the Planets, and in esoteric terms, it represents the galactic starting point on our journey in from the stars. To the observer on Earth, distant Saturn looks like a grayish yellow star and is most easily spotted during the twilight hours when the sky takes on a deep-blue color. It reaches its peak visibility high in the northern sky in the dead of winter.

Experiment 1: The Call of Lead

Pick up a hunk of lead, and the first thing you notice is its weight and its connection to gravity. During the winter months, preferably on some clear night in late January or early February, go outside and find the planet Saturn in the northern sky. Relax and try to focus all your attention on the gray-yellow orb. Let go completely with an open and quiet mind, and then in this empty state, let the planet influence you. Do this until you feel a real connection with the distant orb.

Continue gazing at Saturn and place a piece of lead (such as a lead fishing weight) in your hand. You should feel a strange resonance building. That eerie, cold vibration is not your imagination. It is what alchemists refer to as the "call of lead." You are experiencing the metal's true signature or living correspondence with its planetary source. You might want to record your impressions and feelings during these experiments with the calls of the metals.

The celestial source of lead is the coldest planet and also the slowest moving. While the other planets dance merrily around the warm Sun, lumbering Saturn takes 30 years to complete its orbit. Saturn is the largest planet in terms of mass and exerts the most gravitational pull of any of the planets. It is the second largest (after Jupiter) in terms of size.

The shimmering triple ring of rocks and ten moons circling Saturn are remnants of its greedy attempt to attract more mass with its powerful gravity—its largest moon is bigger than Earth. Had Saturn been able to attract more mass, it would have transformed into a star, and our galaxy would have had two suns. But now ancient Saturn sleeps in darkness, having lost its bid to become a shining star.

With amazing insight, the Babylonians considered Saturn the ghost of a dead sun and the oldest spirit in the heavens. Saturn was considered the place where created matter first manifested and represented its most primitive state. Symbolically, it stands for the cosmic law that limits or defines manifestation. Therefore, Saturn and its metal, lead, represent the principles of contraction, stability, structure, and materialism.

The common icon for Saturn is *Chronos* (Father Time) with his distinctive hourglass and sickle and who personifies the forces of age, death, and transformation. Sometimes, Saturn is shown with a peg leg to indicate his infirmity and incompleteness. The black crow is the messenger of Saturn and symbolizes the beginning of the Black Phase of alchemical transformation—a period of darkness over light and matter over spirit.

In myth, Saturn was imprisoned in a deep cave while still a child by his father. The child conspired with his mother to overthrow his father and ended up castrating his father with a sickle. Saturn then became king and ruled just as ruthlessly as his father had. When he heard a prophecy that his own children would dethrone him, Saturn ate them at birth. But his wife saved one child and fed it to Saturn in the form of a stone, which he later vomited out to become Jupiter. Jupiter eventually overthrew his father and banished him to the darkness of the underworld.

The darkness of Saturn is also the fertile soil of new birth. In fact, the word saturn comes from the Latin *serere*, which means to sow or plant. Also, on the Ladder of Planets, Saturn marks the boundary between the personal and transpersonal (or cosmic) powers. For those reasons, Saturn acquired a dual reputation as both a stubborn protector of the status quo and the initiator of profound transformation.

Astrologically, Saturn is represented by two signs of the zodiac. Capricorn is the tenacious mountain goat that patiently moves toward its goal to reach great heights by remaining firmly grounded. Saturn's other sign, Aquarius, is the herald of a new age and represents the potential of transformation that is part of Saturn's makeup.

Because of its transformative potential, Saturn is surprisingly the most important planet to alchemists. They equated it with the First Matter and considered it both the beginning and the end of the Great Work. Within the darkness of saturnine energies, alchemists saw all the possibilities for change and healing. In fact, an early cipher for Saturn was "Rx," which medieval alchemists wrote on a slip of paper and prescribed as a talismanic cure. Their patients actually ate the piece of paper with the sigil of Saturn, which alchemists had animated with conscious intent. Of course, today, the sigil of Saturn is still written on nearly every prescription issued by medical doctors.

The Exuberant Powers of Jupiter

Jupiter, the second rung on the Ladder of the Planets, is the largest and most impressive planet in our solar system, but it is mostly gas. It has four moons, all of which are more active and larger than our Moon.

Jupiter and Saturn have a similar chemical makeup and are dozens of times larger than any of the other planets. Their cores are made of hydrogen metal—the simplest and purest metal that exists—and they are the true Olympian gods of our solar system.

Jupiter's airy and expansive presence balances the heavy and contractive influence of Saturn. Jupiter is considered the great "benefactor" of the solar system and represents the principle of royalty descended from the gods. Esoterically, Jupiter and its metal, tin, represent the light and energy of spirit without which the soul would remain imprisoned in the saturnic darkness of matter.

Experiment 2: The Call of Tin

Jupiter is usually an easy planet to find in the night sky and is the brightest object after the Moon and Venus. Jupiter shines best in July, when it is brightest and can be seen all night. Go outside one night and gaze on the planet while holding a piece of tin metal. You can use anything made of or coated with pure tin, such as a small tin toy, a piece of costume jewelry, or even the lid of a tin can. Relax completely with an open and quiet mind. Again, become empty and let the planet influence you. Wait until you feel a real connection with the giant planet. You should be able to feel a resonance building between you and the biggest planet. You are experiencing the metal's true signature or living correspondence with its planetary source and confirmation of the Hermetic axiom of "As Above, So Below."

Astrologically, Jupiter is primarily linked with Sagittarius, the centaur with his bow and arrow. The half-man, half-horse centaur symbolizes the person who has grown above his instinctive nature and has gained social values and wisdom. Jupiter is also linked with the compassionate sign of Pisces. In direct opposition to the signatures of Saturn, Jupiter produces a state of spirit over matter in which creativity, music, science, and prosperity prevail.

Jupiter's name is the root of the word *jovial*, which means cheerful, and the energies of this gaseous giant planet are expansive, optimistic, joyful, and sociable. With the combination of growth and a positive attitude, it is not surprising that Jupiter represents the power of healing and regeneration.

In mythology, the biggest planet in our solar system is the rightful home for the heavenly father who was known as Jupiter to the Romans and as Zeus to the Greeks. In India, Jupiter takes the form of Indra, the god of fire and lightning, who in Scandinavian tradition is represented by the thunder god, Thor.

In all these traditions, Jupiter is the great god of thunderstorms and was worshipped as a rain god. In Rome, he was commonly known as *Jupiter Pluvius* ("Heavenly Father Who Rains"), and his function was to fertilize the mother Earth with his seminal moisture.

The Masculine Powers of Mars

The third rung on the Ladder of the Planets is Mars, which is considered the brother of Earth, and the two planets share many characteristics. They both have iron cores, the exact same tilt on their axis of rotation, and they rotate in the same direction at about the same speed. That means they experience nearly identical daily cycles and seasons, although temperature extremes are much greater on Mars.

In alchemy, the red planet, Mars, represents energy and raw power. The metal associated with Mars is iron, which actually gives both the planet and human blood their red color. Mars, the warrior, is aggressive and competitive and governs our animal passions and survival instincts. Martian qualities reinforce the ego, strengthen will, and help us surpass previous limitations. Mars provides us with the willful energy to act, to begin new projects, or to transform any situation.

Experiment 3: The Call of Iron

During the early Spring, preferably sometime in March, go outside and find the red planet, Mars, in the night sky. Relax and try to focus all your attention on the tiny red sphere. Relax completely with an open, quiet mind. Then, become empty and let the planet influence you. Do this until you feel a real connection with the distant red orb. Continue gazing on Mars and place a piece of iron in your hand. A large iron nail is ideal, or you can use iron utensils or tools. Actually, anything that is attracted to a magnet will do.

During your meditation under Mars, you should be able to feel a resonance building. It is what alchemists refer to as the "call of iron." Try to feel the cold, hard strength of the iron. You are experiencing the metal's true signature and living connection with its planetary source. See how your feelings compare to how alchemists felt about this powerful metal.

In the zodiac, the month of Mars (March) is the period when the Sun enters the sign of Aries. In fact, the word "Aries" is derived from the Greek word for Mars, *Ares*. This is the time of year when spring begins, and a new solar cycle of the Zodiac starts. Astrologers believe that the location of Mars in your natal chart is the astrological sign that will be your source of energy for the rest of your life.

Aries is also when the Great Work of alchemy begins, and it is believed that the energy generated during this period is what propels us through the next 12 months of transformation. Mars is also linked with the astrological sign of Scorpio, which carries the signature of masculine consciousness and discernment.

In mythology, Mars is the God of War and is considered an overexuberant cosmic troublemaker. None of the other Roman gods really liked Mars, and in Greek myth, Venus was always getting her consort, Mars, out of trouble.

The Feminine Powers of Venus

The next rung on the Ladder of the Planets is Venus, which is known as the "veiled planet" and has a dense and sultry atmosphere. Thick sulfurous clouds constantly hide the face of Venus, which has an average surface temperature of about 450°F (232°C). Venus has the slowest rotation about its axis of any planet and is twice as close to the Sun as Mars. It is the brightest planet in the sky and appears as both the "evening star" and the "morning star."

Esoterically, Venus represents refinement of the senses, the passion of the arts, mystical love, romantic relationships, and physical desire. The feminine energy of the planet is passive, receptive, magnetic, relating, adapting, nurturing, and gentle.

Experiment 4: The Call of Copper

People like handling copper because of its surprising feeling of warmth and moisture. It is easy to connect with copper, just as its planet (Venus) is easy to spot in the sky. The best time to see it is in the early evening or morning when it is close to the horizon. It is so brilliant, it is often mistaken for a bright star or even a UFO.

On some clear night or morning, go outside and find the planet Venus. Relax and try to focus all your attention on the bright white sphere. Let go completely with an open and quiet mind. Empty your mind of thoughts, and let the planet influence you. Do this until you feel a real connection with the shining orb. Continue gazing at Venus and grasp a piece of copper metal, such as a copper penny or wire. You should be able to feel a warm resonance building. That deep and soothing vibration is not your imagination. It is what alchemists refer to as the "call of copper." You are experiencing the metal's vibratory reaction to the presence of its mother in the sky.

Venus is associated with the astrological signs of Taurus and Libra. Taurus represents the sensual part of Venus, while Libra is focused on relating and connecting with others. In terms of the Earth sign, Taurus, the attracting power of Venus is expressed more in possessions and money, while in Libra, the energetic trend is more toward art and harmony in all things.

In mythology, Venus is the Great Goddess of the Romans, who was known as Aphrodite to the Greeks and mother of Hermes' son. Both Greeks and Romans emphasized her sexual energy, and temples to Venus were actually schools of instruction in ecstatic sexual techniques taught by harlot-priestesses.

The religion of Venus, as well as the Hermetic teachings of alchemy, promised a "sacred marriage" through which the initiate could escape the cycle of rebirth and be reborn on a whole new level. Death was seen as a transformative event that was mimicked in the *le petit mort*, the "little death" of sexual orgasm.

The romantic city of Venice was named for the goddess, and our word "veneration" literally means to pay homage to Venus. Known as the "Lady of the Animals," Venus was often shown naked in the forest with animals, especially deer. Several myths tell of hunters encountering Venus and falling in love with her. In fact, "venison" literally means son or follower of Venus.

Venus is a very meaningful symbol in alchemy. Married to Vulcan, the god of alchemy, she could not resist the virile powers of Mars with whom she shared many romantic trysts. To alchemists, Venus was the goddess of generation, and sexual imagery in alchemy almost always refers to the deeply transformative energies of Venus, her metal copper, and the mysteries of the operation of conjunction.

The Transformative Powers of Mercury

The next rung on the Ladder of the Planets is Mercury, which is the closest planet to the Sun and the fastest moving orb in our solar system. Mercury is in tidal lock with the Sun and always shows the same face toward it, which is similar to the tidal lock that causes one side of the Moon to always face the Earth. Usually, Mercury's reflection is absorbed into the bright light of the Sun, but when it is visible in the twilight of the early morning or late evening, the tiny planet is one of the brightest objects in the sky.

Mercury has a very irregular and eccentric orbit and sometimes even appears to go backward in the heavens—a period known as "retrograde," when astrologers say things on Earth take a turn for the worse. The surface of Mercury looks just like that of the

Moon, and the two bodies have the most reflective surfaces of any of the planets, each reflecting exactly the same amount of sunlight (7 percent).

Experiment 5: The Call of Mercury

Mercury is difficult to see in the night sky because it is a small, extremely fast, silvery sphere that likes to stay close to the Sun. If Mercury appears to be moving east to west, it is in retrograde, a sight that terrified medieval observers. Try to find Mercury in the night sky. If you need help, consult the Internet, or download the free StarChart app, which is recommended for finding all the planets. Once again, relax and try to focus your attention on the fleeting sphere. Relax completely with an open and quiet mind; become empty and let the planet influence you. Do this until you feel a connection with the quicksilver planet.

If you can obtain a sealed sample of mercury (such as a glass mercury switch or thermometer), continue gazing on mercury and place the item containing mercury into the palm of your hand. See whether you can feel a resonance building between the shimmering liquid metal and the silvery orb. The "call of mercury" you are experiencing will probably not emanate from your hand because quicksilver resonates with your nerves. You might feel something in the long nerves in your arm, in your throat ganglia, or behind your forehead. Try to find words to describe the unique signatures of Mercury you are experiencing.

Esoterically, the swiftest planet is known as the "Messenger of the Gods" and governs communication, intellect, writing, speech, and any kind of conversing or commerce. The urge of Mercury is to know truth and to communicate that knowledge to others. In the body, Mercury is associated with the brain and nervous system, as well as breathing and the organs of sense. The god Mercury is usually depicted with winged sandals and a winged helmet to connote the ability to move and deliver information quickly on many levels. Certainly, anyone can feel Mercury's quickening signature in today's data-driven world.

Mercury is influenced by the astrological signs of Gemini and Virgo. Gemini, the third sign in the Zodiac, is associated with discrimination and awareness of duality. Virgo is associated with purified consciousness and the alchemical operation of distillation.

In mythology, Mercury is depicted as an androgenous being because Mercury derives consciousness from the union of the left and right brain. In alchemical terms, Mercury derives consciousness from the marriage of the masculine, rational Sun and the feminine, intuitive Moon.

The Greeks knew the Roman Mercury as Hermes, who was the founder of alchemy. Hermes is the twilight god of boundaries and crossroads, and one of his duties was to conduct souls to the underworld. Hermes has mysterious, magical powers over sleep, dreaming, and altered states of consciousness.

The Soulful Powers of the Moon

The sixth rung on the Ladder of the Planets is the Moon. It seems the ancients were correct in their assumption that the Moon was a planet. It has a completely different mineral composition than Earth, and most modern astronomers believe the Moon is really a small planet that crashed into Earth and was captured by its gravity.

Because of the Moon's synchronous orbit, it always shows the same face to Earth. However, because it shines only by the reflected light of the Sun, Earth casts shadows on its face that make it appear to change shape in a 28-day cycle. The Moon's varying distance from Earth controls the ebb and flow of tides and is thought to influence hormone levels and the female menstrual cycle. Our words for menstruation and menopause are based on the Greek word *meno* ("moonpower").

Experiment 6: The Call of Silver

Go outside on a night of the full Moon and gaze up at the silvery orb. Relax and try to focus all your attention on the surface of the Moon. Relax completely with an open and quiet mind. Try to match the emptiness of the Moon's surface by clearing your mind. Allow our closest planetary body to influence you. Do this until you feel a real physical connection.

Now, pick up a piece of silver (such as silver jewelry or sterling dinnerware), and hold it in your left hand, which links to your creative right-brain hemisphere. You should be able to feel a liquid sensation of cool metallic energy. This is what alchemists refer to as the "call of silver." You are experiencing the metal's living correspondence with the Moon itself. Try to remember how this feels in your body. Silver has unusual effects in the body. Has the taste in your mouth changed? Has your eyesight altered? How does your skin feel? Do this same exercise on the night of the new Moon and note the differences you experience.

The esoteric meaning of the Moon is receptivity, reflection, fertility, and nurturing. In many areas of the world, the 13-month lunar calendar governs the cycle of planting and harvesting. The Moon is said to control the subconscious mind and is the source of magnetic and astral powers. The Moon is the archetypal Queen of alchemy, and lunar magic ritual items are always made of silver.

In mythology, the Moon is associated with the virgin goddess, Diana, and the multi-breasted symbol of fertility, Artemis. Egyptians referred to the Moon as the "Mother of the Universe," and in several traditions, the Moon is where our souls go when we die. The Moon is associated with the astrological Water sign of Cancer, whose traits are deep emotions and moodiness, genuineness, loyalty, and a strong sense of family.

The Spiritual Powers of the Sun

The Sun is the seventh and last rung on the Ladder of the Planets. The alchemists saw the Sun as the King and husband to the Moon Queen. In an amazing synchronicity, the solar King and lunar Queen appear to be exactly the same size in the sky to observers on Earth. Because the Moon's image is 400 times smaller but also 400 times closer than the Sun's, they seem to be the same size from our viewpoint. When a total solar eclipse (or conjunction) occurs, the lunar disc exactly and completely covers that of the Sun.

The Sun is our personal star at the center of the solar system. It emits energy in every conceivable wavelength from x-rays to visible light to radio waves, and all this energy is what makes life on Earth possible. The Sun is the fundamental metaphor of the whole alchemical process. Composed of more than 90-percent hydrogen atoms, it is the simplest and purest form of matter known. It also represents a process of constant purification in which cooler and darker impurities, known as sunspots, rise to the surface and are ejected or burned off in a constant process of calcination.

Experiment 7: The Call of Gold

At sunrise or sunset, face the Sun and try to feel its archetypal presence. Try to gaze into the rising or setting Sun just as it meets the horizon—before it becomes too bright or dangerous to look at. Using proper eye protection or a camera, try to discern the mysterious solar disk (the *Aten*) described by the Egyptians. Relax and try to safely observe the golden sphere of the Sun. Let go completely with an open and quiet mind and feel the warm presence of our closest star influence you.

Continue bathing in the Sun's light as you pick up a piece of gold (such as a gold coin, gold watch, or piece of gold jewelry) with your right hand, which links to your analytical left-brain hemisphere. You should be able to feel an electric warmth building. That eerie, warm vibration is what alchemists refer to as the "call of gold"—the resonation of the metal with its celestial home. You are experiencing the metal's true signature, and for gold, this is the most perfect expression of all the planetary metals. If you can connect with this archetype, you realize that it exists both inside and outside you. You are experiencing the potential perfection of your mind, body, and soul resonating with the telesmatic perfection that is inherent in the universe.

Esoterically, the Sun is an image of wholeness, health, wealth, and happiness. Its metal, gold, has the same associations. The blazing Sun corresponds to logic, ambition, courage, vitality, health, and electric or masculine energy.

In mythology, the Sun is associated with the Egyptian god Osiris, as well as the Greek god Hercules in his aspect of monumental strength. In astrology, the Sun as Leo presides over selfless will, beneficent governing, and shared energy and power. On the personal level, the Sun represents our deepest identity, the true self and inner authority, and the source of personal dignity and integrity.

The Music of the Spheres

To the ancients, the seven rungs on the Ladder of the Planets represented individual notes in the Music of the Spheres, which are vibrations of energy that influence every part of our lives. Pythagoras explained the Music of the Spheres in 550 B.C.E. "Each celestial body produces a particular sound on account of its movement, rhythm, or vibration," he wrote. "All the sounds and vibrations together form a universal harmony in which each part, while having its own function and character, contributes to the whole."

In the following figure, the Pythagorean theory of the Music of Spheres is depicted as a three-headed serpent descending from the heavens to Earth. The tones are generated by the planetary spheres and their mythic archetypes. To the side, Apollo the Sun God grasps his lyre as the Muses gather around him.

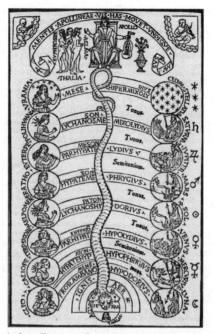

"The power of the mind of Apollo moves these Muses in every way to create celestial music."
(Mentis Apollineae from Practica Musica by Franchinus Gaffurius, 1496)

The Ladder of the Planets is an example of the Law of Octaves. The musical octave is a seven-stepped process that raises the vibration of the first note on the scale to a higher vibration, and it continues rising in frequency with each of the remaining notes. The eighth note repeats the cycle on a higher level. In chemistry, the Law of the Octave is expressed in the Periodic Table, where every eighth element repeats the characteristics of the first on a more complex level.

In alchemy, the Law of Octaves is the overall pattern of harmony in the universe expressed as a seven-stepped formula embedded in our solar system. The first seven notes of the musical scale represent our progress through the planets, while the eighth note of the octave is a return to the first note at a higher level of vibration.

In our solar system, that eighth note is Saturn, the one planet alchemists considered to be both beginning and end, the alpha-omega of our transformation. They considered Saturn and our return to Saturn at a higher frequency to be the most important part of the Great Work. It represents the beginning of a whole new octave of creation that enables our leaving behind the grosser materiality of our solar system and experiencing the more subtle, stellar matter of the spiritual universe. It is our destined return to the stars through Saturn's *Porta Alchemica* ("the Alchemist's Door"), the cosmic exit from duality guarded by two mythic Griffins, which are creatures with the body of a lion and the head and wings of an eagle.

In this chapter, we began our journey up the Ladder of the Planets, an ancient system of spiritual evolution based on the signatures of the planetary bodies and their corresponding metals. By examining the characteristics of the seven planets in detail we acquired a deeper understanding of their archetypal influence in our lives. We also explored the Pythagorean theory of the Music of the Spheres, which so beautifully ties together planetary powers in a dynamic process of universal harmony and steady evolution. In the next three chapters, we will apply the operations of alchemy to perform the transformations necessary at each step to successfully move up the Ladder of the Planets.

CHAPTER 15

The Black Phase: Decomposition

The exact sequence of operations that alchemists used to accomplish their transformations was one of their deepest secrets, and the actual order was often deliberately scrambled to mislead the uninitiated. This random scrambling in the order of operations is evident on the steps leading to the Inner Laboratory shown in the following figure.

The "Mountain of the Adepts" painting was first published in 1616, in a book on Kabbalah and later in 1654, in a book on alchemy. It depicts the steps of alchemical operations on a stairway leading to an inner chamber inside a cavern within a great mountain. The chamber has seven windows, which are symbolic of the seven planetary influences in the work. In the back of the room there is an alchemical furnace or athanor. In the foreground sits the King with his scepter. Across from him is the Queen holding a plant with three roses and three exposed roots.

The floor is laid out in a pattern of square tiles. The canopy of the inner chamber has images of the Sun and Moon on it, and perched at the very top is the Phoenix, which is the symbol of the Philosopher's Stone.

On six terraces on the sides of the mountain are mythic figures representing the planetary powers. On the mountain's left side are Saturn, Jupiter, and the Moon Queen, and on the right side are Venus, Mars, and the Sun King. On a pedestal at the peak of the mountain is the winged figure of Mercury holding the caduceus in his right hand and a five-pointed star in his left. This arrangement tells us that Mercury carries the Quintessence and is the key to the whole process—worth more than any of the other metals in succeeding at the Great Work.

Surrounding the mountain in the heavens are the twelve constellations of the Zodiac. Beyond that lie the Four Elements of *Ignis* ("Fire"), *Aeris* ("Air"), *Aquae* ("Water"), and *Terrae* ("Earth").

The Mountain of the Adepts.
(From Cabala: Spiegel der Kunst und Natur by Steffan Michelspacher, 1616)

The blindfolded person in the lower-right corner of the painting has not yet awakened to the path of alchemy, while the person to his left is trying to tell him that there is life in the underground burrows of the mountain. This hidden life is the subconscious mind, and its contents are symbolized by two prolific rabbits who make their home underground.

Just in front of the entrance to the cave are three rose plants with three blossoms each. This is a subtle clue that the operations listed on the steps to the inner chamber are organized into three groups. Instead of listing specific sequential operations, the alchemists spoke openly only of the overall phases of their work, though each phase contained several different operations.

Three Phases of the Work

The color-coded process of transformation went from an initial Black Phase to an intermediary White Phase and culminated in a Red Phase. This same sequence of colors occurs in working with metals. If the four base metals (lead, tin, iron, and copper) are melted and fused together in a new alloy, its resulting surface color is black. If this black alloy is heated with the noble metal silver and then heated again in mercury, it turns white. With continued heating, a final iridescent reddish violet color appears in the metal. Some alchemists believed they were creating a minuscule amount of genuine gold in the violet-colored area.

We rarely find detailed physical descriptions of the operations associated with the three colors in the writings of alchemists. Instead, the descriptions are veiled in mystical and allegorical language that makes them difficult to understand unless one is an adept. That suggests the alchemists were also talking about spiritual or psychological exercises they performed along with their laboratory work. Just as certain colors appeared during the work in the lab, those same colors dominated the images and visions of the corresponding spiritual work.

Alchemists referred to the three general phases in both practical and spiritual work by their Latin names. They called the work of blackening the *Nigredo*, the work of whitening the *Albedo*, and the work of reddening the *Rubedo*. Jungian psychologists use these same Latin terms to refer to the stages of psychological transformation.

In psychology, the *Nigredo* refers to the depression accompanying the dark night of the soul that underscores the need for deep change in a person. The *Albedo* represents the spiritual purification that results from suffering through the *Nigredo*. And the *Rubedo* is the sense of empowerment and confidence that results from psychological integration in the final phase of personal transformation.

The Black Phase

The work of "blackening" was the longest and most difficult phase in alchemy. Alchemists say that by comparison, the White and Red phases seem like child's play. They consider the Black Phase of *Nigredo* to be a tortuous stage of the work in which the substance at hand suffers and is forced to surrender any superfluous characteristics in order to reveal its true nature.

The goal in this initial phase of transformation is to reduce the subject to its bare essence or most fundamental ingredients. All the impure and extraneous material must be removed, or it will contaminate and destroy the later stages of the work. In general terms, such unwanted material was called "dross" by alchemists. The term originally referred to the scum of solid impurities that float on top of molten metal, but it came to mean any dirt, unwanted compounds, and other waste products, including psychological contaminants that arise in spiritual work.

Alchemists often refer to the overall process that occurs during *Nigredo* as "mortification," a term they used in the literal sense of "facing the dead part." In the lab, mortification results in a pulverized powder or ashes in which the characteristics of the former substance can no longer be recognized. In personal alchemy, mortification is characterized by feelings of worthlessness, humiliation, shame, guilt, and embarrassment that one feels when working with rejected or repugnant material hidden away inside. In initiations into Hermetic fraternities, the Black Phase is characterized by humiliating acts, personal attacks, and forced embarrassment—all to strip the candidate bare of attachments to pride and ego.

The symbol for *Nigredo* is the black crow. If you see one in an alchemical drawing, it means the process shown is taking place during the Black Phase of the work. In Greek mythology, black crows came into being because the white crow maiden, Coronis, had an affair with a young man while she was pregnant with a child from the Sun god Apollo. When he found out, Apollo killed Coronis and her lover, and he then transformed all crows from white to black. Her child was born on her funeral pyre and became the great healer god Asclepius. The myth shows how both death and life arise from the darkness of suffering, and that blackness carries the seeds of light and healing.

The Calcination Operation

The operations that take place during the Black Phase are two destructive processes that involve applying the elements of Fire and Water. After these operations are completed, the purified essences of the matter at hand are separated and saved for further work during the next phases of the work.

The initial fire operation in alchemy is called "calcination," which means literally "reduce to bone by burning." Bone is essentially calcium oxide, and the word comes from an ancient method of obtaining calcium oxide (or lime) by heating limestone. The word *calcination* and related words like *calcify* and *calcium* come from the Latin root *calx*, which means chalk or limestone. In their lab work, alchemists treated any ashes or powdery residue created by heating an ore or mineral as calx, which is now known as an oxide. But alchemists viewed it as an elemental substance that is free of all impurities and a physical expression of the basic essence of a material.

The cipher that alchemists assigned to the process of calcination was the ram horns of the astrological sign for the constellation Aries. Aries is the fieriest of all the signs, and the Great Work of alchemy begins when the Sun enters the House of Aries.

Skulls and skeletons are used as symbols of calcination and represent both pure white calcium oxide and the hidden structure of objects revealed by fire. Other images of calcination include funeral pyres, scenes of hell, torture by fire, crucifixion, birds rising from flames, and frightening confrontations with fire-breathing dragons. Salamanders are another popular symbol for calcination because they were observed scurrying in and out from under bonfires. The cold-blooded creatures sought warmth beneath the burning logs, and the idea took hold that salamanders were born in the fire and frolicked in its flames.

In general, calcining drives off water and other volatile compounds and brings about a decomposition of the material. Alchemists referred to the process of dehydration by fire as the "dragon who drinks the water." Heating ores directly in a fire was an ancient way of obtaining metals. This roasting technique is another kind of calcination in which material is heated in an open flame with plenty of free-flowing air, which also helps oxidize any impurities.

All metals can be calcined and reduced to ashes by adding a calcining agent or combination of chemicals and then applying heat. Lead is calcined by adding sulfur; tin requires the addition of antimony. Iron needs vinegar and *sal ammoniac*. Copper uses sulfur and salt. Mercury needs to be mixed with nitric acid (*aqua fortis*). Silver requires a mixture of table salt and alkali salt, and gold can be calcined with the help of mercury and *sal ammoniac*.

So, any process that involves the heating and breaking up of a solid to drive off water and other volatile compounds can be classified as calcination. In the lab, it usually means heating a substance in an oven, crucible, or over an open flame until it is burnt or reduced to ashes. Sometimes, it might also refer to dipping something in a liquid fire like sulfuric acid.

In their laboratories, alchemists recognized two kinds of calcination, which they called "actual" and "potential." Actual is the typical heating in a fire produced by a fuel such as wood, coal, oil, or gas. Potential calcination used acids and corrosive chemicals that carried the potential or signature of flaming fire within them. Beyond chemical calcination, alchemists recognized what they called "philosophical calcination," which is the reduction of living things to their material basis by application of heat. They associated this phenomenon with the dehydration of living tissue and the loss of life force carried in bodily fluids.

One example of philosophical calcination is human cremation, which results in a dehydration of bodily fluids and tissue that leaves only bone fragments and ashes behind. Another example occurs when animal horns or hooves are suspended over boiling water for a long period. A thick liquid called "mucilage" drips out of the horns or hooves, leaving a dried mass, which is easily reduced to powder by grinding. In both cases, the powdery material resulting from philosophical calcination was considered quite different from the ashes left over from common calcination. The cremains of once-living things were sacred, and it was believed that they still contained a tiny spark of life or Quintessence.

Personal Calcination

At the same time alchemists worked in their labs on the calcination of the metals or other compounds, they also worked to accomplish corresponding calcinations on the personal level. They so closely identified with the substances on which they worked that they felt they were suffering through the same fiery transformations. For them, personal calcination was a similar reduction to ashes as the process in the lab, except the heat was generated by the introspective fires of their own consciousnesses.

If you have ever been embarrassed by your behavior or upset at something you have done, you have experienced the fires of calcination. If you ever hurt someone you cared about or realized your ambitious ego can be your own worst enemy—or anytime you act in ways that do not reflect who you really are—then you have been caught in the calcining flames. So, personal calcination is kindled by the awareness of flaws in our behavior or actions that result in the loss of our integrity.

The alchemists saw personal calcination as a loss of spirit in a person, although modern psychologists view it as a loss of ego or personal identity. The result is the same: Diminished mental energy and an increase of darkness or depression in one's life. It's as if our souls finally despair trying to survive in a world of spiritual drought. This drying up of one's "inner moisture and volatility" during calcination represents the loss of the emotional or psychic energy we invest in the world. After calcination, our personalities are less emotional or "drier." In other words, as we mature and are heated by the natural forces of existence, we tend to be less emotionally invested in life.

What fuels the fires of personal calcination? Our structured ego. In psychological terms, calcination is the destruction of the false ego identity we have built up in response to pressures from our parents, friends, schools, churches, government, and other social institutions. We accumulate the impurities within ourselves, and they become part of the veil that hides the true light of our being.

Personal calcination begins when we realize that the things we have accepted as important might not have any relevance to what we want in our lives. The basic problem is that we identify with our superficial personalities and not with our true essences. We invest all our energy in our egos, which are artificial constructs that often do not reflect who we really are. So, the first step in personal transformation is for us to turn up the fire of consciousness in the inner laboratory and focus it on our thoughts, habits, assumptions, judgments, and relationships to see what is really worth keeping.

The truth is that personal calcination takes place regardless of whether we want it to do so. This natural humbling process takes place as we grow older and are assaulted and overcome by the trials and tribulations of life. Decline of self-esteem, loss of standing in families and at work, personal embarrassments, failure to be loved, loss of material possessions, and all the other harsh realities of life gradually crucify our pampered egos. By the time people reach middle age, many feel they have lost a precious part of themselves and are leading inauthentic lives.

In alchemy, the symbol of the King referred to what we now call ego, and alchemical drawings of personal calcination, as illustrated in the following figure, show the King being boiled alive, cremated, or sitting inside a sweat box or sealed vessel. The idea here is that the ego King must be sacrificed for the good of the whole person. As in the Grail legends, the kingdom of one's personality will wither and decay until the rightful King is restored to power.

Calcination of the King or male ego. "The King is freed from the Black Gall."
(From Atalanta Fugiens by Michael Maier, 1617)

The sacrifice of the King is an important motif in alchemy. In the Middle Ages, there were frequent festivals in which an effigy of the King was burnt, so his spirit could be reborn and multiply for the good of the whole community. The tradition continues today in festivals like "Burning Man" in northern Nevada's Black Rock desert, during which New Age enthusiasts burn a giant wooden effigy of modern man.

In describing the suffering of the King during calcination, the seventeenth-century German alchemist Daniel Stolicus wrote: "The fiery man will sweat and become hot in the fire. Also, will he resolve his body and carry it far through moisture." Stolicus was referring to the conclusion of the fire operation and the promise of healing and cleansing in the next operation, which is an application of the Water Element in the Great Work.

The Dissolution Operation

The next operation alchemists used during the Black Phase is dissolution, which is sometimes referred to simply as "solution." Dissolution is the transformation of a substance by immersing it in water or other liquid. In the lab, it is the liquefaction of a solid or the absorption of a solid into a liquid. It usually involves dissolving the ashes from calcination in water or liquid chemicals. The liquid in which the ashes are dissolved takes on magical properties, and the term *elixir* comes from the Arabic *Al-iksir* that literally means "from the ashes."

Fascination with the powers of the Water Element dates back at least as far as the female alchemists of Alexandria, who developed equipment for performing dissolution and distillation. To the astonishment of ancient experimenters, solids disappeared into solvents as if they had been returned to their original, undifferentiated states. They saw this as reduction to the First Matter, a purification they likened to a return to the womb for rebirth.

The astrological sign associated with the dissolution process is the Water sign of Cancer, which the Egyptians called the sign of the Scarab. Symbols of dissolution include lakes, floods, underground streams, quicksand, reflecting pools, tears, melting, menstruation, washing in tubs, fish swimming on the surface of water, and other allusions to the Water Element. Glass vessels, clay pots, cauldrons, and other womblike vessels of transformation also refer to this process.

Drawings of women riding great fish, taming wild animals or dragons, or naked women walking quietly in the forest are images of dissolution that emphasize the deep connection between nature and the feminine side of our being. While the King derives his powers of light and active energy from the Sun, or solar archetype, the Queen's source of power resides in the darkness and potential energy of the Moon, or lunar archetype. Therefore, psychologically, the King represents the conscious mind and thoughts, while the Queen represents the subconscious mind and feelings.

Understanding the differences between the King and Queen will enable you to more readily recognize these opposing forces in yourself. The King represents the aggressive masculine ego and the powers of reasoning, and the Queen represents the forces of passive acceptance and the feminine ways of knowing, such as feelings and intuition. While the King and Queen represent opposing qualities of our personalities, they are really two aspects or faces of the same thing—our true selves.

Personal Dissolution

Personal dissolution further breaks down the corrupted and artificial structures of the personality by immersion in the dark waters of the unconscious. This is a forbidding realm with slumbering dragons or other monsters guarding great treasures. In alchemy, other symbols of the unconscious realm include depictions of poisonous toads, basilisks (winged serpents), menacing fish, great whales, confrontations with stags, or scenes of rabbits diving down into holes in the ground. Images of dissolution might feature the naked Queen in a bath alone or together with the King, or they might show the King sitting alone in a boiling cauldron or drowning in a lake.

Dissolution of the King or male ego. "He that delivers me shall have a great reward."
(From Atalanta Fugiens by Michael Maier, 1617)

Alchemists sometimes referred to the energies found in this forbidding watery realm of the subconscious as "the water which does not wet the hands." These dissolving waters can take the form of inner voices, visions, dreams, or just odd feelings that reveal a world of shadowy energies existing simultaneously with us in our everyday lives. This buried material and rejected energy surfaces during dissolution because the conscious mind relinquishes control after suffering through the fires of calcination. That is the whole purpose of personal calcination.

Direct confrontation with the primordial energies of the unconscious during dissolution further humbles the beleaguered ego (the King) and results in a surrendering of stubborn beliefs and projections. During these early stages of personal alchemy, projection is a dangerous thing. When we are angered or revolted by things we see in the world, it is because that same negative quality lives subconsciously within us. We end up expending tremendous psychic energy projecting these rejected qualities into other people while keeping them hidden from view within ourselves.

The blackening of the waters of dissolution in the lab was often expressed as the darkness of depression and melancholia within the alchemist. However, alchemists considered personal dissolution to be a completely natural process. Instead of running for Prozac, the true alchemist might try to work with the darkness and suffer through it to emerge transformed. By bringing this threatening material to light in therapy or personal work, the alchemist rises above the "poisonous vapors" of the subconscious and learns to integrate the dark side into a reborn self.

This might seem like a scary process, but it's a necessary step in personal transformation. We all have built-up a personal trash heap of rejected material that is incompatible with our chosen conscious attitudes. Psychologists call this part of our personalities the "shadow," which is the inferior or rejected part of our personalities. Slowing down and paying attention to feelings allows this material to surface and come to light, where we can examine it and transmute its dark energy in positive ways.

How exactly do you transform the threatening darkness of a negative experience? First, you need to stop thinking about the individual incident behind the negative emotion and try to work only with its pure energy—what alchemists would call its "vital principle." If you can dissolve the connection between the emotion and the shadowy material that fuels it, the energy will be free to use for healing or further transformation.

One way of doing this is with a method of dissolution called cibation. Cibation is the addition of water or other fluids to dried-out substances at precisely the right moment in an experiment. Psychologically, this involves coolly and deliberately reviewing painful, hardened memories without letting them upset you and then holding the memories in your mind until the emotions behind them finally break to the surface.

If you let yourself fully re-experience these emotions, sometimes a lump forms in your throat or tears well-up in your eyes. The idea is to let yourself go and cry as long and as hard as you can. Crying therapy is a valid technique used by therapists to overcome eating disorders, sex problems, drug abuse, insomnia, guilt and anger issues, and many other problems.

But the uncontrolled crying must take place at precisely the right time to work. Medieval alchemists were the first to understand the therapeutic benefits of cibation or crying at the right moment. They were so convinced of its effectiveness that they actually believed the salt in tears was the remnant of crystallized thoughts and memories that were broken down by crying.

Other effective methods of personal dissolution include paying attention to dream symbolism, mental images, or slips of the tongue and examining why you feel uncomfortable in certain situations. Keeping journals of your thoughts and feelings also helps bring the shadowy material to light. By applying the operations of alchemy to the human mind, alchemists became the first psychologists.

In this chapter, we learned how alchemists framed their discoveries in terms of their experimental lab work because they believed the principles of transformation to be universal. We introduced the initial operations of Fire and Water that the alchemists named calcination and dissolution. If successful, these first operations have eliminated the dross of the substance, regardless of whether it is of a chemical or psychological nature. The goal of the Black Phase is to eliminate contaminating materials and reveal the most basic constituents or essences of a substance or person. The job of the next phase in alchemy, the *Albedo* or whitening, is to separate these essences and recombine them at higher levels of purity and power.

CHAPTER 16

The White Phase: Purification

In the previous chapter, our matter suffered through the mortifications of the Black Phase of alchemy. However, the blackness is now slowly giving way to light, and a new day is dawning. The matter has nearly died and is being slowly resuscitated. Psychologically, we have experienced the death of old habits, beliefs, judgments, projections, and dependencies, and a new personality is forming.

We have entered the second phase of transformation, the White Phase or *Albedo*, which is a purification of the matter that survived the *Nigredo*. The whitening begins with a washing, or cleansing, of the products and proceeds to their reunion at a new level of purity.

Spiritually, the whiteness of the *Albedo* is the brilliant white light at the end of the dark tunnel between death and the afterlife. The alchemists believed our souls, which are the immortal essences of our beings, follow the same progression through the phases of alchemical transformation, as do substances in the lab or the facets of our personalities.

The White Phase

The *Albedo* emerges from the blackness of the *Nigredo* in a gradual process of filtering and purification. The White Stage is extremely important in the overall progress of transformation because any remaining contamination or impurities that make it through to the third and final phase can ruin the whole experiment.

Albification is the chemical term for the process of whitening. The word comes from the Latin words *albus* ("white") and *fiacre* ("to make"). Albification is accomplished by washing, scrubbing, grinding, or bleaching with chemical agents. The process releases the purified essences from the dross and waste materials of *Nigredo*. The biggest challenge during albification is keeping the purified essences from recombining or picking up contaminants until the alchemist has fully isolated them by filtering them out. The final operation of the *Albedo* is to combine the pure essences into a new incarnation or body.

Another characteristic of the *Albedo* work is that the alchemist discovers the underlying duality of the subject of transformation. The level of purification is so great that the fundamental duality of nature can be observed in the experiment. In other words, the revealed essences almost always turn out to have opposing qualities. In personal transformation, the opposing essences are the masculine and feminine characteristics of the personality, which alchemists referred to as the King and the Queen.

Symbols of the White Phase include the naked King and Queen standing next to one another, as well as more abstract images such as baptismal fonts, silver chalices, fountains from which two streams of water flow into a single basin, or two lions sharing one head vomiting a single stream of liquid.

Other symbols include a white dove, white swan, white dragon, white Queen, white rose, white stone, and white mercury. The full Moon and the morning star Venus are also symbols. In mythology, Aurora, the Roman goddess of the dawn, is often used by alchemists to refer to *Albedo*.

Alchemists believed they could only accomplish the *Albedo* with divine grace through a merging of the powers Above with the powers Below. The actual mechanism of whitening was regarded as a mystery that could not be explained, and during this phase, the alchemist spent more time in prayer and meditation than at any other time.

The Benedictine alchemist Anthony-Joseph Pernety (1716–1796) said of this stage: "When the alchemist sees the perfect whiteness, the philosophers say that one has to destroy his books, because they have become superfluous." As we noted in Chapter 4, that is exactly what happened to the most prolific alchemist of the Middle Ages, Albertus Magnus. After seeing the "perfect whiteness" of Sophia (the Greek word for "wisdom"), he stopped mid-sentence in his writings and never opened another book.

The operations that take place during the White Phase are two processes that involve working with the elements of Air and Earth. They are called separation and conjunction, respectively. After these two operations are completed, the essences of the matter at hand will be fused inseparably to create an exalted matter at a new level of strength and integrity.

The Separation Operation

Separation is the alchemical operation of disuniting, dividing, cutting, or breaking down substances to retrieve their basic constituents or essences. Chemically, it is the isolation of the components of dissolution by filtration and then the discarding of any ungenuine or unworthy material.

To ancient Egyptian alchemists, separation was represented by the compound sodium carbonate, which separated from water and appeared as white soda ash on dry lakebeds. The oldest known deposits are in Egypt. Alchemists sometimes referred to this compound as *Natron*, which symbolized the common tendency in all salts to form solid bodies or precipitates. *Natron* was the primary agent used to preserve mummies in Egypt, and they believed the chemical would act like a catalyst in the birth of a new body in the afterlife.

In the laboratory, the components of the polluted products from calcination and dissolution are usually separated using a process that alchemists called "inhibition" or holding back. The most common method of inhibition is filtration, in which material is separated out by passing it through a screen or porous paper.

Other methods of separation include settling, decomposing, skimming, sifting, or agitation with air. Sometimes, more sophisticated methods such as layered melting or fractional distillation are used. The captured contaminants are discarded, and the saved essences are isolated in separate containers.

The alchemical cipher for separation is the astrological sign of Scorpio. The Egyptians associated Scorpio with a descent into the underworld to bring back knowledge of universal truths, which is a perfect metaphor for the separation process. Other ciphers for separation were stylized filters and funnels, as well as piles of sand used for filtering liquids.

Images of separation include double-edged axes, swords hanging down from above, knights wielding swords, and scenes of dismemberment. The splitting of the Red Sea is sometimes used as a metaphor of separation, as are scenes of the Apocalypse. Alchemical engravings show white birds flying over a burning, blackened countryside. The destruction symbolizes the results of the earlier operations of *Nigredo,* while the white bird represents the essences saved by the separation process.

Personal Separation

Separation on the psychological level is the rediscovery and isolation of your personal essences. During personal separation, you lift yourself out of the quagmire of your broken personality and start to recognize your true Self. The operations of *Nigredo* have broken down your personality into your most basic traits and desires, and during the first stage of *Albedo,* you become aware of the pure essences within and try to isolate them from ego complexes and unwanted subconscious elements.

Alchemists saw separation as the introduction of the Air Element into their work. Air is associated with spiritual energy, divine will, and energies from Above. The Air Element purifies by increasing vibrations, spiritizing, and elevating the matter. In your personality, the Air Element is simply taking the higher road of an enlightened attitude and maintaining an optimistic view of the possibilities that are open to you. The only way to really refine yourself is to raise the noble parts of your personality and bring them into the light.

A typical alchemical drawing of the separation operation is shown in the following figure. Separation requires decisive action, as suggested by the armored male figure with a sword. The process involves cutting into the heart of the subject of the work to reveal the deepest essences of soul and spirit. The great egg that is about to be cut open represents the sealed Hermetic vessel that contains these essences. That vessel can be a retort in the lab that contains a solution from which the essences must be saved, or it could represent the deeper aspects of your own personality or subconscious mind that must be exposed to the light of consciousness to succeed at personal transformation.

Personal separation requires a certain amount of objectivity and honesty about your strengths, weaknesses, and what is worth salvaging from your old personality. Dissecting and discarding what is no longer relevant or useful is an important role of the separation process. The goal is to preserve what is genuine by removing it from contaminating influences and keeping it safe for further alchemical transformation. This stage is about getting beyond the restraints to your true nature, so the real you can shine through. The process involves breaking old habits, replacing them with new behaviors, and doing these things long enough for the new habits to take root.

Separation of the Essences. "Take an Egg and smite it with a fiery sword."
(From Atalanta Fugiens by Michael Maier, 1617)

The Conjunction Operation

If the preceding operations were successful, only the most genuine and essential parts of the matter are left to work with. The next step in the alchemy of transformation is the conjunction, which is the recombination of those saved essences into a new compound or purer substance.

In terms of the Four Elements, conjunction is the union of purified essences to produce a new Earth Element from the operations with the other three elements. Calcination works with the Fire Element, dissolution with the Water Element, and separation with the Air Element.

The conjunction process begins with commixtion, which is simply mixing or commingling the saved essences. Vessels of conjunction sometimes have two glass globes or sections joined by a middle chamber in which the mixing or commingling occurs.

However, just bringing these essences together in the same vessel is not enough to accomplish conjunction. The essences must be attracted to one another and interact to create a new compound, which alchemists called the "Child of the Conjunction."

If the recombination of essences does not produce a new compound, alchemists felt that physical impurities or negative spiritual energies had polluted the process, and the whole experiment had miscarried.

The alchemists saw the coming together of essences during conjunction as a sexual union or mating of chemicals to conceive a child, which was the new compound or alloy. For this reason, many of the drawings of this stage of the work show the King and Queen embracing or making love. Not surprisingly, the symbolic bird of conjunction is the cockerel—the young and licentious rooster.

The alchemical cipher that stands for conjunction is the astrological Earth sign of Taurus, the virile bull. The bull was sacred to ancient Egyptians, who used it to symbolize fertility and growth. They even timed the plowing of their fields and mating of cattle with the rising of Taurus in the heavens.

Other images of conjunction include rams and satyrs, double-chambered furnaces, rope or chains binding opposing entities, birds chained to earthbound animals, and two streams in a forest coming together to form one stream. Drawings of conjunction sometimes show two animals, vessels, or other objects being mixed or joined in some way. Often, drawings show the King and Queen in reconciliation at this stage, with Hermes or Mercury in between or joining them with an embrace or handshake.

Personal Conjunction

Psychologically, conjunction is the union of the opposing sides of our personality—the masculine King and the feminine Queen. Alchemists referred to the result of this conjugal union as the "Lesser Stone" or "Child of the Conjunction." In Rosicrucian alchemy, it is sometimes called the *Parvulus* ("fetus or child"). At this point in the lab or in personal work, all attention is focused on nurturing this new seed of life. *Nil nisi Parvulus* ("Nothing but the child") was the motto of this stage of the work. After this new life stirs within you, you should be able to clearly discern what needs to be done to achieve enlightenment, a state of inner gnosis that can grow into the "Greater Stone," which is also known as the Philosopher's Stone.

In spiritual terms, the essences of conjunction are the soul and spirit of the alchemist, and their union is known as the Sacred Marriage, which is a subject we will explore in some detail in Chapter 20. Alchemical images of this blessed event include the Sun and the Moon uniting high in the sky, an eclipse in a twilight sky, two white birds raising a crown into the heavens, red and white lions or dragons sharing one body, or elaborate outdoor wedding celebrations.

Conjunction of the King and Queen. "He is conceived in Baths, born in the Air, and being made Red, he walks upon the Waters."

(From Atalanta Fugiens by Michael Maier, 1617)

Because the marriage partners in the Sacred Marriage are essences of soul and spirit within the alchemist, many texts described the marriage as an act of incest between a brother and sister, which was considered the purest and closest relationship in a family. To church officials, who took such metaphors literally, this was one more example of the immorality of alchemists.

While the ancients saw soul and spirit everywhere and treated them as two distinct entities, most people today confuse the terms. Spirit, the inner King, is constantly striving for change and betterment, while soul, the inner Queen, is happy with things just as they are and wants only to settle down in a secure place and experience life on a personal level.

Spirit is associated with energy, aggression, expansion, and intellectual pursuits, while soul is associated with matter, passivity, contraction, bodily sensations, and emotions. Spirit craves action and adventure, feeds on abstract concepts, and seeks objective-unifying principles. Spirit is responsible for business, science, technology, and the patriarchal world in which we live.

The soul, on the other hand, craves memories and reflection and prefers storytelling over theorizing. Her language is art and music, and food for the soul comes from subjective feelings about everyday objects and relationships. Spirit is focused on the future but requires the passion of the soul to succeed, and for that reason, spirit must always seek out soul and court her favors.

The union of spirit and soul within an individual produces a third kind of consciousness that combines masculine and feminine ways of knowing into a deeper awareness. The Egyptians called it "Intelligence of the Heart," and medieval alchemists referred to this blossoming of wisdom as the "Philosopher's Child." However we picture it, the Sacred Marriage is the merging of thought and feeling to produce a highly intuitive state that was considered a direct experience of reality. Paracelsus referred to this state of gnosis as stellar or astral consciousness.

What does conjunction feel like on the personal level? Many adepts through the ages have compared it with the development of a spiritual fetus within—something new and unexpected and a wonderfully refreshing presence that emerges from the suffering and darkness of the *Nigredo* and is revealed in the *Albedo*.

In the later stages of alchemy, this golden gnosis becomes an incorruptible "Stone" in the sense that it survives untainted, no matter what happens. No matter how confusing things get in your life, no matter what emotions swell up within you, no matter where your thoughts take you, and no matter how cruel or inconsiderate others are toward you, you will have this solid refuge inside that is very much like a talismanic stone. This spiritual Stone in your personality creates a feeling of deep integrity and confidence in everything you do.

Conjunction is a prerequisite for progressing further in the Great Work. It is the culmination of the work Below in the realm of matter, habits, and thoughts, and it is the beginning of the work Above in the realm of energy, higher consciousness, and spirit.

But conjunction is the operation where most failures occur—both in the lab and on the personal level. The Child of the Conjunction is often stillborn, in which case the work must be abandoned. For example, if the child is the product of an experiment, it might fail to create a viable or useful compound. If it is a tincture, the plant essences might die or lose their life forces when mixed in alcohol. On the psychological level, the child could be a new mental attitude of confidence and optimism that cannot survive in the everyday world of family, coworkers, and stressful responsibilities. For those reasons, conjunction is often called the turning point or pivotal operation in alchemy. If the hermaphroditic Child of the Conjunction survives, it will be nurtured and grow into something entirely new during the operations of the Red Phase.

In this chapter, we explored the White or *Albedo* Phase of transformation and the two operations of separation and conjunction that are associated with it. On the personal level, separation involves finding the essences of the true Self within and protecting them from any contaminating influences. Personal conjunction is about recognizing the inner essences of soul and spirit and uniting them in a new level of consciousness and spiritual awareness. Conjunction is the doorway to spiritual empowerment, the mystery of which is revealed only at the highest levels of initiation. We will return to take a look at the deeper significance of this operation in Chapter 20. For now, we will continue our exploration of the operations of alchemy in the next chapter with the final Red Phase of transformation.

Chapter 17

The Red Phase: Empowerment

The third and final phase of alchemy, known as the Red Phase or *Rubedo,* is a natural continuation of the White Phase. Alchemists believe the deep purification of essences began during the White Phase is what releases the powerful energies experienced during the Red Phase.

The way these two phases complement one another is reflected in the symbols alchemists chose to represent them. The symbol of *Albedo* is the White Queen, and the symbol of *Rubedo* is the Red King. Often, the White Queen and Red King are shown holding hands or clutching a small vessel or container. This was the alchemists' way of saying they work together at this stage. In the laboratory, the white becomes united with the red by increasing the heat in the furnace.

With successful completion of the Red Phase, alchemists believed they would achieve the power of projection and produce the Philosopher's Stone, which would transmute base metals into gold. Psychologically, the Red Phase meant the integration of opposing and rejected elements within the personality and the experience of one's true nature being projected into the world.

Putrefaction of the Matter

A curious thing happens during the transition from the white *Albedo* phase to the red *Rubedo* phase. The work enters another dark phase as the Child of the Conjunction struggles to stay alive in the purified spiritual realm. Alchemists call this stage "putrefaction," and it occurs both in the laboratory work and during the work on the psychological levels.

Putrefaction is a final cleansing of impurities in the work and alchemists sometimes refer to it as the "Purgation of the Stone." Putrefaction is considered a final death to any contaminants or remnants of ego in the matter, and it is a necessary prelude to the resurrection or rebirth of the matter on a more perfect or spiritual level. Things have to die to be reborn.

During the darkness at the beginning of *Rubedo*, alchemists looked for three fleeting signals that they were on the right track. The first was the appearance of a yellow or golden color in the blackened matter. They called it the *Citrinatis* ("Yellow Stage"). This short-lived phenomenon was a sign that the golden stage of transformation was coming. If they were working with a metal, it meant that transmutation into gold was a real possibility.

The second indication of pending success was the appearance of a deep-purple color in the work. Alchemists named it the *Iosis* ("Purple Stage"). The royal-purple hue is the color of gold in solution and is an indicator of pure gold atoms in modern chemistry. To alchemists, it meant the minute quantity of gold revealed by the Yellow Stage was being seeded in the experiment and would eventually grow to transform the entire matter. They also referred to this stage as the "Transmutation of the Venom," and they believed it meant that any contamination or poisons left over from the *Nigredo* were now completely purified and assimilated.

The Peacock Spreads Its Tail

The third indicator of success in the early stages of *Rubedo* appears at the darkest moment of putrefaction, when a sudden and glorious display of many vibrant colors occurs both in the lab and in the alchemist's imagination. Alchemists called this colorful display the *Cauda Pavonis* ("Peacock's Tail"). Again, it was observed in both the laboratory and on the personal levels of transformation.

In mythology, the peacock is sacred to Juno, the Roman goddess and protector of childbirth. In the Middle Ages, peacocks were thought to fight snakes and consume or neutralize their poisons. Medieval people ate peacock meat for its supposed ability to neutralize poisons, but alchemists ate peacock meat ceremoniously, which symbolized assimilating the many colors of the work into themselves.

The rainbow of colors seen in the Peacock's Tail gradually merges into pure whiteness. Because black is the absence of color, the sudden appearance of colors in the Peacock's Tail during putrefaction signaled a fundamental change in the matter. And it's only natural that the Peacock's Tail eventually turned white because white contains all colors together.

Symbolism of the Peacock's Tail include a rainbow appearing in the dark clouds of a thunderstorm, the bursting forth of the colors of spring after the darkness of winter, the colors of the *Aurora Borealis* ("Northern Lights") gleaming against the night sky, and of course, a peacock spreading its tail.

In the lab, the Peacock's Tail is observed in an iridescent oil that floats on the surface of the blackened matter and gradually turns into a white fatty substance. This milky liquid is composed of digesting bacteria that accumulated on the rotting material. Psychologist Carl Jung compared this phenomenon to daybreak, a period of peace and tranquility before the next and final phase, which is the full sunrise of *Rubedo*.

The Red Phase

After suffering through the *Nigredo*, undergoing the intense purifications of *Albedo*, and experiencing the short death of putrefaction, the matter of the work is depleted of energy and life force. It is pure but sterile earth, which alchemists compared to the bleak face of the Moon. To make the work come alive again, alchemists felt it must have fresh blood and undergo reddening in the fire.

German alchemist Franciscus Kieser described this process in his book *Cabalistic Chemistry* (1606): "As the body used to be slow, rough, impure, dark and destructible because it lacked power and energy, so the reddened rebirth unifies soul with spirit, vivified and volatile, light and penetrating, pure, refined and clear, overflowing with energy, indestructible and full of energy. And it is able to maintain this."

The infusion of life into the dead matter is accomplished by the loving union of the White Queen with the Red King, who work together during *Rubedo* in a cosmic process sometimes referred to as the "Marriage of the Sun and the Moon." Obviously, these are profound symbols with universal meanings. According to Hermetic philosophy, these opposing spiritual forces are the basic essences of every created thing in the universe.

The Moon (or White Queen) represents the universal feminine essence of soul; the Sun (or Red King) represents the universal masculine essence of spirit.

Among the operations alchemists used to complete the Red Phase are two dynamic processes known as fermentation and distillation, which combine opposing energies in the work. The third and final operation during *Rubedo* is known as coagulation, which is the ultimate crystallization of energy and matter that becomes the Philosopher's Stone.

The Fermentation Operation

To the ancients, fermentation was a miracle of nature. As early as 7000 B.C.E., Egyptians used their knowledge of fermentation to make mead, wine, and beer. By 4500 B.C.E., the Egyptians and Chinese had learned to ferment milk to make yogurt and cheese. Fermentation requires living cells, such as bacteria or yeast, and is considered a kind of cellular or fetal respiration that usually takes place in the absence of oxygen.

In chemical terms, fermentation is the conversion of organic substances into new compounds in the presence of fermenting bacteria. The most common fermentation is the conversion of sugars into alcohol, which held special meaning for alchemists. They felt alcohol was the actual spiritual essence of a substance, which is why we still refer to liquors and other alcoholic beverages as "spirits."

Some examples of fermentation will make this process clear. Beer is made by germinating grain and then drying and crushing it into pulp. This mash, as it is called, is mixed with warm water. Wine is made by crushing grapes and separating out the juice. In both cases, fermentation begins naturally if the material is allowed to decay, though yeast is usually added to get the process started. After proper aging to allow the alcohol to accumulate, the beer or wine is filtered and bottled.

Putrefaction, whose end was signaled by the appearance of the Peacock's Tail, is actually a natural part of the fermentation process. Putrefaction is the first step in fermentation, when the matter is allowed to rot and decay. Medieval alchemists sometimes added manure to help get that process going. Unlike the hopeless blackness of *Nigredo*, alchemists considered the blackness of putrefaction to be a pregnant darkness that would lead to the rebirth of the Philosopher's Child in the fertile womb of the fermenting vessel.

The cipher used by alchemists to designate putrefaction was the astrological Fire sign of Leo, which the Egyptians associated with the lion-headed Sun god Sekhmet. Images of putrefaction include corpses, graves, coffins, massacres, mutilation, worms, dung beetles, and rotting flesh. Alchemical drawings at this stage depict birds descending from a pitch-black sky, skeletons standing over coffins or black boxes, or a snake crucified on a cross.

The life of dung beetles (scarabs) is an interesting metaphor of the processes of putrefaction and fermentation. The huge beetle makes a ball of animal feces into which it deposits its eggs. Then it rolls the ball back to its underground den, where the natural heat of putrefaction warms the eggs. The esoteric meaning of scarab is "secret enclosed fire." This is the heat generated in decomposing material, as well as the essential Secret Fire that must be generated within alchemists to accomplish their work. As the larvae mature, the beetle rolls its ball toward the heat of the rising Sun, where the newborn beetles emerge and take wing into the light of a new day.

Egyptians worshipped the dung beetle as a manifestation of their god Khepri, the scarab-faced god of the rising Sun who rolls the Sun across the horizon through the day and is thus responsible for the "operation of the Sun" described in the Emerald Tablet. By extension, Khepri represents creation itself and the renewal of life.

When true fermentation begins, the dead material seems to come to life again as movement and bubbling gases emerge from the influx of digesting bacteria. Fermentation drawings sometimes show a bird descending into water where a black toad waits, two birds nesting in a tree, an alchemist waiting patiently for changes to take place in a darkened vessel, or a farmer sowing gold coins in a field.

Other scenes of fermentation feature grapevines, sowing, germination, greenness, and rebirth. Green is often associated with successful fermentation, and other possible green symbols for fermentation include the Emerald Tablet, green gemstones, lush gardens, and the Green Lion stretching up toward the sky. Images capturing the energies of the fermentation process include dark clouds and thunderstorms, lightning, sexual activity in caves or darkened vessels, and angels coming down from heaven.

Alchemists assigned the astrological cipher for Capricorn to stand for the process of fermentation. Capricorn is an Earth sign whose symbols are both the goat and the unicorn. The goat represents the most basic natural instincts, and the unicorn represents the highest or most refined instincts. Alchemists believed that Capricorn encompassed the entire work from beginning to end. It is the first sign of the year, and movement from Capricorn to Capricorn encompassed one alchemical year in which the Great Work could be accomplished.

The primary symbol of successful fermentation is the curious two-headed human figure known as the *Rebis* (from Latin *res bina,* "a double thing"). The Rebis is usually depicted as a hermaphrodite (literally, born of Hermes-Aphrodite) with a male head on its right and a female head on its left. It represents the Philosopher's Child resulting from the union of the King and Queen that took place during the conjunction phase.

Fermentation of the Rebis or Hermaphrodite. "Lying like a dead man in darkness, it wants Fire."
(From Atalanta Fugiens by Michael Maier, 1617)

The naked and purified Rebis is shown being heated by the fires of fermentation in the figure above. This fire is not the direct consuming flames of calcination, but a mild, controlled heat that has been likened to birds sitting on eggs to hatch them. The Rebis is like an embryonic being or intermediate stage in transformation.

Personal Fermentation

Just as chemical fermentation is the introduction of new life into the matter, so is psychological fermentation the introduction of new life into the childlike inner presence created during personal conjunction. Any problems starting the fermentation process to revive the Child of the Conjunction stem from impurities carried over from the White Phase. Those hidden impurities in our character hopefully would have been destroyed during the psychological death of putrefaction.

Fermentation on the personal level starts with the inspiration of spiritual power that reanimates, energizes, and enlightens the blackened ego. Personal fermentation can be achieved using a wide variety of tools, including intense prayer, desire for mystical union, transpersonal therapy, visualization, and deep meditation. In simplest terms, fermentation is a living, loving inspiration from something totally beyond and outside us in the spiritual realm. "Separate the Earth from Fire, the Subtle from the Gross," the Emerald Tablet instructs us at this stage.

Like the colorful Peacock's Tail of its chemical counterpart, psychological fermentation often begins with colorful visions that originate in a higher form of imagination. Alchemists believed the mental images experienced during fermentation were true representations of a greater spiritual reality and not mere fantasy. We should also note that medieval alchemists were natural chemists who were familiar with the psychoactive properties of plants, fungi, and other entheogenic compounds.

The Distillation Operation

In the lab, distillation is the boiling and condensation of a solution to increase its concentration and purity. Alchemists believe that distillation releases the pure essence or spirit of a substance in the evaporating vapors. For example, one can obtain the pure alcohol spirit of wine by distilling a solution of fermented grapes. The liquid essence can then be concentrated by rectification, which is the process of refining or purifying a substance by repeated distillations. In this process, the evaporated distillate is returned to the boiling vessel to be distilled again.

The Emerald Tablet describes the distillation process in terms of Above and Below: "It rises from Earth to Heaven and descends again to Earth, thereby combining within Itself the powers of both the Above and the Below." The typical distillation apparatus consists of a lower boiling vessel (the cucurbit) and an upper stillhead (the alembic), which is a hooded vessel that collects the rising vapors. The hot vapors cool in a long condenser, and the purified condensed liquid (the distillate) is directed by a tube or funnel into a receiving vessel.

An unusual medieval distillation device nicknamed the "Pelican" was a glass retort with two tubes connecting the neck of the vessel with the lower body. The result was a reflux rectification still, in which the mixture was boiled, and vapors condensed in the neck and then flowed back into the boiling liquid through the tubes. This inner circulatory process produced a very pure essence from the original mixture. Alchemical drawings of this operation often show a pelican pecking herself in her chest in order to feed her young, which are gathered at her feet lapping up her fresh blood.

Another kind of distillation is "cohobation," in which solid matter is repeatedly soaked in liquid and distilled to capture its purified essences. In a distillation process known as "sublimation," no liquid is used at all. The solid material gives off vapors that condense directly into an extremely pure powder at the top of the distilling apparatus. The solidified material remains stuck to the sides of the alembic until collected by the alchemist.

Alchemists considered sublimation to be a superior form of distillation that led directly to their treasured Philosopher's Stone. "He who knows how to sublime the Stone," said the Greek alchemist Eudoxus (400–350 B.C.E.), "justly deserves the name of a philosopher, since he knows the Fire of the Wise, which is the only instrument which can work this sublimation."

Distillation is the most important operation in practical alchemy, and some alchemists spent months distilling the same solution over and over. Similarly, on the psychological level, the distillation of wisdom in our lives can take many decades.

Alchemists chose the astrological Earth sign of Virgo as the cipher to signify distillation. The Egyptians associated the alchemical goddess Isis with this sign. The cipher for the operation of sublimation was Libra, an astrological Air sign the Egyptians associated with the divine child, as well as Maat, the goddess of truth.

Drawings of the distillation process sometimes show two-headed creatures rising into the air on wings and then returning to Earth. This repeated circulation between the spiritual forces Above and the material forces Below eventually lead to a concentration and purification of the essences of the substance at hand. Continued cycles of distillation eventually produce a thick and extremely concentrated solution the alchemists called the "Mother of the Stone."

In the following figure, we see the distillation of the Rebis as it nears the final stages. The Rebis stands on a winged stone or globe that is the new Salt or permanent body that coagulates after distillation is complete. Incorporated in the stone are the square of the Four Elements and the triangle of the Three Essentials. The seven planetary forces driving this process are shown as stars surrounding the Rebis. The square and compass it holds indicate that distillation is an objective process of rectification and gradual enlightenment.

Other images of distillation include flowers in bloom, such as the rose, lotus, jasmine, and edelweiss, as well as scenes of fountains, waterwheels, dew, rain, and snow. Animal images include the unicorn, white doves, soaring birds, owls, pelicans, winged serpents, a Green Lion eating the Sun, and a flaming dragon eating its own tail.

Distillation of the Rebis, which rises up on the wings of the dragon,
while the Tria Prima forces rain down from above.

(From Theoria Philosophiae Hermeticae by Heinrich Nollius, 1617)

Personal Distillation

In psychological terms, distillation is a spiritizing process that involves repeated separation and recombination of the subtle or spiritual aspects of the personality with the unrefined thoughts and emotions or gross aspects of the personality. This is actually a very natural process that we can observe simply by paying attention to our everyday thoughts.

We are always recycling thoughts and regurgitating emotions in a never-ending struggle to organize our lives and find direction and meaning. This chaotic process goes on unchecked and unnoticed until a distilled idea breaks through in the form of a new insight or revised judgment.

Successful personal distillation, however, requires mind control. It means being conscious of this mental process and deliberately pursuing it to its distillate conclusion. The deliberate agitation and sublimation of psychic forces is necessary to ensure that no hidden impurities from the inflated ego or submerged shadow are incorporated into the new manifestation of Self in the final stages of transformation.

Tools used in personal distillation include mind control techniques and introspective meditations that raise the content of the psyche to the highest or most objective level possible, free from the emotional energy that often controls our behavior. Almost all types of psychological therapy are methods of personal distillation that seek a reconciliation of subjective and objective realities.

Circulation of the Light

A personal distillation meditation used by Taoist alchemists for more than 5,000 years is known as the "Circulation of the Light." The ancient texts tell the aspirant to "concentrate on the light of the inmost region and, while so doing, to free yourself from all outer and inner entanglements." The light they refer to is the subtle life force scattered throughout the body, and the object of the meditation is to bring all these points of light together in a cauldron visualized in the abdomen just below the navel. This inner boiling vessel is known as the Lower *Tan Tien* ("Elixir Field").

In the first stage of the distillation, the light is gathered by quieting the body and mind through breath awareness and deep relaxation. Life force in the breath called *Chi* ("masculine spiritual energy") is inhaled with a deep breath into the lungs and then exhaled with clear intent downward into the Lower *Tan Tien* in the abdominal cauldron. This cycle is continued until enough *Chi* has accumulated to feel a warmth or sustained tingling there.

In the second stage, sexual life force called *Ching* ("feminine soulful energy") is stimulated by tightening and then releasing the pelvic floor muscles around the *Mons Veneris* ("Mound of Venus"). This causes the *Ching* to melt and pour from the sexual organs into the abdominal cauldron and mix with the *Chi* there. The mixing of the masculine *Chi* with the feminine *Ching* heats up the abdominal cauldron to the boiling point.

During the third stage, concentration is fixed on the abdominal cauldron (Lower *Tan Tien*) as the practitioner wills and feels the light circulate up the "Channel of Control" along the back through the spinal cord to the "precious cauldron" (Upper *Tan Tien*) at the center of the brain. There, the steaming raw energy from below "condenses" into *Shen* ("purified spiritual energy"), and any unconverted energy returns to the cauldron in the abdomen (Lower *Tan Tien*) via the "Channel of Function" that runs down the front through the chest area.

From the chest, the purified energy nourishes all parts of the physical body. Some adepts learn how to "open the heart" in such a way as to direct some of the *Shen* to the sealed heart cauldron (Middle *Tan Tien*) and store it there to share with others for emotional or spiritual healing.

The Coagulation Operation

The final rung on the ladder of transformation is the operation of coagulation, in which the body is made spiritual and the spirit is made corporeal. The motto alchemists have for this operation is *Solvite Corpora et Coagulate Spiritum* ("Dissolve the body and coagulate the spirit."). Successful coagulation produces a new spiritized incarnation that can survive in all realms.

Chemical coagulation is the physical manifestation of the essence created during conjunction, which is reborn during fermentation and purified in distillation. Coagulation is accomplished by the congealing, precipitating, or sublimating of the solidified essence, which is the final maturation of the Child of the Conjunction. This fixation of spiritual forces is what creates the Philosopher's Stone, which embodies the principle of transmutation itself.

With the creation of the Philosopher's Stone, two more operations are now available to alchemists. The first is projection, which is the process of transmuting the base metals into gold. It is said that just a tiny piece of the Stone or a pinch of the red powder of projection made from it is enough to perfect the metals and transmute lead into gold.

The second operation of the Stone is multiplication, which is the process of multiplying or increasing the quantity or volume of something. Just a touch of the Stone or a grain of the red powder is said to cause plants to grow to fruition or cells to be healed and duplicate perfectly. Even the Stone itself and its powers can be magically multiplied. Multiplication provides the raw material for the elixir of life, drinkable gold, and other panaceas that alchemists promised would cure all diseases.

The cipher for coagulation is the astrological Air sign of Gemini, the Divine Twins who to alchemists represent their sacred *Rebis*. The cipher for projection is the Water sign of Pisces. From at least 2300 B.C.E., the Egyptians used two fish to denote this constellation. The cipher used for the multiplication operation is the Water sign of Aquarius, whom the Egyptians associated with Osiris, their god of grain, seeds, and semen.

Coagulation images include brilliantly shining new gold, a balanced set of scales, an egg-shaped stone, the Holy Grail, and a naked androgynous youth emerging from a grave. Scenes of coagulation include such things as wingless creatures being carried away by winged creatures, a lone eagle soaring high in the sky, the serpent and lion united, the King and Queen breaking free of their chains, or the Sun and Moon beaming down proudly over their naked child.

The most popular symbol of coagulation is the Phoenix, a mythical bird that builds its nest in fire and then rises from the ashes reborn as a completely new creature. Alchemists sometimes called the Phoenix the *Ortus* (the "Rectified One"). They described it as a four-legged bird with black eyes, a white face, white forepaws, black hind paws, and a red head with streaks of pure gold reaching to its neck.

The Phoenix and the Emerald Tablet are closely related. Both are said to have been born or first discovered in the ancient land of Phoenicia, and "Phoenix" literally means "of Phoenicia." In most traditions, the original Emerald Tablet was written in Phoenician characters. Some Egyptian writings even refer to the Emerald Tablet as the Phoenix. "I am the Great Phoenix," reads an ancient Egyptian stele, "which is in Heliopolis. I am the rendering of all that is and will exist." The Egyptians also equated the Phoenician bird with their own sacred *Bennu* Bird, which symbolized the completely spiritized Self that rises up from the lower nature of the soul.

Personal Coagulation

Psychologically, the Phoenix is the resurrected personality that rises from the ashes of ego and is fully manifested during coagulation. The alchemists viewed this integrated personality as the divine child of the King and Queen who embodies a new state of awareness beyond either masculine or feminine ways of knowing. Paracelsus named this cosmic essence the *Iliaster*, which literally means "the star in man." He described it as "the completely healed human being who has burned away all the dross of his lower being and is free to fly as the Phoenix."

On the spiritual level, coagulation produces an entirely new body for the alchemist. This second body is often described as a body of light, which is the *Ultima Materia* ("Ultimate Matter") of the soul. Many experience it as a projected golden body of coalesced light that Paracelsus named the Astral Body (literally, the "Star Body"). As one Renaissance alchemist described it: "You break through space, fly to heaven in broad daylight, and shed the flesh-and-bone bag, which is now as useless as the alchemical workshop and vessels once the elixir has been perfected."

In Christian alchemy, the ultimate matter of the soul is the resurrected body of the Apocalypse. In the Gospel of John, the coagulated body is described as the seamless garment that Jesus wore when he said, "I and my Father are one." In the same gospel, Jesus warned that "unless a man be born of both Fire and Water, he cannot enter into the kingdom of God." In Eastern religions, the culmination of the Red Phase corresponds with the formation of the Diamond Body, the resplendent body of crystallized light that began its transformation as a lump of black coal.

"Its inherent strength is perfected if it is turned into Earth," the Emerald Tablet says of the coagulation process. "Thus, will you obtain the Glory of the Whole Universe. All Obscurity will be clear to you. This is the greatest Force of all powers, because it overcomes every Subtle thing and penetrates every Solid thing."

In this chapter, we learned that the Red Phase of transformation is a natural continuation of the purification of the White Phase, and the symbols of this cooperative effort are the Red King and White Queen. Fermentation is an operation of the Red Phase that seeks to revive the dead material left over from putrefaction. Distillation is the next operation that works to purify and concentrate the essences retrieved from fermentation. Coagulation is the final operation of the Red Phase during which the Philosopher's Stone is produced.

Personal fermentation, distillation, and coagulation are operations of the Red Phase of alchemy applied to the psychological and spiritual components of individuals. With our knowledge of the three phases of transformation and the seven basic operations of alchemy, we are now ready to fully appreciate their universal applications. In the next part of the book ("Understanding Alchemical Consciousness"), we reveal the fundamental substratum of reality that gives rise to the planetary archetypes, the operations of alchemy, and the very possibility of transformation.

UNDERSTANDING ALCHEMICAL CONSCIOUSNESS

Alchemy is synonymous in our modern culture with the idea of positive growth and change. Today, people use the word "alchemize" to mean to free one's mind or loosen up a situation to enable for creative transformation. People in all walks of life are discovering that the principles of the ancient Art of Transformation have important applications in the everyday world, and leaders in such diverse fields as science, business, psychology, and the arts are eager to apply the methods of alchemy to release new creative energy in their work. Quantum physicists and scientists in many other fields muse about the New Alchemy, in which consciousness is seen as a force of nature—just as the alchemists always believed.

CHAPTER
18

Mental Alchemy: Creating Integrity

Mental alchemy is the use of alchemical operations on the psychological level in an attempt to perfect one's character and personality. This is different from spiritual alchemy in that mental alchemy focuses on the existing aspects of the personality and deals with psychological forces in personal transformation. Spiritual alchemy, on the other hand, deals with the universal forces of soul and spirit as they are expressed in individuals.

From the alchemists' viewpoint, the mental or psychological work takes place primarily in the material realm in the Salt of the personality. In the work of personal transformation, the psychological operations are usually completed with the conjunction, while the spiritual operations continue in the higher operations that do not culminate until coagulation, which is the fixation of spirit in a new body or incarnation.

Interest in mental alchemy began in the eighteenth century as people realized the operations and matter of alchemy could be interpreted in psychological terms. At the time, there was great interest in curing mental illness and alleviating the day-to-day phobias and neuroses that dominated people's lives.

The Salted Personality

The basic problem in personal alchemy is that people become more rigid and less alive as they grow older. People tend to stubbornly cling to set judgments, prejudices, and outmoded beliefs that limit their range of experience in the world. In simplest terms, everyone turns to Salt as they mature. As we have learned, Salt is the crystallization of energy into set structures. To retrieve that energy, the crystallized Salt in our personality must be dissolved, purified, and reshaped so it better reflects the essence of who we really are.

In other words, as we pass through the trials and tribulations of existence, we form reactionary behavior and unconscious judgments that limit or structure our experiences. We also compromise ourselves and our integrity to conform to the dictates of society, and we end up carrying psychological baggage composed of rejected and suppressed feelings, emotions, thoughts, failed goals, irrational biases, and unfulfilled desires.

In alchemy and psychology, the term for this suppressed or rejected material is the *Umbra* ("the Shadow"). Material in the *Umbra* steals some of a person's life force and can become a threat to complete transformation. It is like a hidden parasite in your personality that feeds on your personal energy to survive. We develop a shadow personality in which the rejected material still lives on in the darkness of our subconscious. That subconscious material has a mind of its own and is the source of many psychological problems when it conflicts with our conscious goals and preferred behaviors.

Of course, this natural process of adulteration is no fault of our own. It is just how we learn to survive in the world and to fit into human society. However, it is also where the work of mental transformation must begin.

The First Matter in People

Psychologically, the First Matter of the alchemists is identical with the dark, irrational forces of the subconscious mind. Like the *Prima Materia* of the universe, the First Matter within us contains all the potential energy and dynamic oppositions necessary to fuel our transformation and achieve the goals of the Great Work.

In the mental work, the First Matter to be transformed is the shadowy and chaotic subconscious mind. It is located in the vessel of the human mind, and that is where we start. However, the awakened subconscious is a surprisingly powerful force that can generate all kinds of negative experiences. That is why the work of mental alchemy must take place in the hermetically sealed vessel of the mind in the Inner Laboratory we created in Part 2 of this book.

The subterranean energies must be contained and worked on without contaminating the personality or interfering with its functioning in the outside world. In analytical psychology, the sealed space of the Inner Laboratory symbolizes the cooperative efforts and confidentiality between the patient and therapist.

The Technique of Active Imagination

In the solitary work pursued by alchemists in the Middle Ages, there was no therapist available to guide them. So, many alchemists created one using the formidable powers of imagination. Carl Jung discovered this technique in his study of alchemy, and it inspired him to create a therapeutic method called "Active Imagination." Active Imagination is a meditative technique in which the contents of the unconscious are personified as separate entities with whom a conscious narrative or conversation is established.

The technique is fairly simple. First, you allow unconscious content, such as dream images or unexplained moods, to become a fantasy that stays connected to its emotional roots. Make the fantasy conscious by acting it out, writing it down, drawing it, or imagining it with your eyes open, as if it were a real scene or person in the room with you.

After the image is firmly established, try to form a respectful relationship with it. Examine it closely and come to terms with it as if it were a real person or situation. Focus only on the real presence in the room with you. Wait patiently for the image to respond to you and to move or change in any way. At that moment, open a dialogue with it. Talk out loud to it, ask it questions, or silently communicate with it like you were conversing with another person.

Insightful information can be gathered this way, and you might be able to establish a continuing relationship like Carl Jung did with his active imagination partner, Philemon. Philemon came to him in a dream in 1913 and played an important role in his personal development. Philemon acted like an inner therapist or guru for Jung for the rest of his life.

Becoming conscious of images, fantasies, and feelings from the unconscious mind through Active Imagination is a useful activity for understanding what is really going on inside you. It is a way of giving the unconscious a conscious outlet, so you do not explode in unexplainable moods and emotional outbursts.

Jung described Active Imagination as a kind of conscious experimentation employing creative images as a tool for perceiving outside your own mental boxes and regaining control of your life. "Until you make the unconscious conscious," he warned, "it will direct your life, and you will call it fate."

The Creation of Consciousness

In his memoirs *Memories, Dreams, Reflections* (1963), Carl Jung summarized what it means to expand consciousness in an individual: "Man's task is to become conscious of the contents that press upward from the unconscious. Neither should he persist in his unconsciousness, nor remain identical with the unconscious elements of his being, thus evading his destiny, which is to create more and more consciousness. As far as we can discern, the sole purpose of human existence is to kindle a light in the darkness of mere being. It may even be assumed that just as the unconscious affects us, so the increase in our consciousness affects the unconscious."

It is not an easy process to bring unconscious elements into the light of consciousness either as individuals or as a species, but that fundamental process will go on with or without our willing participation in both the individual unconscious and in the collective subconscious of our culture. The darkness within will continue to disrupt both our minds and our civilization until brought to awareness. "There is no coming to consciousness without pain", Jung noted. "People will do anything, no matter how absurd, in order to avoid facing their own soul. One does not become enlightened by playing to be figures of light, but by making the darkness conscious."

Sealing the mental workspace in alchemical work confines all the potentially dangerous psychic matter from the unconscious inside, but as heat from the fires of intense introspection increases, the pressure inside the psychic vessel builds. Swiss psychologist Louise von Franz (1915-1998) described this process: "It is the torture of fire, intensifying the psychological process. One is roasted, roasted in what one is—for you roast in what you are yourself and not in anything else; one could say that one is cooked in one's own juice."

Just as in the laboratory work, the matter tends to putrefy with too much liquid at this stage. In mental alchemy, liquid is symbolic of emotions and feelings, so the idea here is to divorce oneself from the intense emotions associated with the contents of the psyche and to work more with dry fire, which is symbolic of objective consciousness. This internal heating results in an evaporative process in which the emotional energy is slowly driven off. This also removes the original impurities, leaving behind a purer inner self with which to work.

This is the general principle behind working with the chaotic and often threatening energies of the First Matter of the subconscious. As we have learned, the process of recognizing, isolating, and interacting with the First Matter is the first step in alchemy, and that work proceeds through the three phases and seven operations of alchemy with which you are already familiar from our work in Part 4 of this book.

The Four Elements in People

In mental alchemy, the structure of one's personality is based on the Four Elements that create the worldly ego from the chaos of the subconscious. This is the same pattern as the fourfold structure of the universe created by the action of the Four Elements that emerge from the *Prima Materia*.

As we know from Chapter 12, the Four Elements were believed to be present in the form of humors that made up a person's temperament or personality. The Fire Element is expressed in the Choleric humor, the Water Element in the Melancholic humor, the Air Element in the Sanguine humor, and the Earth Element in the Phlegmatic humor.

In addition to the humors, the Four Elements are also expressed in people as positive characteristics or virtues and as negative characteristics or vices. For example:

- The virtues of mental Fire are courage, daring, and enthusiasm, while the vices of mental Fire are anger, jealousy, and vindictiveness.
- The virtues of mental Water are compassion, love, and creativity, but the vices of mental Water are instability and spinelessness.
- The virtues of mental Air are diligence, dexterity, and optimism, while the vices of Air are frivolity, boasting, and squandering.
- The virtues of mental Earth are endurance, strength, and patience, but the vices of Earth are laziness, dullness, and boredom.

Carl Jung saw the Four Elements as archetypes existing in the collective subconscious, and thus, they are present in everyone. He called them the "Four Functions." The Fire Element is expressed in the function of intuition; the Water Element is expressed in the function of feeling; the Air Element is expressed in the function of thinking; and the Earth Element is expressed in the function of sensation.

Jung considered Fire and Air to be the active, masculine elements in people, while Water and Earth are the passive, feminine elements. In Jungian psychology, the degree of development of each of the Four Elements in our conscious minds is balanced with the subconscious retention of the remaining elements that determine our personality and attitude.

In both psychology and alchemy, the goal is to develop a balance of the elements within the individual. As far back as Empedocles (490–430 B.C.E.), philosophers noted that those who have near equal proportions of the Four Elements have a deeper sense of personal integrity than others. Such balanced individuals are more resilient, more intelligent, and have truer perceptions of reality.

So, success in mental alchemy requires balancing the elements in one's psyche. And the relationships of the elements within us—whether they oppose or complement one another—determine whether we feel basically happy and balanced or develop neuroses, phobias, or other psychological disturbances.

When two opposing elements encounter each other in the personality, there are three possibilities: 1) They generate psychic energy, 2) They neutralize each other, or, 3) They combine. In alchemy and psychology, the third case is the most important, for it represents the conjunction of opposites that results in a transcendence of conflicting polarities.

The Planets in People

According to the principles of mental alchemy, all the planetary forces filter down into our individual personalities. We reach enlightenment by conquering—understanding and controlling—the archetypal energies each planet represents.

In the cauldron of our personality, the Sun is what gives us the desire to transform in the first place. In a sense, the Sun wants pure spiritual energy and a new, more perfect identity. The Moon, on the other hand, wants physicality and experience. Mercury wants to find inspiration and idealized love. If we were to personify these planetary powers, we might portray the Sun as the Creator, the Moon as the Nurturer, and Mercury as the Thinker.

These three planets represent primordial desires that carry the signatures of the noble metals: gold, silver, and quicksilver, respectively. They also represent the Three Essentials within us: Sulfur (Sun), Mercury (Mercury), and Salt (Moon).

The outer planets and base metals are unbalanced and unperfected. Venus suffers from too much Water and needs focus and intention. Mars suffers from too much Fire and needs compassion and understanding. Jupiter suffers from too much spirit and needs grounding and restraint. And Saturn is too materialistic and structured; it needs growth and expansion. If we were to personify these planetary powers, we might characterize Venus as the Lover, Mars as the Warrior, Jupiter as the Philosopher, and Saturn as the strict Father.

Jung and Alchemy

As you might have noticed so far in this book, it is hard to talk about alchemy without mentioning the work of Swiss psychiatrist Carl Gustav Jung (1875–1961). He has been called the "father of modern alchemy" for his efforts to revitalize the ancient art and apply it to mental alchemy. Jung began a lifelong study of the subject after he discovered the images and principles of alchemy surfacing in the dreams and compulsions of his patients.

Jung accumulated the largest library of original alchemy texts in Europe and spent many years trying to decipher the writings of alchemists. He came to appreciate alchemy as a dynamic system of inquiry into the nature of the subconscious mind. "Alchemy, as a nature philosophy of great consideration in the Middle Ages," he noted, "throws a bridge to the past and their gnosis, and also to the future, in the modern psychology of the unconscious."

Jung's interest in alchemy was kindled not only by the thoughts and dreams of his patients, but also by his own personal experiences. Long before he discovered alchemy, Jung had a series of dreams that held a clue to the structure of the human mind. He dreamed that right next to his house was a huge addition or wing that he had never known about. He was amazed that the strange structure was there all the time, and he had not realized it. In his dreams, Jung explored the mysterious addition to his house and finally realized the rooms contained things from his subconscious that he had rejected or locked away there.

Then, in 1926, Jung had a dream that opened the door to understanding the strange additions to his inner house and shaped the focus of his studies for the rest of his life. He had been intensely searching for a framework for his work with the subconscious but could find no modern discipline—including the psychology of the time—that was powerful enough to encompass the whole subject. In a new and unusually powerful dream, he was being held captive in a time warp in the seventeenth century until he discovered some great secret there. "Later I understood that this dream was referring to alchemy," he wrote, "for in the seventeenth century alchemy reached its height." Jung felt the dream was telling him that the subconscious would reveal itself by an in-depth study of medieval alchemy.

Jung's exhaustive studies in alchemy revealed that its operations were at work in the human mind. It was an astonishing discovery that confirmed the alchemists' teaching that the principles of alchemy were universal and took place on all levels of reality.

Carl Jung was a true philosopher of the ages who introduced alchemy to the modern world. "Only by discovering alchemy," he admitted, "have I clearly understood that the unconscious is a process and that ego's rapport with it and its contents initiate an evolution—more precisely, a *real metamorphosis*—of the mind." Jung saw that the First Matter in people is the subconscious mind, which is the subject of transformation in mental alchemy.

According to Jung, the Philosopher's Stone in mental alchemy is the perfection of the personality. This natural alchemical process is the gradual transformation from a false, fragmented, and distorted personality into a whole or integrated personality in which psychic elements and energies are balanced and functioning at full capacity.

The Black Phase of Mental Alchemy

As in other kinds of alchemy, the *Nigredo* or blackening, is the first sign that the processes of mental alchemy are beginning. The saturnic signatures of depression and melancholia arouse suspicions that all is not right and cause us to slow down and examine our inner life.

On the personal level, the blackening is perceived as a loss of connection to one's core or the removal of life and energy from it. We feel uncomfortable with ourselves and disappointed at what we have become. The suffering leads us to search for a way out, and while there are many paths that offer solutions, only the alchemical tools of the *Nigredo* provide real solutions. These tools lead to the death of old habits, attitudes, prejudices, and unhealthy attachments and dependencies. The first sign of success is the withdrawal of psychological projections in which we blame others for our own predicament.

As we noted earlier, primary among the factions taking shape within the personal First Matter is the shadow or *Umbra*, which is the inferior part of the personality that lives in the darkness. Think of it as those mental elements that are incompatible with our chosen conscious attitude. In mental alchemy, these rejected elements coalesce into a splinter personality, which is a concentration of subconscious energy that alchemists likened to a threatening dragon. To defeat the dragon and keep it from taking control of your life, the shadow and dark aspects of yourself must be brought to light, confronted, and assimilated into consciousness.

Alchemists cooking the mind of a patient in the furnace of heated introspection during the calcination operation.
(From Alchimie by Eugène Léon Canseliet, 1964)

All the unpleasant feelings of guilt and worthlessness must be suffered through during this process of mortification. Both in the lab and in the mind, this is a dangerous period during which poisonous vapors are released and vessels explode due to overheating. On the psychological level, the operations of the *Nigredo* (calcination and dissolution) are necessary to differentiate one's ego from its shadow and to reinvent oneself on a higher level that psychologists refer to as the "integrated Self."

Carl Jung clarified how the mental work proceeded for medieval alchemists: "The profound darkness that shrouds the alchemical procedure comes from the fact that although the alchemist was interested in the chemical part of the work, he also used it to devise a nomenclature for the psychic transformation that really fascinated him." Although alchemists lacked the modern psychiatric system of classification to describe their inner transformations, they invented their own unique terminology that applied to all levels of their work.

The White Phase of Mental Alchemy

The White Phase or *Albedo* begins to unfold with the demise of the shadow and the ashes of personality left after the Black Phase. During *Albedo*, a person rises from darkness and depression and feels suddenly relieved, refreshed, and optimistic.

This is the daybreak of the new personality free of its gross and rejected parts. Psychic energy is no longer shared between the inner forces of light and darkness and is now fully available to the resurrected self. The matter has suffered through the Black Phase and starts coming back to life. This moment is highly rewarding in both the practical lab work and in the Inner Laboratory.

The focus of the White Phase in mental alchemy is a washing, or purification, of psychic contents that are separated from the Black Phase. This takes place entirely in the twilight atmosphere of the mind in a mix of rational thoughts and irrational feelings.

The washing might also occur in free-flowing conversation in the office of a therapist or even with a visualized entity during Active Imagination. There is no longer a reason to hide your dirty linen because you have freed it of its contaminating guilt. During this separation operation, the opposing forces and essences of the psyche are clearly discerned.

If the opposing essences remain separated and generate new energy, the energy will be used up in some sort of creative endeavor, such as an artist giving his inspiration a new form. If these essences merge again and neutralize each other, no new energy is produced, and the result is considered an alchemical stillbirth.

If, however, the opposing essences unite in a fertile marriage of opposites, then a new element is born that incorporates the essences of both. This is the alchemical operation of conjunction, the transcendence of conflicting polarities in the creation of a third reconciliating form that alchemists called the "Child of the Conjunction" or the "Philosopher's Child." This is the product of the operation of conjunction, and if it survives, it can mature into the perfected Philosopher's Stone.

The Red Phase of Mental Alchemy

If the White Phase concludes in a successful conjunction of opposites, then the Red Phase of alchemy begins. This is the true sunrise of the mental work when all forces and elements have been assimilated into conscious awareness.

If, however, there are unassimilated subconscious elements or the ego reacts with stubborn pride, then the matter is still contaminated and cannot proceed without further purification. This often happens both in the lab and in the mental work and initiates a period of putrefaction similar to the darkness of the Black Phase. The length and intensity of the secondary putrefaction depends on the degree of contamination.

If the putrefaction or death of all traces of impurities is successful, then the life-giving operation of fermentation begins. In mental alchemy, fermentation is the introduction of spiritual forces into the personality, which gives us a sense of purpose and new energy for life. Sometimes, the fermenting light enters the mind from intense prayer and meditation, although it is now known that alchemists—as the first pharmacists—had discovered a variety of psychoactive substances that might also have fueled personal fermentation.

In any case, after fermentation, a process of mental distillation begins as the alchemist tries to assimilate the spiritual forces from Above and unite them with the forces of the personality from Below. This is sometimes called the "Vertical Work," and it is exemplified by the "Circulation of the Light" meditation we discussed in the last chapter.

As the Red Phase of alchemy proceeds, the process of coagulation begins naturally. Once the level of purification in distillation reaches a certain stage, the Red Stone will form all by itself. The true key to the Stone—and the last operation over which the alchemist has any control—is distillation. Whether in the lab or in the mind, the operation of distillation is really a process of gradual multiplication of powers and an amplification of energy and wisdom that eventually condenses into a completely new material.

Many works of literature incorporate the three phases of transformation in their plotlines, including *A Strange Story* (1862) by Edward Bulwer-Lytton; *The Solitudes* (1987) by John Crowley; *The Alchemist* (1988) by Paulo Coelho; *Mercurius* (1990) by Patrick Harpur; *Shadow of Night* (2012) by Deborah Harkness; and of course, the *Harry Potter* series (1997-2007) by J.K. Rowling.

The overall plot of the *Harry Potter* books is a three-part drama that follows the three phases of alchemy. The long Black Phase culminates in *Harry Potter and the Order of the Phoenix*, in which everything Harry attempts goes wrong and ends in the devastating death of Sirius Black, his beloved godfather. The White Phase takes place in *Harry Potter and the Half-Blood Prince*, which centers on the death of Albus Dumbledore. "Albus" is Latin for "white." The Red Stage culminates in the final book, *Harry Potter and the Deathly Hallows*, in which Harry's friend Rubeus Hagrid is forced to take part in a death march to celebrate the "slaying" of Harry. "Rubeus" is Latin for "red." At the end of the series, as with the end of the work in mental alchemy, conflict is resolved, and the subject of the work integrated and fully alive.

Distillation of the personality by dissolving the old ego.
(Dissolution: The Alchymist produces an Aetherial Preparation by James Gillray, 1796)

In this chapter, we learned how alchemical principles can be applied to perfect the personality and liberate people from phobias, addictions, neuroses, and other psychic afflictions. The pioneering work of Carl Jung has demonstrated how the operations of the Black, White, and Red phases of alchemy take place on the psychological level. He also showed how the Four Elements are expressed in four mental functions common to all people. Psychologists now interpret the First Matter in the mental environment as the chaotic and powerful subconscious mind. In the next chapter, we will take the psychological work a step further, as we explore the philosophy and techniques of spiritual alchemy.

CHAPTER 19

Spiritual Alchemy: Perfecting the Soul

Spiritual alchemy, which focuses on the perfection of the soul, began in ancient Egypt with efforts to connect the pharaohs with their divine natures. It later developed into the Hermetic teachings that became the basis of alchemy. Spiritual alchemy seeks to transform and perfect the immortal essence that is in all of us.

Some alchemists have argued that alchemy was always a spiritual discipline, which focused on chemistry and metallurgy only to find in nature a universal pattern of transformation that could be applied to mental and spiritual work. Just as alchemists try to awaken the metals to their true nature in gold, so do spiritual alchemists try to awaken the soul and body to their spiritual nature. In spiritual alchemy, the transformation of lead into gold is analogous to spiritual progress. The base metals have yet to mature into the incorruptible flawlessness of gold, just as the common person has not yet awakened to the full glory of their spiritual embodiment.

So, the Great Work, which is the creation of the Philosopher's Stone, is not simply about turning lead into gold, nor is it just about the production of the elixir of life to gain immortality. The Philosopher's Stone represents a level of achievement, a touchstone or proof indicating the alchemist has succeeded in the inner work of spiritual transformation and reached the highest level of consciousness.

The Dragons of Spiritual Alchemy

No symbol in alchemy captures the energies encountered in spiritual work better than that of the dragon. Alchemists both East and West believed in dragons, if not in the real sense, then certainly as archetypal energies embedded in our souls and personalities. In fact, if we do not understand the esoteric nature of the dragon, much of the advanced alchemical symbolism will be beyond our grasp. We have already discussed the Seven Dragons and how they are expressed in the metals. But there are more dragons out there, and the first step in spiritual alchemy is to seek out our personal inner dragons.

Where do we find a dragon? Anywhere—the dragon is in everything. Its scales are in the bark of trees; its claws gouged out the great canyons. The dragon's roar is heard in the thunder, and its forked tongue is the lightning. The dragon is a composite of the features of many animals and represents the chaotic matrix of nature and natural instincts around which our lives are woven.

Dragons derive their power from the primordial First Matter, and unleashing the draconian energies into the world is one of the primary goals of alchemists. To alchemists, the dragon represents boundless unstructured potential energy and the primordial life force, the First Matter within. An old alchemical motto advises: *Opponere draconem est prehendere vitam* ("To face the dragon is to seize life").

Facing the dragon for the first time occurs during the Black Phase of personal transformation. Accepting the dragon beast as a part of yourself is a challenging task for most people. The dragon is the underlying chaos in our lives that is part of the unknown, dark side of the universe. Spiritual leaders, from prehistoric shamans to Buddha and Christ, all began their spiritual journey by realizing how much chaos and suffering are in the world. This unwelcomed awareness of our imperfection is what drives the Great Work.

Our ego blinds us to the existence of our personal dragon or makes us believe we can easily conquer it. In the Azoth drawing that we will work with later in this chapter, we see Sol, the personification of ego, proudly holding his scepter and shield as he confidently looks out over his vast kingdom. But unknown to him, in the entrance to a dark cavern in the mountain on which he rests, a fire-breathing dragon waits for its chance to attack.

Once you we realize the dragon is hidden nearby and you muster the courage to face it, your best choice is just to accept its presence in your life. Challenging or attacking the inner dragon only empowers it. Only the lunar path of surrender will work.

Surrender to the dragon begins in the White Phase of alchemy. During this stage of purification, you must acknowledge both the chaotic powers in the world and the chaos within yourself. Part of this purification is the realization that the dragon is never all good or all bad. You have to suspend judgment to accept the duality of nature and realize that the universe is not just about you or your comfort. A greater pattern exists, and the energy of the wild dragon is what fulfills it.

The last step in dealing with dragons is the most dangerous. It is the act of unleashing the dragon, which marks the Red Phase of alchemy. In personal alchemy, the dragon's fire destroys any structure or "salted thing"—any gross material that exist in a person's spirit. If you are free of falsity, devoid of ego, and pure of spirit, there is a chance the dragon will not notice you.

So, the real trick to unleashing the dragon is not to confront it but to disappear before it notices you. "Be still," the alchemists advised. "Rest in the arms of the dragon." In spiritual alchemy, if you can quietly merge with the primal energies of the universe, the dragon's powers will quietly follow the light of your own mind.

Alchemical Meditation

Meditation is important to alchemists, who consider it one of their most important tools in performing both practical and spiritual work. But alchemical meditation is different from other meditative or relaxation techniques. Alchemical meditations are almost always about harnessing spiritual forces for practical transformation. Alchemical meditation is also different from other forms of meditation because it often has an active goal or a specific application in mind. It seeks to actually work with the transcendental powers and not necessarily just relax the mind.

In general, the meditations of alchemists are marked by three "magisteriums" or accomplishments. Some sources say these three accomplishments made Hermes "Thrice Greatest" and correspond to the three levels of reality—the physical, the mental, and the spiritual.

Distillation of the soul to produce the liquid fire of Vitriol.
(By Italian painter Pier Leone Ghezzi, 1727)

Lunar Meditations

Lunar meditations work on the physical or bodily level. They are about sensing bodily energy and opening up to instinctive wisdom. Lunar work is an introverted journey to the underworld of matter in your own body to seek out the spark of life embedded there that is your essence. During lunar meditations, we plumb the depths of soul in a deeply relaxed state that seeks connection with dormant powers or energy centers. A good example is the Circulation of Light meditation we learned in Chapter 17. Other examples of lunar meditations include progressive relaxation, breath meditation, Chakra meditation, Tantric techniques, and moving meditations like Tai Chi and Sufi whirling.

Solar Meditations

Solar meditations work on the mental or psychological level to encourage a heightened state of awareness. Solar work is a more extroverted journey into the realm of light and consciousness. During solar meditation, we attempt to break the shackles of ego and cultural boundaries to seek higher consciousness. By exposing the self-deception in our thoughts and using mantras and other meditation gimmicks to lull our everyday mind into submission, we can purify and increase our level of consciousness. Solar meditations include mindfulness meditation, Zen, focused intent, ritual magic, mantra techniques, and chanting. The chemicalization techniques we learned in Chapter 6 are solar meditations.

Stellar Meditations

Stellar meditations work on the level of the divine mind or cosmic powers. Stellar work requires the merging of Lunar and Solar consciousness in an integrated superconscious mind that seeks union with the One Mind of the universe. By retrieving the spark of light trapped in our bodies and uniting it with the light of consciousness freed from egotistical control, we create a brilliant beacon to the universe that attracts divine energy. Stellar meditations include intense prayer, Transcendental meditation, Dzogchen, and loving kindness meditation. The Quietist technique we learned in Chapter 6 is a stellar meditation.

Another class of stellar meditations are manifestation visualizations in which you project positive thoughtforms into your life by imaging them, writing about them, or scripting a dialogue in which the desired result has already occurred. A more complex form is tulpamancy, which is the practice of creating mental constructs or thoughtforms that become actual sentient beings. Known as "tulpas" (from the Tibetan word sprulpa, meaning "emanation"), the imaginary beings are said to evolve into autonomous creatures. Similarly, in the sixteenth century, alchemists throughout Europe tried to create a homunculus ("little person") by projecting their thoughts into beakers of various chemicals.

The Azoth of the Philosophers

A popular Solar meditation used by Renaissance alchemists is an alchemical emblem known as the "Azoth of the Philosophers" by the legendary German alchemist Basil Valentine. Circulated privately among alchemists for decades, versions of the drawing started appearing in print in 1616. The emblem is a schematic map to discovering the Azoth, which is the "Universal Mercury" or animating spirit hidden in all matter that makes transformation possible. The "A" and "Z" in "Azoth" convey the idea of something complete and all-encompassing—everything from A–Z or alpha to omega.

The Azoth is a powerful tool of initiation that includes the most important symbols of alchemy and also incorporates the dynamic progression of the alchemical operations. The emblem (see the following figure) is arranged like a mandala, which is a geometric circular design used to focus attention. At its center lies the face of a bearded alchemist at the beginning of the Great Work. Like looking into a mirror, this is where the initiate fixes their attention to begin the meditation.

The downward-pointing triangle superimposed over the face of the alchemist represents Water—in the sense of divine grace pouring down from heaven. This juxtaposition implies that the face of God and the face of the alchemist are the same. Such blasphemous ideas explain why this drawing was circulated secretly among alchemists long before being published openly.

The schematic body of the alchemist is shown in perfect balance with the Four Elements. His right foot is firmly planted on Earth, and his left is in Water. In his right hand is a torch of Fire, and in his left hand is an ostrich feather symbolizing Air.

The alchemist also stands balanced between the masculine and feminine powers in the background. Sol, the archetypal Sun King, is seated on a lion to his right; Luna, the archetypal Moon Queen, is seated on a great fish in the ocean to his left.

Sol wields a scepter and a shield, indicating his authority and power over the visible world, but the fiery dragon of the rejected contents of his subconscious waits patiently in a cave beneath him. Luna holds the reins to a great fish, symbolizing her control of the forces of nature; behind her is a chaff of wheat, which stands for her connection to fertility and growth. The bow and arrow she cradles in her left arm symbolize the wounds of the heart and body she accepts as part of her existence.

Between the legs of the alchemist is a small cube labeled *Corpus,* meaning "physical body." The five stars surrounding it indicate that the body also contains the hidden Fifth Element, which is the invisible Quintessence or life force.

Where the head of the alchemist should be, there is a strange, winged caricature similar to the Behdety, the winged god of the midday Sun from ancient Egypt. This represents the Ascended Essence, the purified soul about to leave the body in a higher incarnation of light. Touching the wings of the Ascended Essence are a salamander engulfed in flames on the left side of the drawing and a standing bird on the right. Below the salamander is the inscription *Anima* ("Soul"); below the bird is the inscription *Spiritus* ("Spirit").

Spiritus, Anima, and *Corpus* (Spirit, Soul, and Body) form a large, inverted triangle that stands behind the central emblem of the alchemist. Together they symbolize the archetypal Three Essentials the alchemists named Sulfur, Mercury, and Salt, respectively.

The Azoth of the Philosophers
(L'Azoth des Philosophes by Basil Valentine, 1659 version)

The Operations of the Azoth

This version of the Azoth shows the true Copernican order of the planets and is the one most popular among psychologists and spiritual alchemists. It reflects the transmutation of the metals from lead to gold along the Ladder of the Planets. The original version reflected the Ptolemaic order with the Earth at the center of the cosmos and the Sun orbiting the Earth in fourth position between Mars and Venus. That traditional version is still used in some Hermetic fraternities.

The seven rays placed in a circular pattern around the face of the alchemist is the Ladder of the Planets and indicate the progressive level of transformation. Numbered from one to seven, each ray contains the cipher of the corresponding planet and metal. Next to each ray is a roundel, which is a circle containing a scene that explains part of a story. In this case, each roundel elaborates on the meaning of the operation performed at that stage. We learned about the operations of alchemy in Part 4 of this book.

The Ray of Saturn

Looking at the figure, you can see that the first ray in the Azoth is the black ray labeled number one. Representing the beginning of the Ladder of the Planets, it is marked by the cipher that stands for both the metal lead and the planet Saturn, which is the archetypal situation at the beginning of the work. Also shown in the first ray is a small square representing Salt, which is one of the Three Essentials. This suggests the Great Work begins in the unredeemed body or imperfect matter.

The first roundel (between rays one and two) shows a black crow perching on top of a skull. Next to it on the outer ring is the Latin word *Visita,* which means "to visit or start a journey." Black crows are symbols of the initial Black Phase of alchemy, during which the subject of transformation is purified by breaking it down during mortification and calcination.

The Ray of Jupiter

The second ray is marked with the symbol that stands for both the metal tin and the planet Jupiter. And the corresponding second roundel depicts the black crow watching itself being dissolved. The word on the outer ring near this roundel is *Interiora,* referring to the "interior or innermost parts." The operation at this stage is a further process of mortification known as dissolution.

The Ray of Mars

The cipher signifying both the metal iron and the planet Mars marks the third ray of the Azoth, which is also marked with a smaller symbol denoting Sulfur, another of the Three Essentials. Iron and sulfur combine naturally in vitriol, a sulfuric acid compound that forms on weathered sulfur-bearing rocks. Sulfuric acid is the aggressive liquid fire of the alchemists.

The third roundel depicts the alchemical operation of separation. The black, earthbound crow splits into two white (or purified) birds of soul and spirit that retrieve the saved remains from the earlier operations. This is the first coming together of soul and spirit and represents the beginning of the White Phase of purification. In the ring above this roundel is written *Terra*, meaning "of the Earth" and refers to the useful essences being separated from the dregs of matter at this stage.

The Ray of Venus

The Azoth's fourth ray is marked with the cipher that stands for both copper and Venus. Its roundel depicts the twin birds of soul and spirit leaving the earth together, lifting a five-spiked crown, which represents the Fifth Element or Quintessence recovered from the preceding operations. At this point in the work, the operation of conjunction begins, which recombines the saved essences of soul and spirit into a new incarnation.

In the ring above the fourth roundel is inscribed the word *Rectificando*, which means "setting things right." This is the turning point in alchemy when the matter begins the spiritizing process.

The Ray of Mercury

In the fifth ray, the cipher for both metallic mercury (quicksilver) and the planet Mercury appears, as well as an identical smaller symbol indicating the principle of Mercury, also one of the Three Essentials.

The fifth roundel is under the inscription *Invenies* ("you will discover"). In this operation of fermentation, the essences of soul and spirit have come together to create a new life, which is the beginning of the Red Phase of empowerment. The corresponding roundel shows the birds of soul and spirit nesting in a tree, brooding over their alchemical egg, the fetal Child of the Conjunction.

The Ray of the Moon

The sixth ray contains the symbol that stands for both the metal silver and the Moon, which is the level of magical manifestation in the Azoth. Distillation is the operation at this stage. Above the roundel is the word *Occultum*, meaning "secret or hidden," because the essences at this stage are carried invisibly by the distilling vapors.

In the sixth roundel, we see a unicorn lying peacefully on the ground in front of a rose bush. According to legend, the unicorn runs tirelessly from pursuers but lies meekly on the ground when approached by a virgin. The virgin is the purified matter at this stage, which has returned to a state of innocence and potential.

The Ray of the Sun

In the seventh ray, the cipher stands for both gold and the Sun. The final roundel shows a naked androgynous youth emerging from an opened grave, with the Latin word *Lapidem* ("the Stone") in the outer ring next to the roundel. This stage of transformation is coagulation, in which the Philosopher's Stone is manifested if all the previous operations were successful. In spiritual terms, the resurrection of the soul is accomplished by bringing together only the purest essences of one's body, soul, and spirit under the guiding light of intense meditative work.

There is a hidden message in the Azoth drawing. The Latin words in the outer ring spell out a summary of what has taken place: *Visita Interiora Terra Rectificando Invenies Occultum Lapidem.* It translates as "Visit the innermost parts of the earth; and by setting things right, you will find the hidden Stone." Also, the first letters of the seven Latin words spell out the word "VITRIOL," which is the aggressive sulfuric acid we discussed in the Ray of Mars. The liquid fire of sulfuric acid is the fundamental agent of change in most alchemical experiments and symbolic of the Secret Fire in the soul that fuels the urge for spiritual perfection.

Your Temperament: The Metals Within

The way the Azoth emblem is used in meditation is very personal. First, you imagine you are at the center where the face of the alchemist is. In some Hermetic initiations, a round mirror is pasted at the center of the emblem. You are now the focus of working with the Azoth. Because the planetary metals are such perfect expressions of archetypal energies, you can learn a lot about yourself by examining how the signatures of the metals are expressed in your personality. Just as heat tempering changes the properties of iron alloys, alchemists referred to the way the inner metals react in a person as their "temperament."

In the following exercise, put your attention on Ray 1 of the Azoth and move sequentially through the rays and roundels until you finish at Ray 7. Each ray on this universal star has visual clues that lead to deeper understanding of what your own inner star looks like. Just be honest and spend at least three minutes on each ray of the Azoth. Use the following general discussion of the metallic temperaments as a guide to your introspective contemplation.

Ray 1: The Lead Temperament

The Saturn-lead archetype in alchemy is the most complicated. It elicits both disdain and elation from alchemists, who see it as both the beginning and end of the Great Work. It is the first step on the Ladder of the Planets and the last step on the return journey from the stars. Similarly, the Saturn-lead component of your personal temperament will take the most effort to fully comprehend.

As soon as bright, silvery lead metal is exposed to air, it forms a dull-gray oxide layer called the "litharge" that resists any further chemical interaction. Air is associated with spiritual energy, and lead reacts to it by instantly forming a barrier blocking any further interaction. Lusterless lead metal born of Saturn is so dead, it is used as containers for acids, like automobile batteries and as a lining in pipes that carry corrosive substances. Similarly, the lead-tempered person is like an acid-proof container that stores up caustic feelings and anger. Such people tend to be "acid tongued" and "vitriolic."

On the psychological level, lead is symbolic of a person's inertness and unwillingness to change. There is a denial of higher spiritual energies, and alchemists often portrayed the leaden person as lying in a grave or hopelessly chained to matter in some way.

Nonetheless, the stubborn, soulful lead core of such people carries all the energy they will ever need to complete their personal transformation. Just as finely pulverized lead in a vacuum spontaneously consumes itself in pure fire, we all carry this deeply hidden potential power within us.

In general, the leaden person is someone who has, like Saturn, lost their bid to become a star. They have accepted their caste in life and are resigned to a mundane physical existence. The black messenger crows of Chronos that haunt such a person bring black moods, depression, and despair, but they also alert us to illusion and fakeness in our lives.

Not surprisingly, there are many negative traits associated with the Saturn-lead archetype. Leaden people seem lazy, stubborn, unyielding, and try to control other people passive-aggressively. Saturnic people must always be right, rarely accept blame or admit to their mistakes, and have no real regard for the truth of a situation. They might be religious but not deeply spiritual. They tend to be suspicious of genius and inspiration, which they often attribute to fantasy. They feel threatened by freedom of expression, and sometimes use ridicule or try to "push people's buttons" to dampen others' moments of inspiration or creativity. On the surface, Saturnic people tend to be unimaginative, judgmental, and smug.

On the other hand, the positive characteristics of the saturnian person are patience, responsibility, somberness, structure, realism, and true knowledge of history and karma. Leaden people are grounded, earthy, and practical, and are good friends during times of bereavement—a rock of support at funerals and deathbeds. They have no illusions about their environment or about the true nature of other people. Because they do not believe people can change, they are surprisingly accepting of faults in friends and family.

Secretly, leaden people crave stimulation, excitement, and drama. They gravitate to reckless people who bring energy and entertainment into their lives. This craving for stimulation sometimes makes the leaden person rely on nervous energy rather than active inspiration. Instead of lethargic, the children of saturnic parents can be anxious and hyperactive, as they try to escape their parental prison.

Ray 2: The Tin Temperament

Jupiter is the largest and most impressive planet in our solar system, but it is mostly gas. The planet's name is the root of the word "jovial" or cheerful, and the energies of Jupiter are expansive, even joyful, but tend to be lacking in depth. That is true of the tin temperament, too.

Jupiterian people are often inflated, expansive, and pompous. They tend to talk endlessly about obvious or mundane things and can be perceived as thoughtless, shallow, and licentious. They are often judgmental and feel they can do nothing wrong. They are aware of spiritual forces but are unable to access them because of lack of depth and integrity. Methods of transforming the tin temperament includes such things as finding their soul mates, working relentlessly with alchemical techniques, learning to relax deeply, and meditating to find their genuine identities.

Psychologically, the focus of the tin temperament is on sensuality, and there is a greater interaction with others than seen in the leaden person. Still, most of the control at this level comes from unconscious impulses. As tin is transformed, a person is dominated by dreams and powerful undercurrents of emotion. Only by integrating the contents of their unconscious can tin people be successfully transmuted into nobler metal.

Jupiterian people tend to suffer from knots or blockages in their bodies that cause symptoms of armoring that are reminiscent of the "tinman." These blockages have both a psychic and a physiological reality, and often it is necessary to seek outside assistance or achieve greater inner flexibility and objectivity in removing them.

Ray 3: The Iron Temperament

Mars and iron rule the aggressive impulses within us—both individually and collectively. Within us, our iron temperaments govern the characteristics of anger, self-assertion, lust for power, ego identity, willpower, passion, and courage. It is our challenge to transform the Mars within us into the expression of spiritual qualities, rather than the selfish fulfillment of personal ambitions or physical desires.

On the positive side, iron loves Air, and the iron temperament naturally seeks higher inspiration and fresh influx of spirit. The Martian archetype reinforces individuality, strengthens will, and helps surpass previous limitations. The red planet governs the animal soul, passions, and the survival instinct.

In psychological terms, the iron temperament is the seat of our will to power, desire to control others, and our concerns about providing for one's physical needs. The iron temperament makes us determined and hard, but like the metal iron, the iron temperament is inflexible and brittle and cracks or breaks if bent.

By transmuting iron, we learn to assert ourselves without dominating or submitting to others, as we become aware of the forces of soul within us. The paradox of iron is that only through iron can we marshal the energies necessary to transmute iron. That is born out in the signature of the most revered arcanum, the ancient chemical of transformation of natural Vitriol, which is a combination of iron and sulfuric acid. It is the willful Vitriol within us that will transform us. Without it, all is lost to illusion and complacency.

Ray 4: The Copper Temperament

The Venus-copper archetype is another complicated constellation of forces in a person's temperament that takes some effort to adjust to. Venus represents the psychological function of judging people and evaluating experience through inner, subjective, feminine ways of knowing. Without the Venusian influence, we would have to rely solely on our objective senses and the concrete mind to evaluate others. Even our intuition would not be able to function correctly without the channel of Venus to bring our insights to conscious awareness. In general, the veiled planet Venus represents refinement of the senses, the arts, mystical love, desire, and earthly relationships.

The copper temperament is associated with the powers of touch and speech, balanced feelings, and a cultured mind. The goal is the creation of a feeling intellect, the union of the female and male aspects of consciousness in a new state of truth-based intuition. Copper needs to work with the Earth Element, but wrong Earth or too much Earth here produces someone who is materialistic and overly practical. It could even produce a "user" mentality or mimic the "take everything I can" licentiousness of Mars in relationships.

Venus is the feminine goddess of love and beauty just as her counterpart, Mars, is thought of as the masculine god of war and strife. These two archetypes complement each other perfectly and work as a polarity, manifesting the tension and desire between the masculine and feminine. Together, these mythic archetypes offer a complete picture of human existence on the material and emotional levels.

In depth psychology, Venus and Mars are often thought of as the *Anima* (feminine soul) and *Animus* (masculine spirit), respectively. Until a person can bring both forces into conscious awareness and learn to balance and accept them fully, he or she cannot be a complete individual. If we repress or deny one of these forces within us, we create a submerged, destructive energy in the shadowy *Umbra* that will manifest in self-defeating extreme behaviors, such as blatant aggression or whimpering passivity.

In developing one's copper temperament, the true heart of the initiate is actualized. In alchemical terms, this is the marriage of the Sun and Moon, the solar and lunar ways of knowing, the coming together of the forces of spirit and soul in consciousness. While there is less self-serving attachment to other people, there is also greater caring and responsiveness exhibited at this level. There arises a giving, optimistic person in place of the previous manipulative one. As the transmutation of copper continues, the alchemist begins to exercise freewill, unencumbered by buried emotions, addictions, impulses, and instincts.

For the work in Venus to succeed, copper must move to the higher frequency or higher octave of unconditional love—a love that embraces all creation and is totally accepting without discrimination or judgment. While many of us strive to attain unconditional love of others and ourselves, we must first travel with Venus and feel copper in our veins to learn love on the personal level. Until we have had the experiences that Venus brings us through relationships, either with people or things, we cannot reach the expanded consciousness that transpersonal love promises.

Ray 5: The Mercury Temperament

As Mercury is transmuted, a sense of trust and sublimity arise in the individual. Initiated people sense a new presence of unlimited sustenance and potential within them. In transmuting from quicksilver into silver, the impression of this inner presence becomes even more solidified. Gradually, a powerful vibration or resonance with the divine can be felt. It is at this level of transformation that personal fermentation begins.

In Eastern alchemy, inner Mercury is said to be transmuted in the Throat Chakra, which is the boundary between the personal and the transpersonal realms in the body. It is the gateway to the worlds of spirit—a new world of divine communication and inspiring movement of spiritual energy. At this stage, Mercury (as Hermes) unites mind, spirit, and matter but gives primacy to intellect and understanding.

Psychologically, the forces of Mercury in a person's temperament yearn for Sulfur, just as quicksilver seeks union with sulfur. But Sulfur here is divine passion and not worldly emotions. The wrong Sulfur at this stage produces someone who is spiritually unyielding and suffers from a superiority complex. It produces someone who uses spirituality for personal gain or practical control of others. This is the classic "guru syndrome" seen in the New Age movement.

Ray 6: The Silver Temperament

After Mercury comes alive or in alchemical parlance is "animated" in an individual, the work of personal transformation usually proceeds at a faster pace. If the work in Mercury was successful, things can come together amazingly fast in the transmutation of the noble metals silver and gold in one's temperament.

Psychologically, the transmutation of silver produces a lasting mystical state absolutely purified of habitual or egotistic forces. Intuition reaches its highest state of perfection, and the mind begins to move beyond the limitations of space and time. The feeling is one of intense connection to the cosmos. In the last stages of transmutation, a sublimation of spiritual forces occurs, which lays the groundwork for the formation of a Second Body in which inner moonlight becomes flesh in the next and final position on the Azoth.

Ray 7: The Gold Temperament

For those who suffer with weaker wills or loss of contact with the divine presence, gold represents a powerful psychological cure. The solar essences encourage hope, ambition, courage, self-reliance, dignity, authority, and the ability to manage oneself and others. The creative light within us, no matter how small and insignificant it is, can be enhanced to a great degree by tapping into the solar archetype. Just as the Sun represents the divine creative force in our solar system, gold represents the same thing in our inner temperament.

For lasting manifestation, the golden temperament needs to be firmly grounded in the world, and the danger now is that the individual becomes too focused on the workings Above and forgets their connection to the real world. Gold and the blazing Sun correspond to higher ambitions, courage, and creative energy and vitality, but without a constant effort to remain pure and alive in the real world, the golden temperament can quickly devolve into the leaden qualities of despair, poor self-esteem, lack of confidence, and impurity.

It is most important for the golden temperament to realize that once you reach this plateau, you have certain personal and karmic obligations. The golden attitude of the solar temperament is what brings the rewards of health, wealth, and happiness through synchronistic responses from the universe. If you go against these archetypal powers at this level of achievement, then even the slightest deviation from the golden path of righteousness and personal integrity can have disastrous and immediate consequences. The gold created at this stage of transformation needs to be planted in the Earth—in noble works and material perfection.

In this chapter, we focused on spiritual alchemy and the perfection of the soul. The primary tools for this kind of work are intense prayer and meditation, which we organized into the three groups of Lunar, Solar, and Stellar. Most of this chapter was devoted to working with the Azoth of the Philosophers emblem, which contains a coded formula for the creation of the Philosopher's Stone. Each ray of this star is a step through the Ladder of the Planets to the level of stellar consciousness that the Philosopher's Stone represents. In the next chapter, we will delve deeper into the mysterious Sacred Marriage in alchemy, where the work on the physical, mental, and spiritual levels unite in unexpected glory.

CHAPTER 20

Mystery of the Sacred Marriage

In alchemy, the compounding of two different substances is known as a *conjunction*, which literally means to "join with." Conjunctions usually yield a new compound with different properties from the original ingredients. For instance, when finely ground charcoal (black carbon) and black copper oxide are heated together, gas is released from the reaction. If the gas is allowed to pass through a solution of lime water (calcium hydroxide), a solid white precipitate (calcium carbonate) appears out of nowhere. Alchemists viewed the white precipitate as the "child" of the conjunction of black carbon and black copper oxide.

So, the combination or conjoining of substances that takes place during a successful conjunction produces a new substance with its own characteristics, and this new compound is called the "Child of the Conjunction." Most often in alchemy, the child is viewed as a hermaphrodite, a gross melding of the opposing characteristics of the original substances. But if the union produces a precipitate or other completely new compound, as in our example, the child may be referred to as a "stone."

The Sacred Marriage and the birth of the Philosopher's Child from the First Matter.
(From Materia Prima Philosophorum in The Circle of Gold and Rosicrucians, 1781)

If the substances involved in conjunction are the primal immortal essences of soul and spirit, then the event is special indeed. Known as the Sacred Marriage, it is the most important event in alchemy. Whether in the laboratory work, the mental work, or the spiritual work, the Sacred Marriage is considered the crucial turning point in the transformation of the matter, and it is generally believed to take place on all three levels of the work at once.

In the *Gospel of Thomas,* Jesus describes the Sacred Marriage in surprisingly alchemical terms: "When you make the two One, and when you make the inside like the outside, and the outside like the inside, and the Above like the Below, and when you make the male and the female one and the same, then you will enter the Kingdom of God."

The Sacred Marriage in You

The Sacred Marriage on the personal level is the marriage of the Sun and Moon within—the union of your spirit with your soul to produce a new presence. Alchemists saw this as a passionate coming together of the Fire and Water elements, an act of inner love that united and balanced all the opposing forces within a person.

Psychologically, the Sacred Marriage is the creation of a whole new personality from the genuine essences of soul and spirit we have discovered within us, and it takes a lot of courage, passion, and devotion to succeed in melding them. Conjunction is what we experience when we fall in love with another person, but it is also the communion we feel with all of nature. Personal conjunction can be a powerfully mystical experience.

Spiritual alchemists realize that no matter how fervently one desires to possess the qualities of soul and spirit recognized in another person, romantic love often fails. However, it is possible to bring together within ourselves those same aspects of soul and spirit that we fall in love with in another person.

"That which failed to become two in one flesh will succeed in becoming two in one spirit," noted one Renaissance alchemist. "Earthly lovers, however greatly they may love," agreed another, "must be distinct and separate from one another. But you can pour yourself so utterly into the soul's essence that no part of you remains outside."

Though they sometimes depicted the Sacred Marriage as outright sexual intercourse, the alchemists were trying to describe inner mystical experiences. Among the most disturbing images of the Sacred Marriage are those that describe it as an act of incest or masturbation, and some medieval churchmen even accused alchemists of advocating such lewd behavior. We now understand that the alchemist's symbolic incest was their metaphor for the act of going into oneself—the descent into the subconscious mind. The mother is the subconscious, the son is the conscious part, and the marriage is a return to the womb of the mother. For most Hermetic writers, such scenes are descriptions of the inner union that takes place between the alchemist's own soul and spirit.

The icon for the Sacred Marriage is the six-pointed star in which the two overlapping triangles signify the union of opposites. The triangle pointing upward is the alchemical cipher for Fire and symbolizes spirit, God, the Sun, or the masculine ego. The triangle pointing downward is the cipher for Water and symbolizes soul, the goddess, the Moon, and the feminine unconscious. Sometimes in their writings, alchemists used the same symbol to stand for the Universal Solvent or Mercury, the child of the Sacred Marriage, or the Philosopher's Stone.

Birth of the Philosopher's Stone

As we have seen, alchemy uses many opposing concepts, such as Fire and Water, Sun and Moon, Mars and Venus, lead and gold, dryness and wetness, warmth and cold, volatile and fixed, matter and spirit. The union of these opposite conceptual qualities constitute a conjunction in the philosophical sense. The new insight or belief created from the conjunction of opposing ideas was considered to be the "Philosopher's Child."

Many medieval laboratory experiments confirmed the idea that something new is born from the conjunction of a wide variety of substances. For example, in an ancient experiment known to Alexandrian alchemists, mixing potassium nitrate and sulfuric acid produces a blue-colored solution of *aqua fortis* ("strong water" or nitric acid) that can be used to separate silver from gold. In the reaction, a solid residue miraculously precipitates out of the solution like a child dropping from an invisible womb.

Potassium nitrate was also known as cubic-saltpeter and was often referred to simply as *Natron*, which stood for the general principle of Salt to alchemists. Sulfur was obtained from vitriol, the highly symbolic chemical also known as the "Green Dragon." That the mixture of these two highly symbolic substances would produce a child precipitate was considered extremely significant to early alchemists.

In the following figure, we see a depiction of the formation of the precipitate or stone from the marriage of opposites. The two dragons represent the opposing lunar and solar forces of conjunction. Their heads are twisted backward as they seek out the complementary solar (masculine) or lunar (feminine) energy that will complete their union. This natural urge to find balance in the embrace of our opposites is what makes the world go 'round. This act results in the birth or precipitation of the stone, which is shown as the round ball on which the dragons perch.

The Dragons of the Stone.
(By Robert Vaughan in Theatrum Chemicum Britannicum by Elias Ashmole, 1652)

In the same way precipitates form in some chemical reactions, the Philosopher's Stone is formed during the Sacred Marriage. This marriage begins with the union of the divine spirit with the human soul and proceeds to their precipitation in physical reality in the body. According to some authors, the Great Work has been accomplished when the divine spirit has been brought down to impregnate the soul with light. This act results in the purification and assimilation of the physical body, so that spirit, soul, and body unite to form a new or resurrected body of pure light.

The Sacred Marriage in Christian Alchemy

Christian alchemy began in the Middle Ages in the writings of alchemists who saw parallels between the Great Work and the life of Christ. Christ was viewed as the Philosopher's Stone and referred to in many treatises as simply the *Lapis* ("the Stone").

Christian mystics view the Sacred Marriage as the union of one's soul with the eternal spirit of Christ. Christ consciousness is born out of that union, and Christ himself, as the Philosopher's Stone, then becomes the magical touchstone that transforms one's life.

In Christian alchemy, every event in the life of Christ is a metaphor for operations in the Great Work. The virgin birth and nativity of Jesus represent the birth of the Philosopher's Child, and his subsequent separation, conjunction, fermentation, and sublimation produced the essence of the Divine Life that is available for all of us to follow.

The Holy Sacrament is believed to contain the most profound secrets of spiritual alchemy and is said to offer anyone a way to experience the transformation of the soul. Out of this ritualistic mystical marriage, Christ as the Philosopher's Stone is born again within the worshipper.

"Transubstantiation" is the Christian term for the process of alchemical transmutation. It is the mystical process of becoming the body of Christ in the sacrament of the Eucharist. Worshippers partake of the bread, which is the body and nature of Christ, they partake of the wine, which is the blood and life force of Christ, and they become one with Him. The accompanying rituals of the sacrament transform the bread and wine into vehicles of spiritual power.

According to Christian alchemy, all three phases of the Great Work were played out in the last three days in the life of Jesus. The Black Phase of alchemy was Christ's suffering on Calvary; the White Phase was his lingering death on the cross; and his resurrection was the perfection of his soul in the Red Phase of alchemy.

In both Gnostic and Christian alchemy, the place where the supreme mystery of the Sacred Marriage occurs is called the "Bridal Chamber," which seems to be a metaphor for the human brain. The *Gospel of Philip* instructs the initiate that he will receive the heavenly light in the Bridal Chamber. "If anyone does not receive the light while he is here," it warns, "he will not be able to receive it in the other place, for when he leaves the world, he has already received the truth."

The experience one receives in the Bridal Chamber has something to do with the resurrection of the soul. For instance, in the Gnostic text "The Exegesis of the Soul," the feminine soul falls from heaven and is trapped in the physical world. She returns to heaven by incest with her brother in the mysterious Bridal Chamber. "And when she had intercourse with him," says the text, "she got from him the seed that is the life-giving spirit, and this is the resurrection from the dead."

The Three Marriages of Hermes

Some alchemists claim that three different conjunctions in alchemy correspond to the Three Magisteriums—accomplishments of the Great Work that were attributed to Thrice Greatest Hermes. The first Magisterium is the Lunar Marriage or *unio mentalis* ("union in the mind"). This marriage occurs when the united soul and spirit separates itself from the body or when the alchemist becomes conscious that soul and spirit have formed a separate entity. It feels like a voluntary rejection or even death of the body in relation to the united soul and spirit.

The second Magisterium or Solar Marriage occurs when the united soul and spirit (of the *unio mentalis*) reunites with the body, which has now been completely purified by the spiritual or solar energies. The third Magisterium or final union is the Stellar Marriage in which the fused body-soul-spirit unites with the One Mind in the *unus mundus* ("the One World") of the universe. The body of light at this level is the Salt of the Starsthe Astral Body or what the theurgists call the *Augoeides*.

The *unus mundus* represents the whole universe called the "One Thing" in the Emerald Tablet. The One Thing (or *plethora*) contains all of the potential of the First Matter on the first day of creation. The One Thing unites with the One Mind in the act of creation. So, at its source, everything is united. This idea is expressed in the alchemical motto "All is One." This is the cosmic marriage or union of "everything we are" with "everything that is."

The Sacred Marriage in Psychology

Carl Jung titled the last book he wrote *Mysterium Coniunctionis* ("Mystery of the Conjunction"). It was published in 1955. He considered it his most important work, and scholars are still amazed at the depth and intuitive grasp of the principles of alchemy he revealed. The book focused on the marriage or archetypal union between the powers of Sol (the Sun) and Luna (the Moon). Jung used the alchemists' Latin term *Hierosgamos* ("Sacred Marriage") for this event.

Jung felt that one alchemical text in particular defined the archetype of the Sacred Marriage. Called the *Rosarium Philosophorum* ("Rose Garden of the Philosophers"), this manuscript first appeared in the 1550 edition of an anthology called *De Alchimia* ("Of Alchemy").

The *Rosarium* depicts the Sacred Marriage in a series of twenty woodcuts showing Sol and Luna in various stages of conjunction. As the Sacred Marriage progresses, the male essence or Sol, representing spirit or energy, merges completely with the female essence or Luna, representing soul or matter.

As depicted in the *Rosarium,* this union is achieved through coitus or the sexual union of Sol and Luna. Their lovemaking symbolizes the mystical union of opposites. The bride represents the soul or incarnate eternal self, and the bridegroom represents the spirit or disincarnate temporal self.

The product of this Sacred Marriage, the child of Sol and Luna, is a new archetype known as the Divine Child or Divine Androgyne. This is a similar but more complete archetype to the alchemical hermaphrodite or *Rebis* we have talked about throughout this book.

In Jungian psychology, the marriage of opposites within the psyche—including all levels of masculine and feminine traits, conscious and subconscious, divine and human forces—gives birth to the "Self." The Self is the archetype of wholeness in a person. According to Jung, the realization of the Self is the real goal of the alchemical quest.

There is no doubt that Carl Jung's interpretation of alchemical symbols proved extremely powerful. His discovery of alchemy completely changed his life and inspired a whole new therapy known as "depth psychology."

In the garden of Jung's home in Bollingen, Switzerland, stands a large cube-shaped monument inscribed by Jung in his own hand with alchemical symbols. This square stone symbolizes Jung's alchemical work in the world. In his last dream before his death, Jung saw a huge round stone engraved with the words "And this shall be a sign unto you of wholeness and Oneness." For him, it was the Philosopher's Stone—a confirmation that he had followed the right path in life.

In this chapter, we pursued the Philosopher's Stone as the product of the Sacred Marriage, which is a conjunction of the essences of soul and spirit. We explored the idea that the mysterious Sacred Marriage takes place on the three levels of the Magisteriums of the Lunar, Solar, and Stellar marriages. We also discussed the importance of the Sacred Marriage in psychology and philosophy and saw how deeply it influenced the work of Carl Jung, who believed the product of the Sacred Marriage is the integrated and actualized Self. We continue to explore what goes on in the privacy of Bridal Chamber of the brain in the next chapter on the Alchemy of Consciousness.

CHAPTER 21

The Science of Consciousness

Alchemy is not only the origin of systematic experimentation and the scientific method, but it is also the first attempt to create a science of consciousness. Those early philosophers of nature treated the contents of consciousness as objective phenomena, and that uniquely empirical approach to the mental realm offers modern researchers a wealth of raw material that sheds new light on the questions of what consciousness is and how it arises from matter.

Alchemists view consciousness as a force of nature that is part of the creation of the universe and is present everywhere in it. For them, the One Mind of the universe is the fabric of reality on which all phenomena play out. The Hermetic philosophy behind alchemy says that our thoughts and feelings are the thoughts and feelings of the whole universe. That is because our thoughts and feelings are not unique to individuals; instead, they grow from archetypal patterns embedded in consciousness itself.

For alchemists, the only way to understand consciousness is to become of One Mind beyond the duality of the manifested world. They tried to do this in the Sacred Marriage by uniting logic with intuition or thoughts with feelings. The union of the masculine and feminine ways of knowing creates a unique and empowered state of consciousness, which is the source of true awareness and infinite wisdom they called the Philosopher's Stone. Like modern seekers of a unified field theory, the alchemists sought one true philosophy of universal principles that were as valid in the laboratory as they were in their own minds and souls—and in the One Mind of the cosmos.

Medieval alchemists expressed mental states and levels of consciousness in terms of the basic materials of their world— metals, compounds, gases, caustic solutions, and acids. Although they spoke of crucibles, retorts, and furnaces, they were really talking about changes taking place in their own minds and bodies. The strange creatures and complex symbols pictured in alchemists' flasks were attempts to identify the archetypal forces churning in the hermetically sealed vessel of the brain. They even tried to influence the outcome of their experiments by purifying their thoughts and taming their emotions to become one with the quantum-like First Matter—the common source of all of things.

The Alchemy of Chaos Magic

Science-fiction writer Arthur C. Clarke noted that any future science will be indistinguishable from magic to those of our present time. The ancient principles of alchemy and magic are merging with modern science and creating a greater discipline that recognizes the mystery inherent in the universe and acknowledges that consciousness partakes in nature. This new alchemy has become the science of magic in modern times.

As we learned in Chapter 3, Egyptian magic (or theurgy) and alchemy developed simultaneously from the Hermetic teachings in Alexandria. Those traditions shared many common beliefs, including the notion of the First Matter as the agent of transformation and the idea that focusing consciousness with will and intention can alter physical reality.

With the development of chaos magic in the last 50 years, the theories of magic approach the same theoretical basis as alchemy and quantum physics. Chaos magic emphasizes the power of the consciousness of the practitioner, as opposed to the ceremonial invocation of elemental forces or spiritual energies.

Developed in England in the 1970s, the discipline teaches that both subjective experience and objective reality can be changed through a highly focused mind. A key belief in chaos magic is that there is no such thing as an objective truth outside of our perception, and therefore, all things are true and possible. This mercurial mindset is very empowering, and the basic philosophy behind chaos magic is extremely alchemical and even fits in the framework of quantum theory.

The basic technique in chaos magic is the development of a highly purified state of one-pointed concentration known as the "gnostic state." This heightened level of awareness is an altered state of consciousness in which a person's mind is focused on knowing only one thing—a single idea or goal—and all other thoughts are thrust out. The gnostic state results in total immersion and perfect knowledge of just one thing.

Then, the highly purified single thought created in the gnostic state is quickly released or forgotten and absorbed into the subconscious mind, where it is enacted into reality through "mysterious means." That is enough explanation for magicians, who are usually focused only on practical results.

The principle is really not that new. The alchemists were quite familiar with the chaotic subconscious mind and viewed it much like the First Matter, which is the source of creative physical change in the real world. They also tried to achieve the gnostic state in their private meditations. "The mind can do all when concentrated upon one sole thing," noted alchemist-monk Antoine-Joseph Pernety (1716–1796), "but nothing when trying to embrace too many."

The Esoteric Nature of Light

Light is the common catalyst that seems to dissolve the boundaries of alchemy, magic, and science. Whenever alchemists, magicians, or scientists talk about the nature of light, it seems they are talking about the same thing.

In ancient India, light was considered a subtle element out of which emerged the gross elements of creation. According to texts dating back to 500 B.C.E., light consists of particles of energy that make up all matter. Indian theorists knew that the Sun was at the center of the solar system and that the Moon and planets shined by reflecting the light of the Sun. They also knew that white light was composed of colors that they called "the seven rays of the Sun." All these ideas have been confirmed by modern science.

About the same time, the Greek philosopher Empedocles postulated his theory of the Four Elements that viewed light as the Fire Element traveling at high speed. This light-fire was carried in humans and shone out of their eyes making sight possible. Around 300 B.C.E., Euclid wrote *Optica*, which was the first scientific study of light. He described the laws of reflection mathematically and postulated that light traveled in straight lines.

In his *Book of Optics,* the Arabian alchemist Alhazen (965–1040) disputed the idea that light originated from the eyes and said instead that sight was caused by light rays emitted from the Sun or lamps that struck the eyes. He theorized that light was streams of minute particles that traveled at an extremely fast but finite speed. He also described the laws of refraction (how light behaves in a lens) and invented a primitive camera.

French philosopher René Descartes (1596–1650) believed light traveled in the unseen *plenum*, which is the subtle substance or etheric First Matter of which the universe is composed. He demonstrated that light behaved like a wave and concluded that refraction could be explained by the varying speed of light in different media. As a result, Descartes is considered the father of the wave theory of light.

Alchemist Isaac Newton promoted the particle theory of light when he postulated that light was composed of corpuscles of matter emitted from a light source in all directions at once. Newton published these ideas in his book *Opticks* in 1704. But as we learned in Chapter 4, Newton's alchemical studies suggested that light might exist in two states at once—both as wave energy and particulate matter—although the idea was too controversial for his time and he never published it. "The changing of bodies into light and light into bodies," noted Newton, "is very comfortable to the course of Nature, which seems delighted with such transmutations."

Newton suspected light was like the alchemical Rebis, the "double-headed thing" that showed two opposite faces to the world at the same time. For thousands of years, alchemists had associated Mercury with light and the paradoxical Rebis. For philosophical alchemists, Mercury represented light in all its forms: the light of the heavens, the light of our fires, and the light of our imagination and consciousness.

Newton was correct in his assumption that the world was not ready for an alchemical theory of light. Endless quibbling over the nature of light dominated physics for the next century. Dozens of experiments that demonstrated the wave nature of light challenged Newton's corpuscular theory. Finally, in the nineteenth century, James Clerk Maxwell (1831–1879) developed a mathematical wave theory of electromagnetic radiation that included light, and numerous experiments verified his work.

The wave theory was accurate at explaining most optical and electromagnetic phenomena, but a few troubling anomalies remained that could not be accounted for. One of these was the speed of light, which could not be calculated from Maxwell's equations. Another problem was that the wave theory failed to explain the levels of electricity produced by the photoelectric effect, in which light striking a metal surface generated an electrical current. Yet another problem was known as the "ultraviolet catastrophe," in which the spectrum of energy emitted by black bodies or thermal radiators could not be accounted for. Wave theory also had a hard time explaining light pressure or the way light pushes objects in a vacuum.

Finally, in 1905, Albert Einstein resolved all these problems by returning to Newton's suspicion that light existed as both matter and energy. Einstein combined the particle and wave theories of light in a "wavicle" concept in which photons exhibit wave-particle duality. His theory stated that light has both a particle nature and a wave nature, and various experiments can be done to bring out one state or the other. In other words, the nature of light—or which face the Rebis shows the world—is determined by the conscious choice of the human observer as to which experiment to use in studying light. Some experiments prove the wave or energetic nature of light, while other experiments prove the particle or material nature of light.

Quantum Alchemy

Einstein's work and that of other physicists led to the development of the truly alchemical new science of quantum physics. The basic premise is that reality is made up of *quanta* or packets of energy from which matter originates. In effect, the efforts of physicists to understand light led to the creation of quantum physics, which is the most comprehensive and accurate theory ever formulated to explain natural phenomena.

The power of quantum physics led to its acceptance by many reluctant physicists. The notion of wave-particle duality was extended to include the electron and all electromagnetic phenomena. According to the field of quantum electrodynamics, when electrons are excited, packets of *quanta* are released as electromagnetic radiation. These packets of energy act the same way as a ball hitting a wall but are, in fact, packets of solidified energy.

Modern physicists have also discovered that every fundamental particle of matter has a shadow energy-carrier particle, and every energy-carrier particle has a shadow matter particle. This relationship between matter particles and their shadow energy carriers is called supersymmetry. The idea is eerily similar to the concept of the energy-carrying shadow (or *Umbra*) of the personality in psychology.

The most startling revelation of modern quantum theory is another alchemical principle that states the origin of the physical world is in unseen spirits, which is how alchemists described the behavior of energy in nature. Today we know that matter does not exist of itself in the universe but emerges from the amorphous "Quantum Foam" or First Matter. Atomic particles, which are the basis of all matter, are created out of underlying strings of pure, wild energy that condense into physical reality when observed.

Even the movement of particles of matter is not what it seems. Particles move in quantum jumps by disappearing from reality and reappearing in another position. The discontinuous motion of atomic particles gets so weird that completely imaginary components must be invented to describe their movement.

It's hard for us to accept such alchemical explanations of the everyday world, but our mechanistic concept of reality is completely false and has polluted all our thinking and beliefs. No scientific experiment in the history of physics has ever proved that hard material particles exist on the atomic level or can even move anywhere. However, now thousands of experiments prove subatomic particles move by being tele-transported through time—disappearing from one place to reappear somewhere else without moving along a continuous path. So, we might as well call them "unseen spirits" like the alchemists first viewed them.

Contrary to what our senses make us believe, the world is not solid and fixed, but it is constantly being created out of a chaotic, formless, and invisible Quantum Foam that is guided by our conscious expectation of what is there. And that is a more perfect description of the First Matter than any alchemist ever put forth.

In his book *The Mysterious Universe* (1944), British astrophysicist Sir James Jeans wrote: "The universe begins to look more like a great thought than like a great machine. Mind no longer appears to be an accidental intruder into the realm of matter. We ought rather hail it as the creator and governor of the realm of matter."

Whether the conscious expectation that creates reality comes from our minds or the One Mind of the universe is still open to debate in modern physics. For alchemists, however, the divine light of mind—the same light we share in purified consciousness and the True Imagination—is the fundamental source of creation.

The Study of Consciousness

We can gain much deeper insight into the problem of consciousness by taking a look at the philosophical alchemists who were first to explore it. Their theories and observations became the basis for the modern discipline of consciousness studies.

Basil Valentine (1394–1450)

The Benedictine monk and alchemist systematized the operations of alchemy and applied them to human consciousness. He summarized the process in a meditative mandala called the "Azoth of the Philosophers," which we explored in Chapter 19. His mandala was designed so the face of the alchemist and the face of God were united in shared consciousness at its center. Most of Valentine's works allude to the importance of purified consciousness in creating the Philosopher's Stone, including his *Twelve Keys*, *Triumphant Chariot of Antimony*, and *Last Will and Testament*. All these centuries-old manuscripts were reportedly found hidden in a salt mine owned by Johann Thölde (1565-1624). He studied the texts and became a noted alchemist in Germany. The texts then circulated privately for decades until Thölde published copies in the early seventeenth century.

Paracelsus (1493–1541)

The great Swiss alchemist believed a person could achieve union with the One Mind by focusing on the infinite nature of their own consciousnesses. According to Paracelsus, a disciplined imagination is the key to transforming physical reality. One could transmute a substance by stripping away its outer form to reveal its First Matter and then projecting the light of True Imagination into it. This is possible because the microcosm and macrocosm are united within the light of One Mind, and the human mind is the focal point through which Nature manifests. "Imagination is a great power," he wrote, "and if the world knew what strange things can be produced by the power of the imagination, the public authorities would force idle people to stop daydreaming and keep busy."

John Dee (1527–1608)

The English mathematician and alchemist revived the Pythagorean notion of the Monad to explain the role of consciousness in the universe. The Monad was the first being or idea that contained the totality of all things. "It is the force behind the evolution of life," he said, "and the universal binding power which unites minds and souls in a human oneness." For seven years, Dee struggled to prove the existence of the divine Monad. Finally, in 1564, he completed a step-by-step proof using Euclidean geometry to create the Hieroglyphic Monad, a symbol that contained all the planetary ciphers in their proper relationship (see Chapter 13). His Monad cipher is a map to the archetypes in human consciousness shown in their proper working relationships.

Giordano Bruno (1548–1600)

The Italian mathematician and alchemist viewed the universe as an infinite living presence that possessed a monadic consciousness. He was fascinated by the nature of consciousness and did groundbreaking research into how memories are formed. He also created a geometric language to clarify thought processes that was a precursor of modern computer coding. Bruno asserted that consciousness exists everywhere in the universe and that stars are distant suns with their own planets, which might harbor intelligent life. Despite years of torture by the medieval Church that led to his being burned alive, he never recanted a single word of his lifelong study of consciousness.

Francis Bacon (1561–1626)

The English alchemist and philosopher accepted the Paracelsian view that all things arise from the interaction of the three archetypal principles of Sulfur, Salt, and Mercury. But Bacon eliminated Salt and theorized it was created later through the interaction of Sulfur and Mercury. This subtle change in the concept of the Three Essentials had important implications and foreshadowed the modern idea that matter is created through the interplay of energy and light (or consciousness). His tireless efforts to prove his theory—"so that all men will accept it"—led him to develop a systematic way of finding the truth behind natural phenomena. In 1603, he published *Of the Interpretation of Nature*, in which he described what we know today as the scientific method.

Robert Fludd (1574–1637)

The English alchemist and mathematician believed consciousness was embedded in the universe. He suggested this could be proven by studying parallel actions that remained linked by sympathetic or synchronistic forces formed at their inception. He argued that two or more identical actions performed simultaneously under the same conditions should share a conscious bond whose effects could be observed. It would be more than 300 years before scientists accepted his theory in what is now called "quantum entanglement."

Inspired by the ancient concept of the Word (*Logos*), Fludd theorized the One Mind emits vibrations to create physical reality. In 1618, he invented two single-string musical instruments (monochords) based on his theory. His Mundane Monochord played microcosmic or terrestrial sounds, while his Divine Monochord played macrocosmic or celestial sounds.

Robert Fludd's map of consciousness.

(From Utriusque Cosmi: Metaphysica, Tom. II, Tract. I, Lib. X, by Robert Fludd, 1624).

Jakob Boehme (1575–1624)

The German alchemist and mystic proclaimed that all things arise from a formless void he called the *Ungrund* ("the place without ground"). It is a perfect description of what we now call the Quantum Foam from which material particles emerge. According to Boehme, this infinite Abyss is brought to manifestation by the primordial urge of the One Mind to become conscious of itself. He said we can experience this deeper level of creation by purifying our consciousness to a supersensual monadic state "before nature and creature." After "extricating our consciousness from all that is the effect of our time and place," what remains is a state beyond duality of absolute simplicity and clarity. "My writings are only for those willing to receive the truth in a simple and childlike state of mind," Boehme summarized, "but I have written only for those who seek truth; to the cunning and world-wise, I have nothing to say."

Robert Boyle (1627–1691)

The Irish alchemist and philosopher tried to free alchemy of its secrecy. He encouraged radical freedom of consciousness based on an open exchange of ideas. He met frequently with fellow alchemists, and his network became known as the "Invisible College," which included Isaac Newton, Gottfried Leibniz, John Locke, and dozens of other alchemists. Then in 1689, Boyle abruptly announced he had made strides in creating the Philosopher's Stone that required he spend more time in his lab. He explained the products of his work were exhibiting properties that should not be discussed openly. "In spite of my previous philanthropy," he said, "I am now engaged to secrecy."

John Locke (1632–1704)

The English alchemist and statesman preached a new era of freedom of consciousness. He believed independent thought was a fundamental human right that should be implemented on all levels of government and culture. Locke insisted that tolerance, respect for ideas, and freedom of speech should become the laws of the land. His writings inspired the Enlightenment, a late seventeenth-century movement that placed objective reasoning as the source of authority beyond the control of the Church and monarchies. Moreover, Locke showed that an understanding of principles of clear thinking was necessary to the scientific investigation of nature. His work led to the birth of formal logic, as mathematicians and philosophers throughout Europe tried to systemize the process of rational thought.

Isaac Newton (1643–1727)

The great English alchemist based his personal philosophy on a literal interpretation of the Bible and wanted to go back before the Fall to a state of perfect knowledge. He was convinced angels came to Adam to reveal a way to return to Garden, and the Emerald Tablet described that path. For Newton, alchemists were holy adepts seeking the Philosopher's Stone, which was a state of higher consciousness that once achieved would enable communication with higher spirits. Newton also believed the spiritual state of the alchemist was intimately connected to the outcome of the experiment. As we noted in Chapter 4, Newton was against his own corpuscular theory of light because it "robbed matter of its divine essence" and speculated light might exist as both particles and waves.

Gottfried Leibniz (1646–1716)

The German alchemist and philosopher believed that mind was present everywhere in the universe in the form of monads—atoms of consciousness created at the beginning of time. All substances can be broken down into smaller units, but at some point in this infinite process, we get to an ultimate essence that can no longer be rationally understood. In his view, the basis of reality is not a material particle but a conscious subjective presence of pure awareness. He theorized that his monads exist on all levels of consciousness, ranging from the highest One Mind that contains all other monads to the lowest, proto-conscious monad at the border between mind and matter. Monads, at the lowest level, are unconscious, unaware, and without memory, but they possess the potential to become conscious.

Johann von Goethe (1749–1832)

The famous philosopher maintained a large alchemy lab in Weimar, Germany. As a youth, he was deeply influenced by alchemy texts from Basil Valentine and Paracelsus, and he channeled his enthusiasm into a stream of poetic, mystical, and scientific works that presented alchemy from a variety of viewpoints. Goethe believed the essence of truth can be found in its contradictions, and he developed a method of cognition based on uniting opposites. He said his method consisted of "holding two opposing truths in two hands and then walking forward in purest contemplation." He also extolled the importance of achieving a beginner's mind and being very selective of the material that filled the mind. Goethe's ideas about the nature and workings of the mind became the basis for modern epistemology.

Modern Alchemists of Science

Alchemical principles continue to inspire philosophers and scientists in modern times. The Perennial Philosophy born in Alexandria has survived even the paradigm shifts in science and technology of the last century. In the writings of many of the world's greatest thinkers of our era, we see the vestiges of the teachings of Thoth/Hermes.

Werner Heisenberg (1901–1976)

The German theoretical physicist was one of the first physicists to show that material things were more like thoughts than physical objects. "The old paradigm of materialism rested on the illusion that the kind of existence we have—the direct actuality of the world—can be extrapolated into the atomic range," he declared, "but the smallest units of matter are not physical objects; they are forms or ideas which can be expressed unambiguously only in mathematical language."

In 1925, Heisenberg proved that exact measurement and precise knowledge in physics is not possible. Specifically, he showed that the position and momentum of an atomic particle cannot both be known exactly. He demonstrated that just the act of consciously observing one magnitude of a particle—whether it be its mass, momentum, velocity, or position—causes the other magnitudes to blur.

It is not that we do not have precise enough instruments to measure the magnitudes of subatomic particles. The blurring of exact knowledge of a single particle of matter is a fundamental property of the universe. It is as if Nature does not want us to know everything at this level of reality. This startling defeat for classical physics became known as the "Heisenberg Uncertainty Principle" and is now a basic tenet of quantum physics.

Kurt Gödel (1906–1978)

The Austrian mathematician is widely considered the most original and important logician since Aristotle. Just six years after Heisenberg formulated his Uncertainty Principle in physics, Gödel did the same thing in mathematics with his famous Incompleteness Theorems.

Before Gödel, mathematicians believed everything that is true in the universe could be proven using mathematics, which is built on a set of basic axioms that are accepted as true and need no proof. Gödel showed that it is impossible to create a set of axioms that is complete and consistent without contradictions. His two theorems state that any formal system of logic, such as arithmetic, is either incomplete or inconsistent:

> Theorem 1. In using a specific set of axioms there will always be questions that cannot be answered and propositions that cannot be solved.

> Theorem 2. A specific set of axioms cannot be proven to be consistent without using another completely different set of axioms. And so on, *ad infinitum*.

Albert Einstein (1879–1955)

The German theoretical physicist was the epitome of the Renaissance scientist-alchemist and never lost sight of the fundamental mystery of the universe. When the youthful Werner Heisenberg came to Einstein for advice, Einstein told him to beware of relying on logic alone. Instead, he told him to follow his intuition and allow the object of his work—his theory—to speak to him through his own imagination, and let it suggest where he should look and what is important.

In his theory of Special Relativity (1905), Einstein proved that space and time are united in a single continuum known as "spacetime," and events that occur at the same time for one observer could happen at different times for another. In his theory of General Relativity (1915), he proved that gravity is not a force, as Newton believed, but it is a curving or warping of space itself.

As we noted earlier, Einstein also proved an ancient tenet of alchemy that was previously unknown in physics: The fundamental equivalence between energy and matter in relation to light. His revolutionary equation of the universe is $E = mc^2$. As we have learned, this theorem is a restatement of the three forces of the alchemists in which Sulfur is energy, Salt is mass or matter, and Mercury represents light. Basically, the equation states that energy and matter are interchangeable and different forms of the same thing, which alchemists called First Matter.

David Bohm (1917–1992)

Another example of an alchemical scientist is nuclear physicist David Bohm, who demonstrated that electrons possess a "proto-mind" or primitive intelligence that seems to read active information in experiments. He developed the "Ontological Interpretation" of quantum mechanics in which mind and matter are aspects of a universal consciousness expressed through light that is part of the fabric of creation. "The Universe," he summarized, "consists of frozen light."

Bohm also introduced the notion of the "Implicate Order," which is the ground or undivided wholeness of the One Mind of the universe from which the manifested world, which he called the "Explicate Order," emerges.

Bohm was a believer in the alchemical principle of "As Above, so Below." Because we are created of the same matter and in the same way as the whole universe, the truths of the cosmos should be found within us. In quiet meditation, Bohm listened to his body and translated sensations of movement and tension into mathematical formulae that provided insights into problems of physics he was working on. He believed that consciousness and the physical brain itself could be transformed by contact with the greater mind of the universe.

Wolfgang Pauli (1900–1958)

The Nobel-prize-winning Austrian physicist, who was one of the founders of quantum physics, spent much of his later life studying alchemy. He felt that the goal of physics and the Great Work of alchemy was the same—to unite mind and matter. He was so impressed by the alchemical work of Carl Jung that he sought him out, and in 1933, he began a lifelong collaboration with the psychologist. Pauli's interest in alchemy had unleashed a torrent of alchemical images in his dreams. Jung documented over 400 of Pauli's alchemical dreams in *Psychology and Alchemy* (1953).

One of the results of their collaboration was the "Jung-Pauli Conjecture," a new worldview that unites mind and matter in a single underlying psychophysical reality. They noted that as scientists probe deeper into the mysteries of matter, they are simultaneously probing into the nature of mind. And as psychologists look deeper into the nature of mind, they discover a deeper psychoid connection to matter. Princeton University later collected and published their discussions in *Atom and Archetype* (1992).

Pauli's "World Clock" dream shows two intersecting circles of the conscious and unconscious realms carried through space-time by the crow of chaos. Four elemental monks orient the mind by setting off in separate directions.

For Pauli, the deeper truths of nature would be revealed, not by logic but through archetypal images. "To achieve a true description of nature," he explained, "it is essential to access the deeper archetypal background of the scientific terms and concepts. When one analyzes the preconscious steps to these concepts, one always finds ideas consist of deeply held symbolic images. We have to postulate a new cosmic order of nature in which material objects are connected to preexisting inner images. The natural laws of matter would then be revealed as the physical manifestation of their corresponding archetypal images."

Pauli spent his life working on a unified field theory in which all the forces of the universe would be explained by one grand theory. He included consciousness as one of the primordial forces of nature. The Grand Unified Theory he was working on is now the Philosopher's Stone of modern science. It is the one theory of everything that will give human beings unprecedented understanding of the forces of nature.

The work of Pauli, Heisenberg, Gödel, Einstein, among others, was extremely unsettling to traditional scientists. Heisenberg showed that the scientist is no longer external and neutral to the experiment but becomes part of it, just as the alchemists believed. Gödel revealed the fallibility of mathematics and suggested the only way to understand the whole universe is from a mind completely outside and yet part of the universe—a perfect description of the One Mind of the alchemists. Einstein described a universe in which the fundamental constants of nature are relative to the conscious awareness of the observer. And Bohm put consciousness right at the heart of physics as the fundamental force of creation.

To modern scientists, it all means that the "facts" of physical reality are no longer objectively verifiable and mathematically treatable. The most important tool of scientific investigation—the consciousness of the scientist—is now somehow part of the experiment. The new paradigm suggests that the scientific method will never be able to achieve complete and ultimate knowledge of the universe. There seems to be something else out there, some pervasive yet separate form of consciousness that does not want to be fully revealed.

In this chapter, we examined the centuries-old science of consciousness based on the works of such respected practicing alchemists as Gottfried Leibniz, Isaac Newton, John Locke, Robert Boyle, Robert Fludd, Francis Bacon, Giordano Bruno, and John Dee. Their work was continued by iconoclastic modern scientist-alchemists, such as Albert Einstein, Werner Heisenberg, Kurt Gödel, David Bohm, and Wolfgang Pauli. The resulting cauldron of ideas on mind and matter leads to a truer understanding of the Philosopher's Stone—not as an object but a state of consciousness. In the next and final chapter, we will formulate a model of alchemical consciousness and see how it applies to our lives in the everyday world.

CHAPTER 22

A Model of Alchemical Consciousness

Alchemical cosmology is based on the idea that consciousness is an intrinsic part of nature and the driving force behind the evolution of the universe. Alchemists treated consciousness as a force of nature that was amenable to experimentation and even manipulation. That is why prayer and meditation were such an important part of their work in the laboratory. For them, consciousness was the fabric of reality from which the universe emerges constantly in every moment.

Renaissance alchemists tried to create a practical science of consciousness based on their lab experiments as well as on their personal observations during psychological and spiritual work. The philosophical framework for their ideas was a new paradigm created from a melding of Hermetic principles with the Pythagorean notion that the universe was created through the emanations of a series of archetypal numbers.

The Pythagorean Model

Pythagoras (570–490 B.C.E.) taught that the universe is more like a conscious organism than an inanimate machine. He believed that the universe is "one whole of wholes"— a single source of all created things. For Pythagoras, the universe grew from a transcendent singularity he named the "Monad" (from Greek *monas*, meaning "one" or "unitary"). The monad was not only the origin of all numbers but also the first being or God.

In his book *Psychology and Alchemy* (1953), Carl Jung described the mystery of the Pythagorean Monad: "The Monad as the first and original number is, strictly speaking, not a number at all. One as unity and totality exists prior to the awareness of numbers which requires a capacity to distinguish between separate, discrete entities. Thus, the Monad symbolically corresponds to the uroboric state prior to the creation and separation of things. Two (the Dyad) is the first real number since with it is born the possibility of discriminating one thing from another. Two symbolizes the act of creation, as well as the emergence of the ego from the original state of unity."

The Dyad (duality) is born through a projective multiplication of the Monad, an act which creates the plurality of all numbers from which are derived two-dimensional objects. The Triad appears as a triplicity of forces that complete or balance duality in a resultant third number from which are derived three-dimensional bodies. The perfect ideals or archetypes of three-dimensional bodies are manifested in space-time through the Tetrad archetype, which is the basis for physical reality.

The Tetractys

The first four numerical archetypes (1,2,3,4) add up to ten, which Pythagoras considered a perfect number and source of the natural base-ten system of counting. The first four archetypes of creation can be arranged in the form of a perfect triangle containing the perfect number. Pythagoreans worshipped that diagram as a divine expression of reality called the "Tetractys."

The diagram of the Tetractys in the first figure depicts the emanations of the divine mind with the associated alchemical cipher. At the top is the unitary Monad from which the universe explodes into the duality of existence. This is the level of the Dyad indicated by the opposing alchemical ciphers for the Moon and Sun, which indicate the original duality of creation. The Triad level follows with the ciphers for the Three Essentials of creation: Salt (matter), Mercury (light), and Sulfur (energy). The final level is the Tetrad of manifestation, which is indicated by the ciphers for the Four Elements (Earth, Water, Fire, Air).

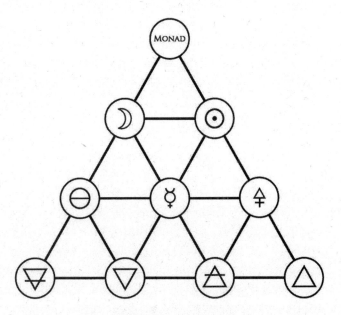

The sacred Tetractys with alchemical ciphers

In their Prayer to the Tetractys, the Pythagorean sect honors this hidden mystery at the root of creation: "Bless us divine number, You who generates gods and men! Oh Holy, Holy Tetractys, You that contains the root and the source of the eternally flowing creation! For the divine number begins with the profound, pure Unity until it comes to the holy Four; then it begets the mother of all, the all-comprising, the all-bounding, the first born, the never-swerving, the never-tiring holy Ten, the keyholder of all."

Alchemists also believe the Tetractys is the key numerical pattern of creation. The so-called "Axiom of Maria," attributed to the third-century female alchemist Maria Prophetissa, describes the movement of the divine mind through the Tetractys: "One becomes Two, Two becomes Three, and out of the Third comes the One as the Fourth."

In *The Psychology of the Transference* (1946), Carl Jung described how the Axiom of Maria is the key to the whole alchemical process: "It begins with the *Four* separate elements, the state of chaos, and ascends by degrees to the *Three* manifestations of Mercury in the inorganic, organic, and spiritual worlds. After attaining the *Two* forms of Sol and Luna, it culminates in the *One* and indivisible eternal nature of the Philosopher's Stone. This progression from the number 4 to 3 to 2 to 1 is the Axiom of Maria."

Jung also described the Axiom of Maria in terms of personal transformation. He defined One as primal "unconscious wholeness" and Two as the conflict of opposites of a wakening consciousness that is resolved in Three. Three is a transcendent function, which he defined as "a psychic function that arises from the tension between consciousness and the unconscious that supports their union." Four is the resurfacing of the One in an integrated state of consciousness, now whole and fully functioning in the world.

The Hermetic Model

From the Hermetic viewpoint, the universe was also created through a series of ten emanations of consciousness from the One Mind. Vibrations of consciousness (known as "the Word" or *Logos*) is what organizes the chaos of the One Thing to manifest in objective physical reality.

Hermetic cosmology is based on the writings attributed to Hermes Trismegistus archived in the *Corpus Hermeticum*. Unlike the mathematical Pythagorean teachings, the Hermetic texts are poetic, story-driven wisdom texts. The symbolic cosmology of Hermes is based on emanations of consciousness from the One Mind in the fiery bright "Empireum," which lies outside the universe.

As in the Pythagorean model, there are ten emanations of the divine mind to create the universe. But in the Hermetic model, these are viewed not as numbers but as celestial "heavens" or spheres of creation. In this geocentric scheme, the Earth is the center of the universe and everything else spins around it in ten concentric spheres. All the heavenly objects exist only to influence life on Earth, and it is a perfect application of the Hermetic dictum "As Above, So Below."

In the Hermetic model, the divine mind descends through celestial spheres made of the thick ethereal matter of the Fifth Element. The spheres of rarefied material are nested, one next to the other, with each sphere in physical contact with the spheres above and below it.

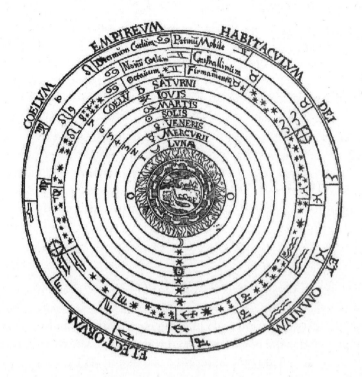

The Heavenly Spheres, from the Empireum outside creation to the Earth at the center.
(From Gemma Frisius Cosmographia by Petrus Apianus, 1539.)

ten. Tenth Heaven: The First Cause

The first emanation of the divine mind from the Empireum creates the Tenth Heaven, which is the highest celestial sphere and most distant from Earth. The Tenth Heaven is the direct creation of the divine Word. After this, the divine Mind outside the universe is no longer active in creation, and the "Mind of Nature" (also called "Mind the Maker") takes over to fulfill the Word. Hermeticists consider the Tenth Heaven the "First Cause," which is the ultimate cause of all subsequent events that itself does not have a cause but issues directly from the mind of god.

9. Ninth Heaven: The First Mover

The ninth sphere surrounding Earth is a spiraling emanation of solidified light that carries all the lower spheres with it in their 24-hour east-to-west rotation around the Earth. The crystallized light is known as the *Primum Mobile* ("First Mover"), the source of all rotation and change in the universe.

8. Eighth Heaven: The Stars

The eighth sphere surrounding Earth is the Firmament of Stars. At the time, it was believed the stars never changed positions relative to one another. For that reason, it was thought the stars were fixed on the surface of a single celestial sphere. These immutable constellations influence life on Earth through their astrological signatures.

Against the background of the fixed stars are the wandering planetary spirits who move in bewildering spiraling patterns across the night sky. To make sense of it, the ancients divided the firmament into twelve equal sectors called "houses" and named them by their dominant constellation. These signs of the Zodiac act as a lens to focus the archetypal light from above into psychic content of the aspects of consciousness they govern. Each of the following seven planets regulates a specific level of consciousness relative to the filtering action of the outer Zodiac.

7. Heaven of Saturn: Contraction

The cold, chthonic emanation of the Seventh Heaven expresses contraction and the totality of dualistic existence—the idea of being bound to time and space. Saturn's mindset is evident in chronologies, timelines, lifecycles, coordinates, timecards, accounting, probabilities, and many other preoccupations with getting by in the everyday world. But Saturn serves as a gateway to the stars in the Eighth Heaven, so it is a two-way street. While Saturn is the condensation of soul at the beginning of manifestation, it is where spirit takes flight to the stars during the return to Saturn on the Planetary Ladder.

6. Heaven of Jupiter: Expansion

This sphere imparts expansion and exaltation. It reveals itself most clearly on the worldly level in the blissful grace and sublime superiority encountered in the courts of monarchs. But the Jovian impulse to mingle and be popular is also present in any social gathering from Viennese ballrooms to Facebook. The Jupiterian identity tries to hold on to its transcendental origin while individuating in material reality. Yet without Jupiter, there would be no Ladder of the Planets, for it forces the stubborn Saturn archetype to transform and grow.

5. Heaven of Mars: Aggression

The emanations of Mars are aggressive ego, discipline, laws, and rigor but also the essential alchemical attributes of purification and forging changes in the environment.

Mars checks the expansive and sometimes superficial signatures of Jupiter and demands a re-examination of what is real. The Martian sphere also balances the solar impulses of over-confidence and complacency by exposing the tribulations of existing in a dualistic world in which both good and evil exist.

4. Heaven of the Sun: Stability and Growth

The warm emanations of the solar sphere provide a healthy and stable environment for growth. Solar consciousness stimulates transcendental awareness and an appreciation for the non-duality of the monadic Mind. The Sun establishes a balancing or neutralizing force between the masculine spheres above it (Saturn, Jupiter, and Mars) and the feminine spheres below it (Moon, Mercury, and Venus).

3. Heaven of Venus: Beauty and Love

The impulses projected by Venus include emotions, feelings, beauty, and sexual desire. Venus tempers Mercury's discipline with the desire to just live, love, and be happy. Venus not only reveals the power of pleasure but also gives an appreciation for the complexities and rewards of interpersonal relationships. Venus serves to ground both the expansive energy of the Sun and the cohering energy of Mercury.

2. Heaven of Mercury: Mind and Imagination

Mercury inspires thought, mental clarity, imagination, and constraint to emotional decision making. The objectivity and lightning-fast response of mercurial consciousness build confidence in the personality and provides the capacity to intellectualize complex situations to find quick solutions. The mental structure and discipline provided by the sphere of Mercury determine the boundaries of the personality, and the mercurial gift of imagination determines a person's creativity. Mercury balances the settled feminine aspects of the Moon with the sometimes reckless, whimsical impulses of Venus.

1. Heaven of the Moon: The Subconscious Mind

The lunar influence encourages reflection and balance in a person or situation. It focuses our attention on physical form and natural cycles of growth and decay. The Moon filters the reflected light from the higher celestial spheres through the darkness of the subconscious mind, and this information is presented to us in dreams, fantasies, intuition, psychic impressions, and mystical feelings. Because of the Moon's position between earthly existence and the distant planets, it serves as a filter or balancing force between the powers Above and the powers Below.

The Heavenly Spheres in the Tree of Life

In the Jewish map of consciousness known as "Kabbalah" (or "Qabalah") we find similar heavenly spheres known as "sephirot" (singular "sephira"), which are arranged in the form of a three-pillared Tree of Life. Each sephira is seen as having a light burning within it that signifies divine consciousness.

In this scheme, the monadic mind of the Empireum is also located outside our universe in what is called the "Atzmus" ("Essence Beyond"). Atzmus is outside our reality, yet it permeates all levels of the Tree of Life though the divine Word, which strikes the Tree like a bolt of lightning from the "Ein Sof" ("the Infinite above").

The lightning bolt enters the Tree of Life in a celestial sphere called Kether ("Crown"), which is the divine will (or Word) expressed in pure light. This is the Tenth Heaven or First Cause in the Hermetic system. At this point, the divine emanations split into duality forming two branches, a feminine alignment called "Jachin" ("Pillar of Mercy") and a masculine alignment called "Boaz" ("Pillar of Severity").

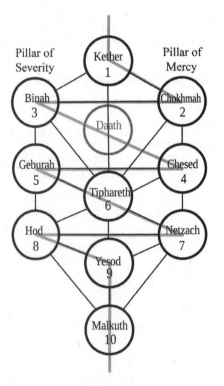

Sephirot of the Tree of Life with the Lightning Bolt of creation entering Kether and grounded at Malkuth.

The next emanation from Kether is "Chokmah" ("Divine Wisdom") on the Pillar of Mercy. From Chokmah, comes Binah ("Humility of Understanding") on the Pillar of Severity. Conscious creation continues in the Tree of Life in the pattern of the Lightning Bolt.

The flash of light alternates from the Pillar of Mercy to the Pillar of Severity creating "Chesed" ("Loving Kindness") and "Geburah" ("Strength and Punishment"). Next on the Pillar of Severity is "Hod" ("Splendor in Withdrawal"), then "Netzach" ("Eternal Endurance") on the Pillar of Mercy.

At this point, a third middle pillar emerges reconciling all the previously opposing sephirot. It is known as the "Pillar of Equilibrium" centered on the sephira of the heart known as "Tiphareth" ("Beauty"). This middle pillar originates in the crown sephira of Kether and passes through a mysterious hidden eleventh sephira called "Daath" ("Unifying Knowledge"), which is associated with the dark wisdom of the subconscious mind. The Pillar of Equilibrium continues from Tiphareth to the ninth sephira "Yesod" ("Foundation of Memory") and culminates in the tenth sephira "Malkuth" ("Kingdom of the Manifested Realm").

The sephirot on the Tree of Life correspond exactly to the Hermetic model of heavenly spheres. Ein Sof is the Tenth Heaven or First Cause. Kether is the Ninth Heaven or First Mover. Chokmah is ruled by the Zodiac in the Eighth Heaven or Firmament of Stars. Binah (humility) is ruled by the Seventh Heaven of Saturn, and Chesed (mercy) is ruled by the Sixth Heaven of Jupiter.

The downward-spiraling emanations in the Tree of Life continue to bear the fruit of Atzmus. Geburah (strength) is ruled by the Fifth Heaven of Mars, and Tiphareth (beauty) is ruled by the Fourth Heaven of the Sun. Netzach (endurance) is ruled by the Third Heaven of Venus, and Hod (splendor) is ruled by the Second Heaven of Mercury. Yesod (foundation) is ruled by the First Heaven of the Moon. The one exception to the Hermetic model is that Malkuth (kingdom of manifestation) is ruled by the Four Elements, which is closer to the interpretation found in the Pythagorean model.

The Alchemical Model

The Alchemical Model of Consciousness is a union of the principles of Hermetic cosmology and the Pythagorean format of the Tetractys. It follows the Axiom of Maria in its cosmological development but adds important alchemical and scientific insights into the nature of consciousness and the creation of the universe.

The Monad: The Singularity

At the top of our cosmological diagram (see the following figure) is a chaotic circle containing a singular point at its center. This singularity is the indivisible Monad or One Mind, which is the source of everything that follows. The Monad point is surrounded by the chaotic Abyss from which it emerges. To alchemists, this is the One Thing—the boundless darkness into which the universe unfolds.

Alchemists sometimes interpreted the One Thing as the *Prima Materia*, the zero-state plethora of potential from which all things emerge through the projection of consciousness. This idea is clearly restated in modern physics with the notion of Quantum Foam, a roiling sea of virtual particles that exist briefly in the etheric fabric of spacetime. Atomic particles exist in a state of pure potential until observed or acted upon by the field of consciousness.

In the Hermetic tradition, the first projection of thought into the chaotic *Prima Materia* is the divine *Logos* that causes the explosion of light and consciousness we now call the Big Bang. Alchemists believe that burst of creative forces—the condensation of light and mind from nothingness—still happens on both the physical and spiritual levels in their laboratories and in their souls.

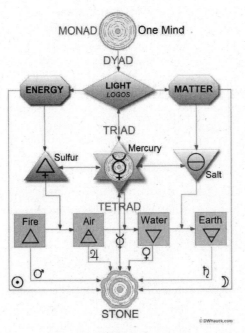

Model of Alchemical Consciousness

The Dyad: The Necessity of Duality

In Hermetic philosophy, the monadic One Mind, the ineffable source of creation, lies outside our understanding, and there is nothing we can say about it. We only know it because its consciousness is mirrored in our universe and within ourselves.

The first and only act of the One Mind is the utterance of the Word or *Logos*, the first thought that causes the Big Bang and sets the universe in motion. After that, only the *Logos* remains, as depicted in our model by the crystallized light in diamond-shaped emanation from the One Mind. It echoes through spacetime in the Mind of Nature or what Hermeticists called "Mind the Maker." This primal emanation is embedded in our reality in the laws of physics and mathematics. The *Logos* as the Mind of Nature can only be expressed in terms of the Dyad or duality, which is depicted in the diagram by the two opposing positive and negative poles shown with the first created opposites of energy and matter.

But why can the divine Word only be expressed in duality? Because the universe was created from nothing, it must always add up to zero. This is a fundamental law of both Hermetic philosophy and science. So, every positive thing must be neutralized with its opposite negative thing, and every particle of matter must have its corresponding particle of antimatter. Everything must add up to zero. Thus, the first principle of natural law is this oppositional duality in the universe.

How did the universe come into existence if everything adds up to zero? The answer is the "God Particle." In 1930, Wolfgang Pauli (our alchemical physicist from Chapter 21) solved this existential problem when he postulated a new subatomic particle called the "neutrino," which is an invisible building block for atomic particles. Pauli predicted the neutrino would have zero electric charge, zero mass, and the ability to pass through matter without being stopped. It would be more than 25 years before anyone could actually detect neutrinos.

The neutrino is known as the God Particle because for some mysterious reason during the first seconds of creation, just a few more matter neutrinos were created than antimatter neutrinos. Because of that, the universe did not quite add up to zero and atomic particles, stars, planets, and people can exist. Nonetheless, duality is still the dominant principle behind the creation and the origin of energy and change in the universe.

As we noted earlier, the primal opposites in the universe are energy and matter connected through the *Logos* of light, as shown in the previous figure. Energy is expressed in fields of force or waves, while matter is expressed in particles and solid objects. Psychologically, energy is associated with the masculine archetypes of aggressive expansion and spirit, while matter is associated with the feminine archetypes of passive contraction and soul. These opposite archetypes are conveyed in the alchemists' images of the Solar King and Lunar Queen.

Energy and matter are constantly changing into one another, and they are really just one thing, but we will never know what that looks like, because we see everything through the lens of duality. Alchemists tried to capture this idea in the Rebis, the two-faced thing with one body.

Duality appears on every level of our existence—physically, biologically, psychologically, and spiritually. There is a never-ending series of opposites that determine our reality—male and female, wave and particle, light and dark, hot and cold, virtue and vice, love and hate, war and peace, conservative and liberal, good and evil, life and death.

The Triad: Three Creative Forces

The third level of emanation in our model is the Three Essentials, the three forces of Sulfur, Mercury, and Salt. These forces of creation are engendered through the primal opposites of energy and matter through the intermediary of light. Thus, Sulfur is a manifestation of energy, Salt is a manifestation of matter, and Mercury is a manifestation of light. We studied the Three Essentials in Chapter 11, where we discovered that these ancient concepts have the mathematical relationship of $E = mc^2$.

The third generation of consciousness in the universe is depicted in the Triad level of the previous figure. Sulfur as energy and Salt as matter are shown as opposing forces balanced by Mercury as light at the center. Sulfur is carried in the upward-pointing triangle of Fire, and Salt is carried in the downward-pointing triangle of Water.

Mercury is represented by the star-shaped figure made by merging the triangles of Fire and Water that is also a symbol for the Philosopher's Stone. This symbol in three dimensions forms an eight-pointed star that is associated with an ancient Egyptian symbol for the astral body called the *Merkabah* ("light spirit body"). Early Jewish mystics taught the *Merkabah* was the throne-chariot in which Ezekiel ascended into heaven.

Just as Dr. John Dee placed Mercury at the center of his elegant *Hieroglyphic Monad* cipher (see Chapter 13), Mercury stands at the heart of our model. The point at the center of Mercury is a repetition of the singularity in the Monad. In other words, Mercury shares the same kind of consciousness as the first mind of creation.

Furthermore, Mercury sits at the center of the vertical axis of reality or *Axis Mundi* ("World Axis"). This reflects the Hermetic concept that Mercury can access all levels of reality from heaven Above to the myriad of manifested things Below and everything in-between. That is to say, our reflected consciousness can reach any level of the embedded divine consciousness in the universe using contemplation, concentration, meditation, imagination, and other tools of mind.

The Tetrad: Four Kinds of Manifestation

The Four Elements (Fire, Air, Water, and Earth) are shown in the previous figure in four boxes of manifestation. They are created from the interaction of the Three Essentials. Fire and Air are influenced by the force of Sulfur (energy). Air and Water are influenced by Mercury (light), and Water and Earth by Salt (matter).

The fourth level of the Tetractys is where Maria's Axion tells us "out of the Third comes the One as the Fourth." That is to say that the original thought or divine Word is fulfilled at this level in physical reality. In modern physics, the classic Four Elements have been reinterpreted as the Four Fundamental Interactions in matter. These interactive forces control everything that happens in the material universe. By far, the strongest interactions in matter are with the cohesive Strong Nuclear Force, which is associated with the alchemists' primary agent of change, the Fire Element.

The next strongest interactive force is Electromagnetism, which is the source of visible light and the spectrum of invisible frequencies carried in the air. Alchemists associated light and other "invisible spirits" with the Air Element.

The so-called Weak Nuclear Force is responsible for the dissolution of matter in the decay of atomic particles. It is also responsible for the fluid fusion reactions that power everything from life on Earth to the heat of the Sun. Alchemists would associate this force with the Water Element.

While the final interactive force of Gravity pulls galaxies, stars, and planets together, it is the least powerful force on the atomic level. Alchemists would view it as an expression of the static Earth Element.

Recently, physicists have proposed a new fifth interactive force, appropriately named the Quintessence. It has been variously described as a pervasive etheric force associated with ether antigravity or dark matter, and scientists around the world are trying to detect it.

No matter how you look at it, the universe manifests in reality through four elemental (or interactive) forces. The original thought or Word of the One Mind is fulfilled in materialization. Or as the Emerald Tablet puts it: "Its inherent strength is perfected if it is turned into Earth."

Seven Forces Shape the Stone

To the basic concept of the creation of material objects through the projection of consciousness, the alchemistic philosophers added preexisting patterns that further shape the characteristics of matter. They postulated that the emanations of the Four Elements were filtered through seven planetary archetypes culminating in a new embodiment of consciousness or "stone." In their geocentric cosmology, the first stone was the Earth itself. Remember, a stone is what alchemists called any precipitated or crystallized matter. It could be a planet, a rock, a flower, an animal, a human, a new personality, or even a resurrected soul.

The precipitated Stone at the bottom of the previous figure is the manifestation of thought in our model. The multilayered object represents the cosmological completion of the first thought that originated outside our universe. Matter in our universe still contains the original spark or point of consciousness that created it, but it is also shaped by the external forces around it.

The seven archetypal forces harnessed to create the Stone in our diagram represent the seven planetary influences of Hermetic philosophy. These are indicated by their corresponding alchemical cipher. The primal opposites of energy and matter are the Sun and Moon, while the Four Elements are expressed archetypally as Mars (Fire), Venus (Water), Jupiter (Air), and Saturn (Earth).

The seventh planetary archetype in the creation of the Stone is Mercury, which is the light of consciousness that originated in the One Mind Above and is reflected in Mercury Below—in the personal reality each of us of us creates for ourselves. That original spark of light from the level of the unitary Monad is projected through the *Logos* and transmitted by the light of Mercury in all sentient beings. In other words, we create our personal realities in much the same way the universe was created.

The Alchemical Big Bang

Astrophysicists divide the birth of our universe into four events of creation similar to the emanations of consciousness in our model. The first event was the singularity, which occurred about 13.8 billion years ago when an infinitesimally small point appears out of nothing that inflates to the size of a golf ball in less than a trillionth of a second.

This monadic singularity from outside our reality and its immediate inflation is the ultimate mystery that cannot be explained with the current laws of physics. This is the level of the Monad in our model and the One Mind outside the universe that originates in the higher dimensional Hermetic Empireum or Atzmus in the Tree of Life.

During the next three minutes of the Big Bang, there is a violent explosion of light and heat at an unimaginable temperature of 100 nonillion (10^{32}) degrees Kelvin. This is the power of the *Logos* emerging from the Tenth Heaven (the First Cause) in the Hermetic model or in Kether in the Tree of Life.

As the temperature cools to 1 billion (10^9) degrees Kelvin, the universe enters a dyadic period of creation of opposing subatomic particles and their antimatter counterparts. Only the unexplainable fact that there was about one extra matter neutrino created for every billion antimatter neutrinos keeps the early universe from disappearing into oblivion. This is the level of the Dyad, the origin of the Prime Mover of the Ninth Heaven or the duality indicated by the opposing pillars of the Tree of Life.

For the next 380,000 years, the universe is in a sealed state of pure radiation that creates a super-dense plasma, which blocks the light like a dense, dark cloud. This is the sealed cauldron of creation, the churning Three Essentials expressed in the Triad level of our model.

Finally, the triadic plasma begins to condense into atoms, which allows the original light from the Big Bang to escape in a brilliant flash that is so intense it can still be detected in the cosmic microwave background radiation. As the flash of energy and light dissipates, the cosmos is plunged into utter darkness. This is the explosion of the three primal forces of Sulfur (energy), Mercury (light), and Salt (matter) that is projected into the heart of the universe.

About 400 million years after the Big Bang, the Three Essentials have done their work, and the universe begins to emerge from the pregnant darkness in a period of macrocosmic materialization. For the next half-billion years, elemental atoms in clumps of gas collapse to form the first stars and galaxies.

This period of creation represents the level of the Tetrad in our model—the rendering of the Four Elements in the Firmament of Stars of the Hermetic Eighth Heaven. As the evolution of the universe continues, the planetary spheres of the next seven Heavens (or seven levels of sephirot on the Tree of Life) come into play. Finally, the Earth materializes, and human civilization is possible. The creation of stellar matter continues to expand into empty space to its current size of more than 100 billion galaxies.

Mercury: Key to the Mysteries

The key to all the models of creation and consciousness we have discussed in this chapter is the primal force of nature the alchemists called Mercury, which they associated with light and mind. The concept of Mercury as the force of consciousness and source of matter is everywhere in alchemy. Mercury is the mother of all the metals, the carrier of archetypes, and the First Matter at the heart of every created thing.

In *Psychology and Alchemy*, Carl Jung noted that when alchemists speak of Mercury, readers assume they are talking about the liquid metal, but in fact they are usually referring to Mercurius, which is the world-creating spark of consciousness concealed in all matter. This spirit of pure consciousness—like a quicksilver mirror that reflects the world and takes the shape of any container—is the most important tool in all of alchemy and the essential ingredient in any transformation.

"Mercurius stands at the beginning and end of the Work," Jung explained. "It is the *Prima Materia* and *Caput Corvi* ("Raven's Head") of the *Nigredo* at the beginning. As the dragon Mercurius, it devours itself, and as the dragon it dies, only to rise again in the *Lapis* ("Stone"). Mercurius is the play of colors in the *Cauda Pavonis* ("Peacock's Tail") and the reason for the division into the Four Elements. It is the Hermaphrodite that was at the beginning, who splits into the classical male-female duality that is reunited in the conjunction to appear once again at the end in the radiant form of the *Lumen Novum* ("New Light") of the androgenous child that becomes the Philosopher's Stone. Mercurius is all—metallic yet liquid, cold yet fiery, poison yet healing, male yet female, matter yet spirit—a symbolic force uniting all the opposites."

Although many Renaissance alchemists recognized consciousness as a necessary component of the universe from the beginning of creation, modern scientists have been slow to accept the creative sea of consciousness that surrounds us. Erwin Schrödinger (1887–1961), Nobel prize-winning pioneer of quantum physics, was one of the first of a growing number of alchemical scientists who recognized this concept.

"Our science has cut itself off from an adequate understanding of the Subject of Cognizance—of the mind," Schrödinger noted. "Consciousness cannot be accounted for in physical terms. For consciousness is absolutely fundamental to the universe. It cannot be accounted for in terms of anything else."

The Mercurial Light of Imagination

Freedom of consciousness is essential for doing alchemy. Not just political and religious freedom, but also personal freedom—freedom from our own inner bureaucracy that tries to keep us in line. Alchemists recognized that the most important tool of the Great Work is the unfettered light of consciousness they called True Imagination, which is the ability to envision what transformation looks like and establish it in the light of mind. "The True Imagination," Paracelsus noted, "leads life back to its spiritual reality, and it then takes on the name of meditation."

Alchemists believed imagination was a piece of heaven concealed within us, a direct connection to the cosmic Mind. When Hermetic writers speak of the "mind's eye" or "seeing with the eyes of spirit," they are describing a process that penetrates the deeper reality of things beyond their outward appearances and attempts to capture the "Seed of the World" as the divine mind dreams it.

The *Lexicon of Alchemy* (1612) defines "imagination" as "the Star in Man, a celestial or supercelestial body." Carl Jung elaborated on this definition in his *Psychology and Alchemy.* "The alchemists' concept of imagination is the most important key to understanding the Opus. We have to conceive of their imaginal processes not as the immaterial phantoms that we take fantasy pictures to be, but as something corporeal—a subtle body."

"The act of imagining," Jung continued, "was like a physical ingredient that could be fitted into the cycle of material changes in the lab. The alchemist related himself not only to his unconscious but directly to the substance he hoped to transform through the power of imagination. The alchemical act of imagining is therefore a concentrated extract of life forces that produces a subtle body, a psychoid hybrid of the physical with the psychic."

You can practice freeing the True Imagination within you by following the operations of alchemy we have described in this book and understanding the subtle relationships revealed in our Model of Alchemical Consciousness. In our model, we placed the light of Mercury—the True Imagination—at the heart of our diagram. It is the key to the projection of consciousness, and the best way to practice it is to become an alchemist in the modern world.

Become Mercury!

In this chapter, we developed a model that concisely summarizes more than 3,500 years of Egyptian and Greek thought on cosmology and the role of mind in the universe. We discovered clear connections to the diverse traditions of Pythagoreanism, the Hermetic teachings, astrology, Kabbalah, and other traditions. We have also found startling confirmation of our model in modern psychology, astronomy, and quantum physics.

We must not forget that while Mercury—and the patterns of consciousness it contains—originates from the One Mind, it is an independent force in our world. Each of us carries our own Mercury, like a hidden star within shining with mind and imagination. With those divine gifts, each of us creates our own world in the same way the whole universe was created. This microcosm is the "little world" that each of us creates out of the beliefs and desires of our personal *Logos*.

The problem comes when that microcosm within becomes salted and frozen in time, when the mercurial Quintessence that enlivens it fails to shine.

If there is one last admonition against living in the prison of a salted world—that also summarizes this entire book—it is simply "Become Mercury!" Let your consciousness flow again like a child's by desalting yourself. Alchemize your life and live with imaginative integrity. Be active, alive, and shimmering with inner light like Mercury.

Clarify your mind by finding the thoughts that matter. What you do *not* think about will determine the power of your projection in the world. Be singular in thought and action. Get out from under the constant cascade of irrelevant thoughts that pollute your mind and focus on the One Thing in your life your heart knows is true.

Develop a mercurial nonchalance in the game of life as it is being played out in our current culture. The game is never the same from one generation to the next, so rise above it. Extract your consciousness from supporting the worldview of others whose vision you do not share and focus on the greater reality of the alchemical universe within you.

When combined with an attitude of free-flowing movement through the world, an enlightened mind that is free of temporal customs and shifting politics will release unexpected novelty in your life that fuels transformations that are in line with your deepest desires and spiritual destiny.

Be mindful and reflective and flow freely into life with the light of Mercury surging unobstructed through your body, mind, and spirit—as it does in the universe.

Recommended Resources

Books

Aromatico, Andrea. *Alchemy: The Great Secret*. Harry Abrams, 2000. An illustrated history exploring alchemy's mix of science, philosophy, art, religion, and magic.

Ash, Heather, and Vicki Noble. *The Four Elements of Change*. Council Oak Books, 2004. Using the Four Elements to create a solid foundation to support your mind, body, and spirit.

Cavalli, Thom. *Alchemical Psychology*. Tarcher, 2002. Ancient alchemical recipes for living in the modern world.

Dee, John. *The Hieroglyphic Monad*. Red Wheel Weiser, 1975. Dr. Dee's Euclidian explanation of his magical cipher for the Philosopher's Stone.

Eason, Cassandra. *Alchemy at Work*. Crossing Press, 2004. How to use the ancient arts to enhance your life at work.

Edinger, Edward. *Anatomy of the Psyche: Alchemical Symbolism in Psychotherapy*. Open Court Publishing, 1991. In-depth description of the operations of alchemy in psychological terms.

Goddard, David. *Tower of Alchemy*. Samuel Weiser, 1999. Filled with Hermetic principles that are meant to be applied at the spiritual level.

Green, Mindy, and Kathi Keville. *Aromatherapy: A Complete Guide to the Healing Art*. Crossing Press, 1995. Shows how to use, blend, and prepare essential oils at home.

Hauck, Dennis William. *Emerald Tablet: Alchemy for Personal Transformation*. Penguin Arkana, 1999. Definitive history of the Emerald Tablet and the application of its principles to personal transformation.

———. *Sorcerer's Stone: A Beginner's Guide to Alchemy*. Athanor Press, 2013. Makes alchemy come alive with clear explanations, fascinating anecdotes, and hands-on experiments.

Linden, Stanton. *The Alchemy Reader: From Hermes Trismegistus to Isaac Newton*. Cambridge University, 2003. Basic writings of the alchemists ranging from Alexandria to the end of the seventeenth century.

Marlan, Stanton. *Black Sun: Alchemy and Art of Darkness*. Texas A&M Press, 2005. Examines the alchemical stage of *Nigredo*, which is the blackening or mortification from which the true light emerges.

Martin, Sean. *Alchemy and Alchemists*. Chartwell Books, 2007. Basic review of the history and methods of alchemy.

Melville, Francis. *Book of Alchemy*. Barron's, 2002. Presents the seven operations of the Emerald Tablet, as well as an illustrated overview of alchemy.

Miller, Richard, and Iona Miller. *Modern Alchemist*. Phanes Press, 1994. Guide to personal transformation using the principles of alchemy.

Moring, Gary. *The Complete Idiot's Guide to Theories of the Universe*. Alpha Books, 2001. Guide to modern cosmology and quantum physics that lays the foundation for the ideas of modern alchemy.

———. *The Complete Idiot's Guide to Understanding Einstein*. Alpha Books, 2004. Great introduction to modern physics that contains an interesting section on alchemy.

Reich, Wilhelm. *Secret of the Golden Flower*. Harcourt Brace, 1988. Taoist alchemy treatise with a wonderful commentary by Carl Jung.

Rolfe, Randy. *The Four Temperaments*. Marlowe & Company, 2002. Understanding the Elements as alchemical humors that allow you to fine-tune your health, career, and relationships.

Roob, Alexander. *Alchemy & Mysticism*. Taschen, 1997. Stunning pictorial presentation of the spiritual practice of alchemy.

Stavish, Mark. *Path of Alchemy: Energetic Healing and the World of Natural Magic*. Llewellyn, 2006. Guide to the teachings of Hermes and their applications in alchemy and healing.

Von Franz, Marie-Louise. *Alchemical Active Imagination*. Shambhala Publications, 1997. Details how alchemists practiced a kind of meditation that Carl Jung called "active imagination."

Von Franz, Marie-Louise. *Alchemy: An Introduction to the Symbolism and the Psychology*. Inner City Books, 1980. Inspiring guide to spiritual wholeness that follows the Jungian interpretation.

Whitmont, Edward. *Alchemy of Healing: Psyche and Soma*. North Atlantic Books, 1996. Challenges the methods of mechanical medicine and emphasizes the importance of consciousness in healing.

Wolf, Fred Alan. *Matter Into Feeling: A New Alchemy of Science and Spirit*. Moment Point Press, 2002. Examines the science behind consciousness, memory, dreams, and the "One Mind" concept of the alchemists.

———. *Mind Into Matter: A New Alchemy of Science and Spirit*. Moment Point Press, 2000. Interprets modern physics in terms of ancient spiritual texts from alchemy, the Qabala, and the Eastern traditions.

———. *The Spiritual Universe*. Moment Point Press, 1998. Presents one physicist's vision of spirit, soul, matter, and self in the universe.

Yudelove, Eric. *Tao and the Tree of Life: Alchemical and Sexual Mysteries of the East and West*. Llewellyn, 1996. Decodes the mysteries of the Tao and Kabbalah to show their underlying bases in alchemy.

Internet Resources

Alchemy Museum in San Jose, California, features historic artifacts and books about Western alchemy.
Website: www.rosicrucianpark.org/alchemy-museum
Facebook: www.facebook.com/Alchemy.Museum/

Alchemy Web Site is Adam McLean's huge resource of original texts, drawings, and articles on practical and spiritual alchemy.
Website: www.levity.com/alchemy

Alchemy of Consciousness is Dennis William Hauck's alchemy resource website.
Website: www.DWHauck.com
YouTube channel: www.YouTube.com/user/alchemergist

Alchemy Study Program features certification courses in both practical and spiritual alchemy.
Website: www.AlchemyStudy.com and www.AlchemyStudy.org
Facebook: www.facebook.com/groups/studyalchemy/

Alchemy Conferences has lecture videos from conferences held by the International Alchemy Guild.
Website: www.AlchemyConference.net

Alchemy Guild is the official website of the International Alchemy Guild (IAG) with more than 500 members around the world.
Website: www.AlchemyGuild.org
Facebook: www.facebook.com/groups/guildalchemy

Alchemy Lab is dedicated to personal transformation and has been described by the *London Times* as a stunning archive of alchemical philosophy.
Website: www.AlchemyLab.com

Alchemergy is devoted to modern alchemy films and filmmaking as it applies to personal, social, and global transformation.
Website: www.Alchemergy.net
Facebook: www.facebook.com/groups/alchemergy/

Planetary Charts for Spagyric work can be downloaded from AlchemyStudy.com/download/Planetary_Charts.pdf.

Spagyric Theory is a free eBook on Spagyrics that includes all the Planetary Hours charts.
Website: cdn.fs.teachablecdn.com/nL3kL5LBTKKy8n8u3T0Q

Glossary of Alchemical Terms

adept   Someone who is initiated into the secrets of alchemy or has completed an alchemical apprenticeship.

albification   Whitening of a substance by washing, scrubbing, grinding, or bleaching (using chemical or spiritual processes).

alchemy   The art and science of transforming substances, situations, or living things to perfect them.

alembic   The upper or heavenly part of a still; a still head or type of retort. *See* distillation.

aludel   A pear-shaped vessel that is open at both ends. Used as a condenser in the sublimation process, it came to signify the end stages of transformation. Also called the Hermetic Vase or the Philosopher's Egg.

amalgamation   The formation of an amalgam or alloy of a metal with mercury. Any union of opposing archetypal forces.

archetypes   Elementary ideas rooted permanently in one's consciousness. They are the divine ideals or spiritual essences from which existing objects, ideas, or situations arise.

athanor   From the Arabic word *al-tannur* (oven), the furnace used by the alchemists. Built of brick or clay, it usually was shaped like a tower with a domed roof. It was designed to keep an even heat over long periods of time.

Azoth   Formed from the first and last letters of the English alphabet, which stand for the Greek alpha and omega or the beginning and end of all creation. The Azoth is the ultimate solvent and coagulant that can reduce anything to its perfected essence.

baths   In alchemy, baths symbolize the dissolution process in which metals are cleansed and purified.

brimstone   From a German word meaning "burning stone." Also called sulfur.

caduceus   The staff of Hermes with two serpents entwined in opposite directions around it. The serpents represent the life force, and the caduceus is often shown with two wings that represent the purified or ascended life force.

calcination   An operation in alchemy in which a substance is dehydrated and reduced to ashes in a fire.

cibation   The addition of liquid to the contents of the crucible at precisely the right moment.

cipher   A stylized symbol or glyph used to signify fundamental principles or universal archetypes.

circulation   The purification of a substance by a circular distillation in a pelican or closed distillation apparatus.

coagulation   An operation in alchemy in which a solution thickens, congeals, or crystallizes into a solid material or body.

coction   The cooking or heating of a substance at a moderate heat for an extended period.

cohobation   A method of distillation in which the distillate is poured back into its residue.

conjunction   The marriage or union of two substances.

crucible   The melting vessel used by alchemists that is made of inert material such as porcelain and can withstand great heat.

cucurbit   The lower or earthly part of a still that contains the original liquid. Made of glass or earthenware, it was also known as a "gourd" because of its shape. A receiver.

digestion   A kind of putrefaction in which the nutrients or essences are reabsorbed; the slow modification of a substance using gentle heat.

dissolution   To turn a solid into a liquid, or a process by which something is mixed with a liquid.

distillation   The process of purifying a liquid by boiling it and condensing its vapors; an operation of alchemy in which volatile essences are separated from solutions. A vertical union of heavenly and earthly forces.

dross   Scum formed by oxidation at the surface of molten metals; any worthless material that should be removed. From the Old English word *dros*, meaning dirt or dregs.

essential oils   The volatile oily components of plants, trees, and grasses. They are found in tiny sacs or glands located in the flowers, leaves, roots, bark, or resins of a plant.

exaltation   An operation by which a substance is raised into a purer and more perfect nature. It usually involves the release of a gas or air from a substance.

fermentation   Transformation of an organic substance into new compounds by the action of a ferment such as yeast. In general, the introduction of new life, agitation, excitement, or inspiration into a substance or situation.

filtration   A kind of separation in which material is passed through a sieve or screen designed to allow only pieces of a certain size to pass through.

First Matter   The primordial chaos out of which the universe originated; the first principle or soul of a substance.

fixation   To change a volatile subject so that it is fixed, stable, or solid and so that it remains permanently unaffected by fire.

Four Elements   The four archetypal principles that emerged from the First Matter: Fire, Water, Air, and Earth.

head   The top of the retort flask used in distillation.

Henosis   Greek word for mystical oneness, union, or unity. The goal is union with the fundamental source of reality, the One Mind or Monad.

Hermetic   Secret; referring to the teachings of Hermes. "Hermetically sealed" means sealed airtight so no outside influences might corrupt the contents.

Iatrochemistry   The use of chemicals or drugs in medicine as pioneered by Paracelsus. Iatrochemists believe that health depends on chemical reactions in the humors or fluids of the body.

impregnation   To saturate thoroughly in order to produce a crystallization or new compound.

inhumation   To bury under the earth; sometimes used to mean any process that buries the active substance in a dark earthy material. Also refers to placing a flask in the warm heat of a dung bath.

litharge (or **letharge**)   The leftover scum, spume, or ashes of a metallic operation; reddish-yellow crystalline form of lead monoxide formed by fusing and powdering massicot.

magnesia   A mystical term used by alchemists that denoted the primordial transforming substance in the universe.

matrass   A round-bottomed flask with an exceptionally long neck that is sometimes called a "bolt-head."

menstruum   An alchemical term meaning a solvent or alkahest having both the power to dissolve and coagulate at the same time. Based on the belief that the ovum takes its life and form from the menses, the menstruum was also referred to the as the Mercury of the Philosophers.

mental alchemy   The use of alchemical techniques and operations on the psychological level to perfect one's character and personality.

microcosm and macrocosm   The "little universe" of human physiology, psychology, and society as opposed to the "greater universe" of planetary, cosmic, and spiritual processes.

mortification   A process during which the substance undergoes a kind of death and seems to have been destroyed but is revived eventually.

multiplication   A process of distillation and coagulation in which the power of transmutation is concentrated; an increase in the amount of the Stone obtained from its pristine form.

Perennial Philosophy   The belief that there are certain universal truths sensed by all sentient beings; this belief is common to all cultures and systems of knowledge.

Philosopher's Stone   A magical substance or catalyst that would immediately turn any base metal into gold. A powder or elixir made from the Stone could perfect or cure anything. A perfected state of consciousness.

precipitation   To cause solid matter to separate from solution or suspension; to cause a vapor to condense and fall or deposit residue.

projection   The final stage of coagulation in which the power of transformation is directed toward a body; the final process in making gold in which the Stone is tossed upon the molten base metal to transmute it.

pulverization   The breaking down of a substance to smaller fragments by repeatedly striking it with a blunt instrument, such as a hammer or mallet.

purgation   Purifying a substance by casting out a gross part of it.

receiver   The flask attached to the outlet of the condenser tube during distillation that contains the distillate or distilled product.

rectification   The purification of the matter by means of repeated distillations, the distillate being again distilled.

retort   A spherical container (usually glass) with a long neck or spout that is used to distill or decompose solutions by the action of heat or acids.

reverberation   To reflect or radiate heat or light. The action of a reverberatory furnace or kiln in which heat is radiated from the roof.

separation   An operation of alchemy in which useful essences are removed from materials by filtration, sifting, ceration, and chemical binding.

signatures   The characteristics plants and other objects share with the planetary powers and astrological events in the heavens.

social alchemy   The application of alchemical principles and operations in relationships and for the general welfare of society.

spagyrics   The applied alchemy of isolating the essences of plants and herbs.

spiritual alchemy   The application of the principles and operations of laboratory alchemy to mental and spiritual processes of transformation.

sublimation   The vaporization of a solid without fusion or melting, followed by the condensation of its vapor in the resolidified form on a cool surface.

Tantra   A form of Asian alchemy that combines elements of Hinduism and mystical teachings to transform bodily energies using mantras, meditations, and erotic rites.

Theurgy   A system of meditations, rituals, and magical ceremonies invoking the actions or presence of divine energies in human affairs, especially with the goal of perfecting oneself.

Three Essentials   The trinity of forces that make up creation, named by the alchemists as Sulfur, Mercury, and Salt.

transmutation   The permanent change of one substance into another at the physical or atomic level, as in the transmutation of uranium into lead by radioactive decay.

transubstantiation   The mystical process of becoming the body of Christ in the sacrament of the Eucharist. Worshippers partake of the bread (the body of Christ) and of the wine (the blood of Christ), becoming one with Him.

transudation   A process that occurs if the essence appears to sweat out in drops during a distillation or when heated.

trituration   The reduction of a substance to a powder, not only by the use of grinding but also by the application of heat.

volatile   Changing readily from a solid or liquid into vapor. Anything characterized by erratic changeability or tending to erupt suddenly or violently.

volatilization   To cause a substance to pass off into a vapor.

Index

B

Bacon, Francis, 272, 279
Bacon, Roger (wizardry of), 44–45
Balinas, 17
Bartholomew the Englishman, 43
basilisk, 115
Behdety, 246
Big Bang, 290–291, 294–295
   dyadic period of, 295
   emerging power of *Logos*, 295
   Three Essentials, expression of, 295
Binah, 289
bioenergetics, 7
birds of alchemy, 114–115
black antimony, 66
Black Death, 47
Black Dragon, 51, 118
Black Lion, 117
Black Phase, 191–202
   blackening, perception of, 236
   calcination, 195–198
     actual, 196
     calcining agent, 195
     cipher, 195
     dehydration by fire, 195
     personal, 196–198
     philosophical, example of, 196
     potential, 196
     symbols, 195
   dissolution, 198–202
     astrological sign associated with, 199
     definition, 198
     images of, 199
     opposing forces, recognition of, 199
     personal, 199–202
     Water Element and, 199

facing the dragon during, 242
   goal in, 194
   mortification, 194, 237
   Mountain of the Adepts(quotes) painting, 191–193
   nomenclature (Jung), 237
   saturnic signatures, 236
   splinter personality, 237
   symbols, 194, 248
   three phases of work, 193
Blue Vitriol, 103
Boaz, 288
bodywork, 6
Boehme, Jakob, 273
Bohm, David, 277, 279
Bolos of Mendes, 28
bolthead, 62
Book of Adjustments, 36
Book of Balinas the Wise on Causes, 17
Book of Breathings, The, 14
Book of the Composition of Alchemy, 42
Book of Concentration, 38
Book of the Dead, The, 14, 16
Book of Enoch, 12
Book of Images, The, 29
Book of the Kingdom, 38
Book of Lambspring, 144
Book of Mercury, 38
Book of Optics, 267
Book of the Secrets of Creation, 17
Book of Thoth, 17
Boyle, Robert, 50, 54, 274, 279
Brief Lives, 163
brimstone, 125
Bronze Age, 99
Brothers of Purity, 37
Bruno, Giordano, 46, 271–272, 279
Buddha, 242
Bulwer-Lytton, Edward, 239
Burkhardt, Titus, 102

C

Cabalistic Chemistry, 215
caduceus (staff of Hermes), 19
Caesar, Julius, 32
calcination, 195–198
   actual, 196
   calcining agent, 195
   cipher, 195
   dehydration by fire, 195
   personal, 196–198
   philosophical, example of, 196
   potential, 196
   symbols, 195
call of copper, 183
call of gold, 187
call of iron, 182
call of lead, 179
call of mercury, 185
call of silver, 186
call of tin, 181
carmot, 161
cast iron, 100
Catholic Church, 42, 74
Cauda Pavonis, 296
Celestial Fire, 156
Central Fire, 157
chakras, 177
chaos magic, 266–267
Characteristics of Chemicals, 54
chemicalization (spiritual), 78–80
   (stage 1) sealing, 79
   (stage 2) agitation, 79
   (stage 3) combustion, 79–80
   (stage 4) withdrawal, 80
   (stage 5) manifestation, 80
chemicals, 63–66
   ancient origins of, 64
   colorful names of, 64
   liquor, 65
   natron, 64–65
   pulvis solaris, 65–66
   vitriol, 64

F

G